A Layman's Guide to Negro History

Compiled and Edited by

Erwin A. Salk

A Layman's Guide to Negro History

New, Enlarged Edition

a *R*amparts book

McGRAW–HILL BOOK COMPANY
New York   Toronto   London   Sydney

Library of Congress Catalog Card Number: 67-22967

NEW, ENLARGED EDITION

Third Printing

54470

FRONTISPIECE:
*General Moses: A Study of 19th Century
Heroine Harriet Tubman,* by Charles White.
From the Golden State Mutual Negro Art
Collection, Los Angeles, California

*To my parents, Gertrude and Harry Salk,
who pointed the direction, and to my wife,
Evelyn, and children, Justin, Anthony and
Jonathan, who are my inspiration and one of the
major reasons for this work.*

CONTENTS

INTRODUCTION

Chained in a foreign land he stood,
A man of giant frame
Amid the gathering multitude
That shrunk to hear his name—
All stern of look and strong of limb
His dark eyes on the ground—
And silently they gazed on him
As on a lion bound.

Vainly, but well that chief had fought—
He was a captive now;
Yet pride that fortune humbles not
Was written on his brow.
The scars his dark broad bosom wore
Showed warrior true and brave;
A prince among his Tribe before,
He could not be a slave.
—William Cullen Bryant, "The African Chief"

This compilation pertaining to the history of the Negro in the United States is intended to show the depth of the Negro's contribution to the history of our country. This is intended not as a scholarly work but as a layman's guide, and therefore it is perhaps not as complete as that required for the professional scholar.

There are many fields related to the history of the Negro people in the United States to which there may be only occasional reference, but no attempt has been made to cover all fields in detail. Slavery, the struggle for emancipation and the abolitionist movement, the civil rights movement, the African colonization movements, the history of Africa in terms of the heritage of the American Negro, race relations—each of these is an integral part of the history of the

United States as well as the history of the Negro in the United States, but each is a study in itself.

Many of these listings and compilations are partial, only a sampling—a touchstone here and there—to provide introductions, indications, and guidelines for use by individuals and organizations. The scholar may find fault, but this book was visualized as having greater meaning and importance to those lay people and organizations desiring access to sources of information and material on the history of the Negro in the United States.

Innumerable U.S. history books contain discussions, materials, and observations on various phases of Negro history. Although there are also many unpublished theses and articles which delve into much of the subject matter referred to above, no attempt here is made to survey these sources. Leon Litwack's *North of Slavery;* "The Negro in New York, 1783-1865" (*Journal of Negro History,* XVI, 1931); "The Negro in Ohio" (*Journal of Negro History,* XXXI, 1946); "The Providence Negro Community, 1820-1842" (*Rhode Island History,* VII, 1948); the *Journal of the Illinois State Historical Society,* VLI, No. 3, Autumn, 1963, an entire issue devoted to the 240 years of history of the Negro in Illinois; the many references to Negro pioneers in California, as, for example, the murals at the Golden State Mutual Life Insurance Company—all are good examples of publications and bibliographies covering the above mentioned subjects.

The various bibliographies herein do not necessarily repeat themselves. The general bibliography, for all practical purposes, excludes all listings contained elsewhere, with the exception of those books also available in paperback. The paperback listing, of course, brings together titles currently available in paperback form.

Often, it is difficult to determine whether or not adults will be interested in publications intended for children and young adults. The adult reader, therefore, may frequently find that such matter can be covered with profit and, on occasion, younger readers may reap benefit from adult-directed writings.

The selected bibliography on Negro history is not intended to be exhaustive nor necessarily to list the most definitive works in the field. It is simply a suggestion for a beginning, an attempt to set forth a representative, readily accessible list of books which can form the basis of an individual or group library on an adult level. The books—some in paperback and therefore not too expensive—

are relatively easy to obtain.To this selected bibliography can be added books from the young adult and children's list. I realize full well that this list, as well as many of the others, can be subject to criticism for omissions as well as for inclusions. But once again, the purpose of this work is only to provoke exploration of an area in the history of our country that has suffered virtual exclusion.

Paperback books on Negro history represent an important resource. With the high cost of books and the relatively low budgets of many educational institutions, libraries, and organizations, there are available at relatively low cost a wide variety of titles for mass consumption and distribution. These books can be easily exhibited and readily presented on paperback racks and literature displays in airports, railroad terminals, hotel lobbies, newsstands, book stores, libraries, schools, churches, community organizations, and the like. To date most of these readily available books are not known to either the general public or through educational channels. They represent an important tool by which to dispel myth and create understanding.

Other interesting listings include the recordings released by the Pepsi-Cola Company, entitled "Adventures in Negro History." Many educational book publishers are developing series in Negro history. Also available are the works of a number of school districts, such as the syllabi of the Washington, D.C., and New York City school systems and the extensive works of the Oakland, California, schools.

The section on Negro slave revolts indicates that Negroes were not docile, childlike people. Like all other oppressed peoples in bondage, such as those under colonialism, they struggled for their independence and freedom, a reflection of motivation and desire basic in all men. Yet this piece of history, like others, has been systematically excluded from our history books, a censorship of omission which nurtured and sustained the myth and stereotype of a backward people, which eliminated the record of struggle and contribution, and thus, negating the human picture, rendered discrimination not only digestible but palatable.

For the first time in the history of our country, major consideration is being given in our public schools to teaching the history of Negro people in the United States of America. Too many responsible people, educators and lay leaders, are unaware of the abundant material covering the participation and contribution of Negro people to the development of our country over some 300 years, that is available (some of it for many years) on bookshelves and in publishers' warehouses.

Numerous studies indicate that there has been a virtual exclusion of this history from our textbooks—not only of the Negro people but of virtually all minority groups. The majority of our U.S. history textbooks have been written from an Anglo-Saxon point of view, and a great many of the problems that exist, particularly in race relations, have been created and have been promulgated not only by misinformation but, what is even worse, by no information at all: censorship by commission and omission. In an article in the *Saturday Review* (September 11, 1965), Elinor Sinette, District School Librarian for the Central and East Harlem Area of New York, is quoted as follows:

> Publishers have participated in a cultural lobotomy. It is no accident that Negro history and Negro identification have been forgotten. Our society has contrived to make the American Negro a rootless person. The Council for Intercultural Books for Children has been formed to relieve this situation.

Also indicative of this problem is a study that was made a few years ago for the Anti-Defamation League of B'nai B'rith, entitled "The Treatment of Minorities in Secondary School Textbooks." The summary of the findings of the Anti-Defamation League in its chapter "Textbook Treatment of American Negroes" states:

> The Negroes' position in contemporary American society continues to be very largely ignored. There is a tendency to treat racial inequality and attempts at its eradication with complacent generalizations, not hard facts. In most cases, the presentation of the 1954 Supreme Court decision on public school desegregation bypasses any consideration of the underlying principles and of the subsequent ongoing attempts at both compliance and evasion. The achievements of living Negro Americans are mentioned in only a small minority of books. Residential segregation by race is seldom discussed.

> Historically, American Negroes continue to be portrayed primarily as simple, childlike slaves and as uneducated, bewildered freedmen. Most textbooks do not chronicle the achievements of this people in the years from 1876 to the present. Where attention is given to outstanding Negroes in American history, the presentation is insufficient to counterbalance the previously created stereo-

type of a racially inferior group.

The scientific knowledge underlying sound understanding of the basic similarity and equality of the races of mankind is absent from the great majority of the textbooks.

With few exceptions, photographs and other illustrations in textbooks continue to portray America as an all-white nation, not as an interracial and increasingly integrated one.

Other general conclusions were:

A majority of the texts still present a largely white, Protestant, Anglo-Saxon view of history and of the current social scene. The nature and problems of minority groups in America are still very largely neglected.

Treatment of the Jews continues to suffer from an overemphasis on their ancient past and on the theme of persecution.

Nazi persecutions of minority groups are inadequately treated.

The Negro's position in contemporary American society is very largely ignored.

Immigrants to the continental United States receive considerable attention in American history and social-problems texts. A more sympathetic portrayal is generally accorded to the post-1880 immigrants from Southern and Eastern Europe than was reported in 1949. Similarly, the history of restrictive legislation is now seldom couched in terms that place an onus on the immigrant. But there is virtually no improvement in textbook treatment of the Asiatic immigrant, who is still shown, in most cases, as a strange, unassimilable outsider presenting a threat to the living standard of native Americans.

Little attention is paid to America's increasingly significant Spanish-speaking immigrant and migrant groups. Little is said in favor of these groups; in several cases, negative stereotypes are still presented. A few textbooks continue to refer to all groups of immigrants as outsiders, but more accounts now reflect the realization that the United States is made better by the richly diversified heritage of its pluralistic citizenry.

Lowell P. Beveridge, Jr., an architect by profession and educational director of the Brooklyn Association for the Study of Negro Life and History, also commented on this situation in an article entitled "Racist Poisons in School Books," which appeared in

Freedomways:

There is in the United States today a national conspiracy to in-
doctrinate our children with white supremacist propaganda. This
conspiracy operates quite openly; it is condoned by most parents'
organizations, officially approved by most school boards and in-
directly subsidized by federal, state, and local governments. It is
able to reach every school child in the country with its insidious,
chauvinist literature. I refer to the multi-million dollar textbook
publishing industry.

In particular, the social science and history books used in our
schools today are, with painfully few exceptions, primers in white
supremacy. We should not be surprised that the children of a
racist society are taught racism. The reasons for this have been
clearly summarized by author John O. Killens: "In order to
justify slavery and oppression in our times, the enslavers through
their propagandists have to create the illusion that the enslaved
people are subhuman and undeserving of human rights and sym-
pathies. The first job is to convince the outside world of the in-
herent inferiority of the victims of oppression. The second job is
to convince the citizens of the country where the enslavers hold
forth. And the third job, which is the cruelest of all, is to convince
the slaves themselves that they deserve to be the victims. This was
the task the propagandists for American slavery tackled with
alacrity and with great measure of success, the effects of which
remain with us even till today, almost a hundred years after the
Emancipation Proclamation.

Beveridge ends his article by saying:

As in so many other areas, the white south is the worst offender,
but the "liberal north" is also guilty. The campaign for honesty in
textbooks must be carried on in the north as well as the south on
every possible level: in local elections, in the school boards, in
parent and teacher organizations, in the universities, in the class-
rooms, in professional organizations and in trade unions. While
not detracting from the duty and necessity for people of African
descent to publish and teach the truth about their own heritage, it
is necessary to carry out a parallel campaign against those who
would perpetuate lies and distortions about this heritage. This is
basically a political problem.

Most of these books, pamphlets, and periodicals have not been
made readily available, nor have they been used on any large scale.
As a consequence, many of the stereotypes have continued to exist
in the minds of the people, and children are educated on the basis

of myth rather than fact. Therefore, important publications dealing with these subjects must be made available on a mass basis to as many people and groups as possible.

These materials should be made available on literature tables through community organizations. Certain local organizations should become repositories for books, pamphlets, periodicals, and other sources of information on Negro history, and should have them available for sale to any and all peoples or groups.

Packets of books and pamphlets on Negro history should be assembled to be given to public and parochial schools, libraries, churches, synagogues, YMCA's, YWCA's, Jewish community centers, Boys' Clubs, teachers or groups responsible for preparation of the curricula of schools, etc. An attempt should be made to have these packets subsidized and distributed by individuals and such organizations as local PTA's, women's clubs, Kiwanis, Rotary, Urban League, NAACP, B'nai B'rith, American Jewish Congress, National Conference of Christians and Jews, Conference on Religion and Race, American Jewish Committee, business concerns, cousins clubs, civic groups, churches and synagogues, and any other organizations interested in making a responsible contribution to the real education of the community. As much of this material as possible should get into the homes of both Negro and white families, as part of the family's own educational program on United States history.

Traveling portable exhibits can be developed on the theme of the Negro in America and made available and/or presented to schools, public forums, and all types of community and other organizations.

Out of all this can also develop essay contests in schools, churches, etc., on the theme of Negro history and/or the Negro contribution to the United States, with prizes awarded for the best essays.

Evening courses can be offered in the community, with perhaps five sessions on the history of the Negro people in the United States, utilizing prepared lectures and open to the public.

Small study groups can be established on neighborhood levels for study and discussion on Negro history and race problems, similar to those that have been set up in the past for the Great Books and World Politics. These discussion groups could also be a basis for the discussion of day-to-day problems in the field, and could develop into local groups for action and support on the neighborhood and community level.

book. I wish to extend my deepest appreciation to the Evanston–North Suburban Urban League. Some five years ago I was afforded an opportunity through this organization to develop a forum series and a literature sales apparatus on Negro history in the United States. This program was put into effect and later published in the *Negro History Bulletin* (February, March, April, 1962).

I am greatly indebted to all those writers of books and compilers of various types of bibliographies from which a great deal of this material has been drawn. Many of these references and sources are listed, and I apologize for any omissions.

My sincere appreciation is especially extended to John Hope Franklin, Langston Hughes, Arna Wendell Bontemps, Herbert Aptheker, and Ben Burns, who were kind enough to read the manuscript before publication and offered valuable criticism and comments. Also my sincere appreciation to my secretary, Mabel Carter, whose patience and cooperation helped make this possible. I take full responsibility for any errors or omissions.

E.A.S.

Part One: A Fact Book on the History of the Negro People in the United States

1. IMPORTANT DATES IN NEGRO HISTORY

I've known rivers:
I've known rivers ancient as the world and older than the
flow of human blood in human veins.
My soul has grown deep like the rivers.
I bathed in the Euphrates when dawns were young.
I built my hut near the Congo and it lulled me to sleep.
I looked upon the Nile and raised the pyramids above it.
I heard the singing of the Mississippi when Abe Lincoln went
down to New Orleans, and I've seen its muddy bosom turn
all golden in the sunset.
I've known rivers:
Ancient, dusky rivers.
My soul has grown deep like the rivers.

—Langston Hughes, "The Negro Speaks of Rivers"

Here is an attempt to provide a partial listing of important dates
in the history of the Negro people in the United States. These dates
clearly show the record of omission in our history books. The original
intent was not to list dates after World War I, since there are so many
day-to-day struggles occurring—each important, each significant, each
contributing. There are obviously many omissions of dates particularly
since the 1920's. It was with a great deal of hesitation that any dates
after World War I were listed, for virtually every day brings a record
of change and development.

1492 - Negroes with first explorers, such as Columbus, Balboa, Ponce
de Leon, Cortes, Pizarro, Menendez; Pedro Alonso Nino of
Columbus' crew identified as a Negro.
1526 - Negro slave revolt in first settlement in U.S. (now South
Carolina) to contain Negro slaves.

1538 - Estevanico credited with discovery of what is now Arizona and New Mexico.

1619 - Twenty Negroes land at Jamestown, Va., August 20.

1624 - William Tucker, first Negro child born in America, baptized at Jamestown.

1661 - Early Negro petition for Freedom to Colony of New Netherlands (later New York).

1663 - First serious slave conspiracy of Negro slaves and white indentured servants, September 13, Gloucester County, Va.; betrayed by house servant.

1688 - First formal protest against slavery made by Germantown Quakers, February 18.

1704 - School for Negro slaves opened in New York by Elias Neau, a Frenchman.

1709 - Joint conspiracy to revolt of Negro and Indian slaves uncovered and crushed in Virginia.

1712 - Slave revolt, New York, April 8; 21 slaves executed, six committed suicide.

1720 - Extensive slave revolt in area of Charleston, S.C.; many slaves banished, some hanged, others burned alive.

1730 - Suppression of three serious slave outbreaks in Virginia, South Carolina, and Louisiana.

1731 - November 9, birthday of Benjamin Banneker, inventor and one of planners of city of Washington.

1739 - Slave revolt, led by Cato, starts on a plantation at Stono, S.C.; approximately 30 whites killed as are many slaves; some escape to freedom.

1760 - February 14, Richard Allen, founder of African Methodist Movement and A.M.E. Church, born a slave in Philadelphia. Jupiter Hammon, Negro slave, one of first Negro poets, publishes *Salvation of Christ with Penitential Cries*, December 25.

1762 - James Derham, generally recognized as first Negro physician in America, born a slave in Philadelphia.

1770 - Five Americans killed on March 5 by British troops in Boston Massacre; first to fall is Crispus Attucks. Quakers, led by Anthony Benezet, open school for Negroes in Philadelphia, June 28.

1773-1779 - Massachusetts slaves petition legislature for freedom, January 6, 1773; record of at least eight petitions during this period.

1773 - Publication of Phillis Wheatley's book, *Poems on Various Subjects, Religious and Moral.* First Negro Baptist church organized at Silver Bluff, S.C.

1775 - First emancipationist society in United States organized in Philadelphia, April 14.

Negro and white minutemen fight at Lexington and Concord, April 19, and throughout Revolutionary War.

(For more detailed information on the Revolutionary War see section on The Negro in American Wars.)

1776 - Continental Congress approves enlistment of free Negroes, January 16.

In the original draft of the Declaration of Independence, Thomas Jefferson denounces slavery.

African Baptist church organized at Williamsburg, Va.

1777 - Vermont is first state to abolish slavery; in 1783, Massachusetts and New Hampshire; in 1780, Pennsylvania (gradual); in 1784, Connecticut and Rhode Island; in 1799, New York (gradual); in 1804, New Jersey.

1778 - Rhode Island authorizes enlistment of slaves.

1780 - February 10, seven Negroes of Dartmouth, Mass., including Paul Cuffe, petition against taxation without representation.

1785 - September 28, David Walker born free in Wilmington, N.C., author of *Appeal to the Coloured Citizens of the World, 1829.*

1787 - Richard Allen and Absalom Jones organize Philadelphia's Free African Society (April 12).

Continental Congress excludes slavery from Northwest Territory, July 13.

Prince Hall establishes first Negro Masonic lodge in America, African Lodge No. 459 (September 12).

Jupiter Hammon publishes *An Address to Negroes in the State of New York,* September 24. Exhorting Negroes to be faithful and obedient to their masters.

October 17, Negroes petition Massachusetts State Legislature for equal educational facilities.

First free school in New York City, the African Free School, opens November 1.

1790 - Jean Baptiste Point du Sable first permanent settler in Chicago.

1791 - Free Negroes of South Carolina protest to their state legislature against inequities before the law.

The Bill of Rights, first ten amendments to the Constitution, take effect December 15.

1792 - Joshua Bishop named pastor of First Baptist Church for whites, Portsmouth, Va.

1793 - Fugitive Slave Act passed.

1793-1794 - South Carolina free Negroes protest against state poll tax.

1794 - First African Church of St. Thomas in Philadelphia dedicated on July 17.

Richard Allen and followers organized the Bethel A.M.E. Church.

1796 - Zion Methodist Church organized in New York City.

Boston African Society established.

1797 - Earliest extant Negro petition to U.S. Congress, January 30; refused.

Sojourner Truth, first Negro woman anti-slavery lecturer and leading abolitionist; born a slave on estate in Hurley, N.Y.

1800 - Antislavery petition presented to Congress on behalf of free Negroes of Philadelphia, January 2.

John Brown born in Torrington, Conn., May 9.

October 2, Nat Turner, leader of major slave revolt, born a slave, Southampton County, Va.

Gabriel slave revolt. Gabriel Prosser, a slave, organizes several thousand slaves and makes plans to attack Richmond, Va., August 30; revolt is betrayed and Prosser is hanged with 15 of his followers, October 7.

1804 - July 24, birthday of Ira Aldridge, famous Shakespearian actor.

1805 - Death of Benjamin Banneker, October 9.

1808 - January 1, Federal law barring African slave trade goes into effect.

1810 - February 1, Charles Lenox Remond born in Salem, Mass., leading Negro abolitionist.

November 29, birthday of Robert Purvis, leading Negro abolitionist.

1811 - Slave revolt led by Charles Deslandes in Louisiana, approximately 35 miles from New Orleans, January 8-10; suppressed by U.S. troops.

1812 - May 6, birthday of Martin R. Delany, army officer and Civil War hero.

(War of 1812. For more detailed information see section on The Negro in American wars.)

1815 - December 23, Henry Highland Garnet, minister, abolitionist, and diplomat, born a slave in Kent County, Md.

1816 - Negro church achieves legal separation and independence; African Methodist Episcopal Church organized at Philadelphia convention.

Two major troop expeditions against large settlements of outlawed fugitive slaves, in South Carolina and at Fort Blount on Apalachicola Bay, Fla.

American Colonization Society organized to transport free Negroes to Africa.

1817 - Frederick Douglass born a slave at Tuckahoe, Talbot County, Md., in February. -

October 17, Samuel Ringgold Ward, minister and active abolitionist, born a slave, eastern shore of Maryland.

1818 - Andrew Jackson defeats force of Indians and Negroes at battle of Suwanee, ending First Seminole War which Jackson called "this savage and negro war," April 18.

Negroes form "Pennsylvania Augustine Society for the education of people of colour."

Negroes in Connecticut disfranchised.

1821 - A.M.E.Z. Church formally organized at New York City, June 21; James Varick first bishop.

Birth of William Still, leader in Underground Railroad.

1822 - Denmark Vesey, slave who had purchased his freedom and was a carpenter, carefully organizes one of the most elaborate slave revolts on record, involving thousands of Negroes in Charleston, S.C., and vicinity. Revolt betrayed; authorities arrest 131 Negroes and four whites; 37 hanged.

September 27, Hiram R. Revels, first Negro U.S. Senator, born free, Fayetteville, N.C.

1826 - John Russwurm, first Negro college graduate, receives degree at Bowdoin.

1827 - First Negro newspaper, *Freedom's Journal,* published in New York City, March 16.

Slavery abolished in New York State, July 4.

1829 - September 28, publication of *David Walker's Appeal to the Colored People of the World,* a radical anti-slavery pamphlet published in Boston by David Walker, a free Negro.

Publication of *The Ethiopian Manifesto, Issued in Defense of the Black Man's Rights in the Scale of Universal Freedom,* written and published by Robert Alexander Young, a free Negro, in New York City.

Race riot, Cincinnati, Ohio, August 10; more than 1,000 Negroes leave the city for Canada.

1830 - April 6, birthday of James Augustine Healy, first Negro Roman Catholic Bishop in America.

First National Negro Convention, chaired by Richard Allen, meets at Philadelphia's Bethel Church, September 20.

1831 - Nat Turner leads largest Negro slave revolt, Southampton County, Va., August 21-22. Some 60 whites killed; Nat Turner captured October 30, hanged in Jerusalem, Va., November 11.

June 6-11, first annual Negro Convention held in Philadelphia.

1833 - Negro library founded in Philadelphia.

April 10, London acclaims Ira Aldridge in "Othello."

American Anti-Slavery Society organized in Philadelphia by Negro and white abolitionists, December 4.

1837 - Negro newspaper, *Weekly Advocate,* established in New York.

May 10, birthday of P. B. S. Pinchback, elected to U.S. Senate, 1873.

1838 - March 14, mass meeting of Negroes in Philadelphia to protest disfranchisement of Negroes in Pennsylvania.

First Negro magazine, *Mirror of Liberty,* published in New York City by David Ruggles.

Charles Lenox Remond is first Negro lecturer employed by an anti-slavery society.

1839 - April 5, birth of Robert Smalls at Beaufort, S.C., Civil War hero and U.S. congressman.

June 13, *Slavery as It Is* published by Theodore Weld.

The ship *Amistad* is brought into Montauk, L. I., by African slaves who, on the seas, had revolted against their captors. Rebels are freed by U.S. Supreme Court.

Liberty party, first anti-slavery political party, organized at convention in Warsaw, N.Y., November 13; two Negro abolitionists, Samuel Ringgold Ward and Henry Highland Garnet, are among earliest supporters of the new political party.

1840 - World Anti-Slavery Conference, London.

August 18-20, New York State Convention of Negroes in Albany.

1841 - March 1, Blanche Kelso Bruce, U.S. Senator, born a slave in Prince Edward County, Va.

August 23-25, Pennyvania State Convention of Negroes, Pittsburgh.

November 7, slave revolt on slave trader *Creole,* en route from Hampton, Va., to New Orleans; slaves overpower crew and sail vessel to Bahamas where they are granted asylum and freedom.

1842 - August 11, birth of Robert Brown Elliott, U.S. Congressman.

1843 - August 22, National Convention of Colored Men in Buffalo, N.Y.; Henry Highland Garnet calls for a slave revolt and a general strike.

August 30, Negroes Henry Highland Garnet, Samuel W. Ward, and Charles B. Ray participate in national political gathering for the first time at meeting of Liberty party convention in Buffalo, N.Y.

October 23-27, first state convention of the Negroes of Michigan held in Detroit.

1844 - June 24, Boston Negroes hold series of mass meetings protesting Jim Crow schools.

1845 - May 3, first Negro formally admitted to bar; Macon B. Allen passes examination at Worcester, Mass.

Negroes of New England form "Freedom Association" to carry on work of assisting fugitive slaves.

1846 - January 16, convention of New England workingmen at Lynn, Mass., adopts resolution against Negro slavery.

1847 - Dred Scott files suit for his freedom in Circuit Court in St. Louis, Mo.

December 3, Frederick Douglass publishes first issue of news-paper, the *North Star*.

Liberia declared an independent republic, July 26.

1848 - July 20, world's first Women's Rights Convention held; women's rights and anti-slavery causes linked.

August 9-10, Free Soil party organized at Buffalo, N.Y.; convention attended by several Negro abolitionists.

1849 - Harriet Tubman, famous "conductor" on Underground Railroad, escapes from slavery in Maryland.

Ellen and William Craft escape from Georgia—one of the most dramatic escapes in history of the Underground Railroad.

January 10-13, Ohio State Convention of Negroes held in Columbus.

New Jersey State Convention of Negroes.

September 12-13, Connecticut State Convention of Negroes held in New Haven.

Wisconsin disfranchises its Negro residents.

First school integration suit filed in Boston by Benjamin Roberts; Massachusetts Supreme Court rejects case and establishes "separate but equal" precedent.

1850 - William Still starts Underground Railroad passenger record, August 2.

Harriet Tubman makes first Underground Railroad trip. During 30 years before Civil War it is estimated that about 75,000 slaves escape to freedom.

September 18, strong fugitive-slave bill passed, requiring all people to become slave-catchers; mass resistance throughout the nation.

October 21, Chicago City Council announces its refusal to enforce the federal fugitive-slave law.

1851 - Sojourner Truth attends Women's Rights Convention, May 28.

Negroes disperse group of slave-catchers in Christiana, Pa., September 11.

Negro and white abolitionists smash into courtroom in Syracuse, N.Y., and rescue a fugitive slave, October 1.

Abolitionist William C. Nell publishes *Services of Colored Americans in the Wars of 1776 and 1812*, the first extended work on the history of the American Negro.

1852 - March 20, *Uncle Tom's Cabin*, Mrs. Harriet Beecher Stowe's anti-slavery novel, is published; a story of the Underground Railroad, it helps arouse anti-slavery sentiment the world over.

The Condition, Elevation, Emancipation and Destiny of the

Colored People of the U.S., Politically Considered, written and published by Martin R. Delany.

Frederick Douglass' famous 4th of July speech in Rochester, N.Y., raising the question of why the Negro people should celebrate this holiday.

1853 - William Wells Brown publishes *Clotel,* the first novel by an American Negro.

May 31, first Negro YMCA organized in Washington, D.C., by Anthony Bower.

July 6-8, National Negro Convention in Rochester, N.Y., one of the most representative of pre-Civil War National Negro Conventions.

August 1, Negroes petition Massachusetts Constitutional Convention for right to join state militia. (From end of War of 1812 to middle years of Civil War, the Army of the United States banned Negroes as soldiers.)

General Convention for the Improvement of the Colored Inhabitants of Canada, Amherstburgh, C.W.

1854 - January 1, first Negro college, Lincoln University, founded as Ashmum Institute in Chester County, Pa.

Anthony Burns, famous fugitive slave, arrested by U.S. deputy marshal in Boston, but mobs attack the federal courthouse in an attempt to free him; 2,000 U.S. troops needed to return him to his master; people so aroused that no fugitive slave is ever again returned from Massachusetts.

June 10, James Augustine Healy, first American Negro Roman Catholic bishop, ordained a priest in Notre Dame Cathedral, Paris.

August 24, John V. DeGrasse admitted to Massachusetts Medical Society.

August 24-26, a Negro Emancipation Convention held in Cleveland, Ohio.

1855 - John Mercer Langston is first Negro to win an elective office—clerk of Brownhelm Township, Lorain County, Ohio.

Boston's Jim Crow schooling ended.

November 20-22, first California Negro Convention in Sacramento.

1856 - April 5, Booker Taliaferro Washington, famous educator and Negro leader, born a slave in Franklin County, Va.

August 30, Methodist Episcopal Church founds Wilberforce University.

1857 - Dred Scott decision by the U.S. Supreme Court, upholding the Fugitive Slave Law, and the idea that Negroes could never become citizens.

1858 - Charles Waddell Chesnutt, outstanding novelist, educator, and attorney, born June 20.

The Oberlin-Wellington Rescue Case: Negro fugitive John Price is seized by slave-catchers but rescued by students and a professor of Oberlin College, Ohio; Price sent safely to Canada.

The Escape, first play by an American Negro, published by William Wells Brown.

1859 - The last slave ship, the *Clothilde,* lands shipment of slaves at Mobile Bay, Ala.

Arkansas legislature requires free Negroes to choose between exile and enslavement.

Henry Ossawa Tanner, renowned artist, born June 21.

August 1-2, New England Colored Citizens' Convention held in Boston.

John Brown, with 21 followers including five Negroes, attacks arsenal at Harpers Ferry, Va., October 16; John Brown and Negroes—Shields Green, Dangerfield Newby, Sherrard Lewis Leary, and John A. Copeland—his co-conspirators, executed at Charlestown, Va., December 2. Osborne P. Anderson escapes to serve later with distinction in the Civil War.

1860 - New York Negroes appeal for equal suffrage rights.

1861 - September 17, predecessor to Hampton Institute established at Fortress Monroe, Va.

September 25, Secretary of Navy authorizes enlistment of Negro slaves.

1862 - Robert Smalls (born April 5, 1839), Civil War hero and Reconstruction congressman from South Carolina; while a seaman on converted Confederate gunboat, escapes with other Negro crew members to Union jurisdiction and turns the ship, a prize of war, over to Union forces.

April 10, Congress declares that U.S. should cooperate with any state that adopts gradual abolition, by paying for the slaves.

April 16, estimated 3,100 slaves freed in District of Columbia.

July 16, birthday of Ida B. Wells-Barnett, Negro leader who edited newspapers in Memphis and Chicago and initiated anti-lynching campaign of the 1890's.

July 17, Congress authorizes President Lincoln to accept Negroes for military service; first Negro Civil War regiment, First South Carolina Volunteers, made up chiefly of ex-slaves.

August 25, Secretary of War authorizes General Rufus Saxton to arm up to 5,000 slaves.

September 27, First Louisiana Native Guards, first Negro regiment to receive official recognition, mustered into Army; regiment composed of free Negroes of New Orleans.

1863 - President Lincoln signs Emancipation Proclamation, January 1. January 26, War Department authorizes Massachusetts governor to recruit Negro troops; Fifty-fourth Massachusetts Volunteers, first Negro regiment raised in North, included two sons of Frederick Douglass.

May 22, War Department establishes Bureau of Colored Troops. William H. Carney, Negro sergeant, wins Congressional Medal of Honor.

Mary Church Terrell, women's leader, born September 23.

1864 - Congress passes bill equalizing pay, arms, equipment, and medical services for Negro troops.

Negro sergeant Decatur Dorsey wins Congressional Medal of Honor.

August 5, John Lawson, Negro gunner on flagship of Admiral David Farragut in Battle of Mobile Bay, wins Congressional Medal of Honor.

September 29-30, 13 Negroes win Congressional Medals of Honor in series of battles around Chaffin's Farm in suburb of Richmond.

Negro sailor Joachim Pease wins Congressional Medal of Honor, June 19.

October 4, *New Orleans Tribune,* first Negro daily newspaper, begins publication in French and English.

December 3, largest all-Negro unit in history of U.S. Army, Twenty-fifth Corps, was established in Army of the James.

December 15-16, In one of the decisive battles of war, two brigades of Negro troops help crush one of the South's finest armies at the battle of Nashville.

(For more detailed information on Civil War see section on The Negro in American Wars.)

1865 - January 17, General Lee says it is "not only expedient but necessary" that Confederate Army use Negro slaves as soldiers.

January 31, Congress passes the Thirteenth Amendment which, on ratification, abolishes slavery in America.

February 1, John S. Rock becomes first Negro admitted to practice before the U.S. Supreme Court.

February 12, Henry Highland Garnet, first Negro to preach in the Capitol, delivers sermon on abolition of slavery.

October 19-21, first annual meeting of the National Equal Rights League in Cleveland, Ohio.

March 3, Congress establishes Freedmen's Bureau to aid refugees and freedmen.

Freedmen's Savings and Trust Company, first bank for Negroes, chartered by U.S. government.

March 13, Jefferson Davis signs bill authorizing use of Negro slaves as soldiers in Confederate Army.

Negroes in Norfolk, Va., hold mass meeting and demand equal rights and ballots, May 11. Other equal rights mass meetings held by Negroes in Petersburg, Va., June 6; Vicksburg, Miss., June 19; Nashville, Tenn., August 7-11; Raleigh, N.C., September 29-October3; Richmond, Va., September 18; Jackson, Miss., October 7; Charleston, S.C., November 20-25.

July 26, Patrick Francis Healy, first U.S. Negro to win Ph.D. degree, passes final exams at Louvain, Belgium.

Tennessee State Convention of Negroes, Nashville, August 7, submits to U.S. Senate a petition protesting the seating in Congress of the delegates from Tennessee until the state legislature secures the rights of the Negro as freemen.

Shaw University founded, Raleigh, N.C.

1866 - First Negroes elected to an American legislative assembly— Edwin G. Walker, son of abolitionist David Walker, and Charles L. Mitchell elected to Massachusetts House of Representatives.

January 9, Fisk University opens in Nashville, Tenn.

April 9, Civil Rights Bill passed over presidential veto.

August 8, birthday of Matthew Henson, only man to accompany Admiral Robert E. Peary on all of his polar expeditions; co-discoverer of North Pole.

December 2, birthday of Henry T. Burleigh, singer and arranger of Negro spirituals.

Illinois State Convention of Colored Men held in Galesburg.

1867 - January 8, bill giving suffrage to Negroes in District of Columbia passed over President Johnson's veto.

February 7, Negro delegation, led by Frederick Douglass, calls on President Johnson to urge ballots for ex-slaves.

February 14, Augusta Institute, later Morehouse College, opens in Atlanta, Ga.

Talladega College opens in Talladega, Ala.

Atlanta University opens in Atlanta, Ga.

Congress passes First Reconstruction Act, inaugurating an era of democracy and equal rights for Negro and white in the South which lasts about a decade.

May 1, Howard University chartered by act of Congress.

1868 - January 14, South Carolina Constitutional Convention meets in Charleston; first assembly of its kind in the West with a majority of Negro delegates (76 of 124).

February 23, birthday of William Edward Burghardt Du Bois, famous scholar and Negro leader, born in Great Barrington, Mass.

Hampton Institute opens in Hampton, Va.

June 13, Oscar J. Dunn, an ex-slave, formally installed as lieutenant governor of Louisiana, the highest elective office held by an American Negro.

July 6, first General Assembly of South Carolina Reconstruction government meets at Janney's Hall, Columbia. Eighty-four of 157 legislators are Negroes.

July 28, Fourteenth Amendment becomes part of Constitution, making the Negro a citizen.

1869 - April 16, Ebenezer Don Carlos Bassett becomes minister to Haiti; first Negro to receive an appointment in diplomatic service.

May 3, Isaac Myers, early Negro labor leader, addresses Fourth Congress of National Labor Union.

December 6, first National Negro Labor Convention meets in Washington, D.C., and creates Colored National Labor Union.

New York Negro State Convention held in Utica.

1870 - February 2, Jonathan Jasper Wright becomes associate justice of South Carolina Supreme Court.

February 25, Hiram R. Revels, first Negro in U.S. Senate, takes oath of office.

Founding of National Medical Society of the District of Columbia (antecedent of oldest Negro medical society, Medico-Chirurgical Society) in protest against Jim Crow practices of medical society of the District.

Convention of the Negroes of Indian Territory (later Oklahoma).

March 30, Fifteenth Amendment becomes part of Constitution; bars voting discrimination on "basis of race, color, or previous condition of servitude."

July 1, James W. Smith of South Carolina enters West Point. Smith, first Negro student, did not graduate; he was separated June 26, 1874.

December 12, Joseph H. Rainey, first Negro in House of Representatives, sworn in as congressman from South Carolina.

December 16, Negro Methodist Episcopal Church organized in Jackson, Tenn.

January 13, *The New Era* newspaper founded; edited by J. Sella Martin; Frederick Douglass, corresponding editor.

Robert H. Wood elected mayor of Natchez, Miss.

Jefferson Franklin Long elected to Congress from Georgia.

1871 - June 17, birth of James Weldon Johnson, poet, composer, and lawyer.

October 6, Fisk Jubilee Singers begin first tour.

1872 - Charlotte E. Ray, first Negro woman lawyer, graduates from Howard University Law School, February 27; she is admitted to practice April 23.

June 27, Paul Laurence Dunbar, famous poet, born in Dayton, Ohio.

September 21, John Henry Conyers of South Carolina, first Negro to enter Annapolis; later resigned.

December 11, P. B. S. Pinchback becomes acting governor of Louisiana upon the impeachment of the governor.

1873 - January 15, P. B. S. Pinchback elected to U.S. Senate.

April 13, Colfax Massacre, Easter Sunday morning, Grant Paris, La.; more than 60 Negroes killed.

August 11, birthday of J. Rosamund Johnson, composer of Negro national anthem, "Lift Every Voice."

October 7, Henry E. Hayne accepted as student at University of South Carolina.

November 16, William C. Handy born in Florence, Ala.; Negro composer, arranger, "Father of the Blues."

Richard T. Greener, first Negro graduate of Harvard University, named professor of metaphysics at University of South Carolina.

Richard Harvey Cain elected to Congress from South Carolina.

A. K. Davis elected lieutenant governor of Mississippi.

1874 - July 31, Patrick Francis Healy, S.J., Ph.D., inaugurated president of Georgetown University, oldest Catholic university in America.

August 26, 16 Negroes taken from jail in Tennessee by hooded men and shot.

August 30, Coushatta Massacre, Coushatta, La.; several Negroes and Republican office-holders slain; governor declares martial law.

December 7, race riot, Vicksburg, Miss.; 35 Negroes killed.

December 21, President issues proclamation on violence in Mississippi.

1875 - March 1, Civil Rights Law, prohibiting discrimination in hotels, theatres, and on public carriers, signed by President Grant.

March 5, Blanche Kelso Bruce, U.S. Senator from Mississippi, becomes member of the Senate, the only Negro to serve full term in Senate.

June 2, James A. Healy, first Negro Roman Catholic bishop in America, consecrated in Cathedral at Portland, Me.

July 10, Mary McLeod Bethune, educator and founder of Bethune-Cookman College, born in Mayesville, S.C.

September 1, race conflict at Yazoo City, Miss.; ten to 20 Negroes killed.

September 4, race conflict, Clinton, Miss.; 20 to 80 Negro leaders and Negro Republicans killed.

September 8, Mississippi governor requests federal troops to protect rights of Negro voters; request refused.

November 2, conservatives win Mississippi election. ("The Mississippi Plan"—staged riots, political assassinations and massacres, and social and economic intimidation—was later used to overthrow Reconstruction governments in South Carolina and Louisiana.)

First convention of Negro newspapermen; representatives present from *Lexington* (Ky.) *American Citizen, Memphis Planet, San Francisco Elevator, New Orleans Louisianian, Carroll Parish* (La.) *True Republican, Baton Rouge Grand Era, Los Angeles Pacific Appeal, Galveston Spectator, Concordia* (La.) *Eagle, Philadelphia Christian Recorder, Cincinnati Colored Citizen, New York Progressive American,* and *Terre Bonne* (La.) *Republican.*

1876 - Senate, after three years of debate and controversy, declines to seat P. B. S. Pinchback by vote of 32 to 29, March 8.

Edward A. Bouchet receives Ph.D. degree in physics at Yale University, the first Negro awarded Ph.D. by an American university.

1877 - June 15, Henry O. Flipper graduated from West Point, the first Negro graduate.

1879 - Exodus of some 50,000 Negroes to the North.

Convention of Louisiana Negroes in New Orleans discusses the migrations.

May 6-9, National Conference of Colored Men of the United States, Nashville, Tenn.

Los Angeles Eagle (newspaper) founded; oldest Negro newspaper in U.S.

1880 - Allen University founded. Columbia, S.C.

1881 - May 17, Frederick Douglass appointed Recorder of Deeds for District of Columbia.

May 19, Blanche Kelso Bruce appointed Register of Treasury by President Garfield.

July 4, Booker T. Washington opens Tuskegee Institute.

Tennessee begins modern segregation movement with Jim Crow railroad car law; Florida follows in 1887; Mississippi, 1888; Texas, 1889; Louisiana, 1890; Alabama, Kentucky, Arkansas, Georgia, 1891; South Carolina, 1898; North Carolina, 1899; Virginia, 1900; Maryland, 1904; Oklahoma, 1907.

1882 - Birthday of R. Nathaniel Dett, American Negro composer.

Lane College, founded in Jackson, Tenn.

April 27-28, Convention of Colored Men held in Parsons, Kans.; requests distribution of public lands in Oklahoma to Negro people.

1883 - March 20, Jan Matzeliger obtains a patent on a "lasting machine," considered to have made the manufacture of shoes by machine possible.

July 10-12, state convention of Colored Men of Texas held in Austin.

September 24, National Convention of Colored Men held in Louisville, Ky.

November 26, death of Sojourner Truth, Battle Creek, Mich.

Spellman College organized in Atlanta, Ga.

1884 - June 3, John Roy Lynch, former Congressman, elected temporary chairman of Republican convention, first Negro to preside over deliberations of national political party.

August 9, death of Robert Brown Elliott, Congressman, in New Orleans.

1885 - *New York Age* (newspaper) founded.

1886 - March 17, Carrollton Massacre, Carrollton, Miss.; 20 Negroes killed.

April 24, Augustus Tolton, first American Negro priest ordained in Rome.

North Carolina (Negro) State Teachers' Association raises demands for Negro higher education, federal support of education, and establishment of uniform requirements and salaries for Negro and white teachers.

Livingstone College, Salisbury, N.C., founded.

1887 - June 3, birthday of Roland Hayes, Negro concert artist.

1889 - April 15, A. Philip Randolph, labor leader and founder of Sleeping Car Porters' Union, born, Crescent City, Fla.

Graduation of Charles Young from West Point. At start of World War I highest ranking Negro officer.

1890 - January 15-17, Afro-American National League founded to combat all forms of attack and discrimination and to establish organization and governmental unit to assist in the advancement of the Negro; leading organization of its day; program foreshadowed the NAACP.

Mississippi Constitutional Convention begins systematic exclusion of Negroes from political life of South, August 12-November 1. (Mississippi literacy and "understanding" tests later adopted with embellishments by other states: South Carolina, 1895; Louisiana, 1898; North Carolina, 1900; Alabama, 1901; Virginia, 1901; Georgia, 1908; Oklahoma, 1910.)

1891 - January 23, Chicago's Provident Hospital incorporated with first training school for Negro nurses.

Colored Farmers' Alliance has organizations in 20 states and nearly 1,250,000 members.

1892 - August 13, first issue of Baltimore Afro-American newspaper.

First annual Tuskegee Negro Conference.

1893 - July 1, Walter White, executive secretary of NAACP, born in Atlanta, Ga.

July 9, Dr. Daniel Hale Williams performs "world's first successful heart operation" at Chicago's Provident Hospital.

1895 - February 20, death of Frederick Douglass, Anacostia Heights, D.C.

February 21, North Carolina legislature, primarily Negro Republicans and white Populists, adjourns to mark the death of Frederick Douglass.

May 11, birthday of William Grant Still, American Negro composer.

June 10, I.B.P.O. Elks of the World organized.

July 29, first National Conference of Colored Women held in Boston, leading to founding of National Association of Colored Women, oldest women's organization still in existence.

September 18, Booker T. Washington delivers "Atlanta Compromise" address at Cotton Exposition in Atlanta, Ga.

September 28, National Baptist Convention organized.

1896 - *Plessy vs. Ferguson* decision by the U. S. Supreme Court upholds doctrine of "separate but equal" as it relates to civil rights of American Negroes.

National League of Colored Women and National Federation of Colored Women combines to form National Association of Colored Women. (In 1900 it affiliated with the National Council of Women of the United States.)

1896-1907 - Atlanta Conferences for the Study of the Negro Problem.

1898 - March 17, death of Blanche Kelso Bruce, Washington, D.C.

April 9, birth of Paul Robeson, singer, actor, and leader in fight for Negro equality.

June 24, American troops, including Tenth Cavalry, drives Spanish forces from entrenched positions at La Guasimas, Cuba.

Tenth Cavalry makes famous charge at El Caney and relieves Theodore Roosevelt's Rough Riders, July 1. Four Negro regiments in regular Army are conspicuous in fighting around Santiago in Spanish-American War; 16 regiments of Negro volunteers also raised during the war.

Reign of terror directed against Negroes and white radicals in and around Phoenix, S.C.

November 10, race riot, Wilmington, N.C., eight Negroes killed.

Bob Cole's "A Trip to Coontown," first musical comedy written by a Negro for Negro talent, produced.

1899 - March 15, eight Negroes massacred in Palmetto, Ga.

April 4, birth of composer and orchestra leader Edward Kennedy

("Duke") Ellington, Washington, D.C.

1900 - July 4, Louis Armstrong, famous jazz musician, born in New Orleans.

July 24-27, race riot, New Orleans; several persons injured, Negro school and 30 Negro homes burned.

August 5, death of James Augustine Healy, Negro Roman Catholic bishop, Portland, Me.

August 23-24, National Negro Business League organized in Boston.

8,800,000 Negroes in U.S., of whom all but 900,000 are in the South; 1910, total number 9,800,000 — outside the South, 1,000,000.

1901 - January 16, death of Hiram R. Revels.

March 4, term of George H. White, last of post-Reconstruction congressmen, ended.

October 16, Booker T. Washington dines at White House with President Roosevelt, who is criticized in the South.

1903 - April 27, Supreme Court decision upholds clauses in Alabama constitution which disfranchise Negroes.

Publication of W. E. B. Du Bois' *The Souls of Black Folk* crystallizes opposition to Booker T. Washington's program of social and political subordination.

Countee Cullen, famous poet, born.

1904 - Formation of the National Liberty Party, an all-Negro national political organization.

1905 - July 11-13, group of militant Negro intellectuals, opposing appeasement policies of Booker T. Washington, organized Niagara Movement, forerunner of NAACP, at meeting near Niagara Falls; delegates from 14 states, led by W. E. B. Du Bois, William Monroe Trotter, J. Max Barber, John Hope, and others, demand abolition of all distinctions based on race.

November 29, *Chicago Defender* begins publication; now one of the largest Negro papers in U.S.

1906 - February 9, death of Paul Laurence Dunbar.

February 13-14, Georgia Equal Rights Convention held in Macon; 500 local delegates attend.

August 13, group of Negro soldiers raid Brownsville, Tex., in retaliation for racial insults; one white man killed, two wounded; President Roosevelt orders discharge of three companies of 25th Regiment.

September 22-24, race riot, Atlanta, Ga.; ten Negroes and two whites killed, martial law proclaimed.

1908 - August 14-19, race riot, Springfield, Ill.; troops called out; riot led to founding of NAACP.

August 25, National Association of Colored Graduate Nurses, first professional organization of Negro women, founded.

December 26, Jack Johnson defeats Tommy Burns at Sydney, Australia, to become first Negro heavyweight boxing champion.

Twenty-five bishops of A.M.E., A.M.E. Zion and Colored Methodist Episcopal churches conferred in Washington D.C., issued "An Address to the American People."

1909 - February 12, founding of NAACP on 100th anniversary of Lincoln's birthday.

April 6, Matthew Henson, Negro explorer with Commander Robert E. Peary, places U.S. flag on North Pole; Henson is first to reach the pole.

1913 - March 10, death of Harriet Tubman, leader in Underground Railroad and woman suffrage movement.

1915 - Death of Booker T. Washington, November 14.

Association for the Study of Negro Life and History founded by Dr. Carter G. Woodson.

1916 - Initial publication of the *Journal of Negro History* by Dr. Carter G. Woodson.

1917 - July 1-3 race riot, East St. Louis, Ill. Many Negroes killed.

July 28, New York City, 10,000 Negroes paraded in protest against lynchings and discrimination.

August 23, Houston, Tex., race riots between soldiers of 24th Infantry Regiment and white citizens.

(For detailed information on First World War see section on The Negro in American Wars.)

1919 - First Pan-African Congress, organized by W. E. B. Du Bois, meets at Grand Hotel, Paris, France, February 19-21.

November 6, Supreme Court decision strikes down Louisville ordinance requiring Negroes and whites to live on separate blocks.

National Urban League founded.

Twenty-six race riots occur during the summer of this year. Scenes of racial violence occur in the states of Texas and Arkansas, and the cities of Chicago and Washington, D.C.

1920 - August 1, Marcus Garvey's black nationalist movement, Universal Improvement Association, holds national convention in Liberty Hall, Harlem.

The play, *Emperor Jones,* opens at the Provincetown Theater with Charles Gilpin in the title role.

1921 - The first Doctor of Philosophy degrees for Negro women awarded to Eva B. Dykes, English, Radcliffe; Sadie T. Mossell, Economics, U. of Pennsylvania; Georgiana R. Simpson, German, U. of Chicago.

1922 - Death of Colonel Charles R. Young, West Point graduate and highest-ranking Negro officer at time of World War I.
Death of Bert Williams, famous Negro performer.
1923 - Negro migration from South numbers almost 500,000.
1925 - Clarence Darrow successfully defends Ossian Sweet, Detroit doctor, against murder charges when white mob rioted in front of Sweet home in an all-white area.
1926 - Negro History Week initiated by Dr. Carter G. Woodson and other leaders of the Association for the Study of Negro Life and History.
1927 - *Nixon vs. Herndon,* Supreme Court decision, strikes down white primaries.
1929 - January 15, birth of Martin Luther King, Jr., president of Southern Christian Leadership Conference.
Oscar DePriest enters Congress as first Negro Representative since 1901.
1930 - Death of Negro actor Charles Gilpin.
1931 - Scottsboro Trials begin. Nine Negro youths framed on charges of "rape"; their defense becomes of national and international interest, and the boys are eventually freed.
1933 - NAACP initiates court attacks on segregation and discrimination in education; first suit filed against U. of North Carolina on behalf of Thomas Hocutt.
Angelo Herndon sentenced to 20 years for organizing Negro and white workers in Atlanta.
1934 - Arthur Mitchell elected to U.S. Congress as the first Negro Democratic Congressman.
1935 - Langston Hughes' play *The Mulatto,* begins Broadway run.
1936 - Olympic champion Jesse Owens wins four gold medals in Berlin.
Gibbs vs. Board of Education suit to equalize salaries in Montgomery County, Md., is first in series of suits between Negro and white teachers.
1937 - First Negro federal judge, William H. Hastie, appointed judge of Federal District Court in the Virgin Islands.
Joe Louis wins heavyweight championship, defeating J. J. Braddock.
Death of Bessie Smith, famous blues singer.
1938 - Death of Joe (King) Oliver, pioneer Negro jazz star.
Crystal Bird Fauset, first Negro woman state legislator, elected to Pennsylvania House of Representatives.
Joe Louis knocks out heavyweight champion Max Schmeling, June 22.
1939 - April 9, the famed contralto Marian Anderson, denied the use of Constitution Hall by the Daughters of the American Revolu-

tion, sings to 75,000 at an Easter concert at the Lincoln Memorial in Washington.

Jane M. Bolin, first Negro woman judge, appointed to New York City Court of Domestic Relations.

1940 - *Native Son* by Richard Wright published.

Virginia legislature chooses "Carry Me Back to Ole Virginny," written by Negro composer James A. Bland, as State Song of Virginia.

Death of Marcus Garvey, leader of Black Nationalist Movement.

Benjamin O. Davis, Sr., promoted to brigadier general; first Negro general in U.S. history.

1941 - Dr. Charles R. Drew, developer of blood plasma, directs blood donor stations for armed forces.

Dr. Robert Weaver appointed director of government office in charge of integrating Negroes into the national defense program.

Supreme Court rules in case brought by Congressman Arthur Mitchell that separate facilities in railroad cars must be substantially equal.

A. Philip Randolph and other Negro leaders threaten a march of 100,000 Negroes on Washington, D.C., protesting racial discrimination in all government and civil defense programs.

President Franklin D. Roosevelt, on June 25, issues Executive Order No. 8802 establishing Fair Employment Practices Commission to prohibit discrimination in defense industries because of race, color, creed, or national origin.

Dorie Miller, messman aboard *USS Arizona,* shoots down four enemy planes during Pearl Harbor attack; he later received the Navy Cross.

Adam Clayton Powell, Jr., elected first Negro Councilman in New York City.

(For detailed information on Second World War see section on The Negro in American Wars.)

1942 - February 28, anti-Negro riots in Detroit.

Negro seaman admitted to Naval Reserve.

Bernard W. Robinson commissioned first Negro ensign in the U.S. Navy.

Launching of *Booker T. Washington* at Wilmington, Delaware, September 29; the ship was commanded by Hugh Mulzac, a Negro captain.

Chicagoan William L. Dawson elected to Congress.

1943 - Death of George Washington Carver, leading scientist, January 5.

Porgy and Bess opens on Broadway with Anne Brown and Todd Duncan.

William H. Hastie, civilian aide to Secretary of War, resigns in protest against Army's policy of segregation and discrimination.

Congress of Racial Equality (CORE) organized.

99th Pursuit Squadron flies first combat mission; the Negro fliers attack Pantelleria in the Mediterranean, June 2.

Series of serious race riots in Los Angeles, Detroit, Harlem, and Beaumont, Tex.

Theater Guild presents *Othello* at Shubert Theater with Paul Robeson in title role, October 19; production ran for 296 performances, set record for Shakespearean drama on Broadway.

Benjamin J. Davis, Jr., member of National Committee of Communist party, elected to New York City Council; re-elected in 1945.

Death of Fats Waller, leading jazz musician, December 15.

1944 - Adam Clayton Powell, Jr., elected to Congress; first Negro from the East ever elected.

Supreme Court bans white primaries.

War Department abolishes segregation in Army posts.

1945 - New York state FEPC law signed.

Irvin C. Mollison becomes U.S. Customs Court Judge in New York City, November 3.

Georgia repeals poll tax.

1946 - Death of Countee Cullen, poet, January 9.

William H. Hastie named governor of Virgin Islands.

Race riots in Columbia, Tenn., Athens, Ala., and Philadelphia result in many injuries.

Segregated interstate bus travel banned by Supreme Court, June 3.

Committee on Civil Rights organized by President Truman's executive order, December 9.

1947 - According to the conservative figures of the Tuskegee Institute, 3,426 Negroes were lynched in the U.S. from 1882 through 1947. Of this total 36 per cent, or 1,217, were lynched from 1890 to 1900. These figures are taken from *We Charge Genocide*.

Jackie Robinson, first Negro in organized baseball, signs with Brooklyn Dodgers, April 10, plays first game April 11.

Archbishop Joseph E. Ritter threatens excommunication of St. Louis Catholics who continued to protest integration of parochial schools.

NAACP petition on racial injustices in America, "An Appeal to the World," presented to United Nations, October 23.

1948 - Mrs. Rosa Lee Ingram, Negro mother of twelve children, sentenced to die in the electric chair for having defended herself against the advances of a white man; sentence later changed to life imprisonment.

Supreme Court *(Shelley v. Kraemer)* rules that federal and state courts may not enforce restrictive covenants, May 3.

Death of Claude McKay, poet, May 22.

President Truman issues Executive Order No. 9981 establishing as a policy for the armed forces "equality of treatment and opportunity for all persons, without regard to race, color or national origin," July 26.

Herman Sweatt applies to University of Texas Law School.

California Supreme Court holds that state statute banning racial intermarriage violates Constitution.

Ralph J. Bunche named as Acting U.N. Mediator in Palestine, September 18.

1949 - Congressman William L. Dawson becomes first Negro to head a congressional committee; he was appointed chairman of House Committee on Government Operations.

Wesley A. Brown, first Negro graduate from Annapolis Naval Academy.

William Hastie nominated for U.S. Circuit Court of Appeals.

Death of Bill Robinson, dancer, November 25.

1950 - Death of Charles R. Drew, developer of blood plasma, April 1.

Death of Carter G. Woodson, founder of Association for the Study of Negro Life and History, April 3.

Death of Charles H. Houston, one of the greatest constitutional lawyers, April 22.

Gwendolyn Brooks, Chicago poet, awarded Pulitzer Prize for poetry; only Negro so honored.

Attorney Edith Sampson appointed alternate delegate to United Nations, August 24.

Ralph J. Bunche awarded Nobel Peace Prize, September 22.

1951 - First Negro student admitted to University of North Carolina, April 24.

Racial segregation in Washington, D.C., restaurants ruled illegal by Municipal Court of Appeals, May 24.

Pfc. William Thompson posthumously awarded Congressional Medal of Honor; first to a Negro since Spanish-American War.

Ralph Bunche appointed Under Secretary of United Nations.

Delegation headed by Paul Robeson and William L. Patterson presented petition to United Nations charging U.S. government with a policy of genocide against the American Negro people.

1952 - U. of Tennessee admits first Negro student, January 12.

First time in 71 years that a year had passed without one lynching occurring, Tuskegee Institute reported.

Violence erupts in Cicero, Ill., when 3,500 whites converge on building into which Negro family was moving.

1953 - Supreme Court ruling bans discrimination in Washington, D.C., restaurants, June 8.

Hulan Jack sworn in as borough president of Manhattan, December 31.

President Eisenhower appoints Government Contract Compliance Committee to investigate discrimination among employers with government contracts.

1954 - J. Ernest Wilkins, Sr., named Assistant Secretary of Labor by President Eisenhower, March 4.

Supreme Court decision (*Brown vs. Board of Education*) rules unconstitutional racial segregation in public schools.

Dr. Peter Murray Marshall, first Negro to head unit of American Medical Association, installed as president of New York County Medical Society.

Death of Mary Church Terrell, once president of the National Association of Colored Women, life-long leader in anti-discrimination fights, July 24.

Benjamin O. Davis, Jr., appointed first Negro general in Air Force, October 27.

Defense Department announces complete abolition of Negro units in the armed forces, October 30.

Charles C. Diggs, Jr., elected Michigan's first Negro Congressman.

1955 - First Negro to sing with Metropolitan Opera, Marian Anderson, makes debut in Verdi's *Masked Ball.*

Death of Walter White, writer and for many years executive secretary of NAACP, March 21.

Death of Mary McLeod Bethune, founder of Bethune-Cookman College, May 18.

E. Frederic Morrow appointed administrative aide to President Eisenhower.

Fourteen-year-old Emmett Till kidnapped in Money, Miss.; body found four days later in river; two white men tried by all-white all-male jury, acquitted.

Segregation in public recreational facilities banned by Supreme Court in Baltimore case, November 7.

Interstate Commerce Commission bans segregation in buses, waiting rooms, and travel coaches involved in interstate travel, November 25.

Mrs. Rosa Parks arrested in Montgomery, Ala., after refusing to take back seat in bus, December 1, resulting in famous bus boycott which began in Montgomery, December 5.

A. Philip Randolph and Willard S. Townsend elected vice presidents of AFL-CIO.

1956 - Autherine Lucy, Negro student, admitted to U. of Alabama, February 3; suspended and expelled after rioting began.

Racial segregation on Montgomery city buses ruled unconstitutional by federal court, June 5.

Louisville, Ky., public schools integrated, September 10.

Montgomery buses integrated on December 21 after year-long boycott.

1957 - Southern Christian Leadership Conference organized on February 14 with Rev. Martin Luther King as president.

Supreme Court rules Jim Crow buses unconstitutional.

Prayer pilgrimage held in Washington, May 17.

Archibald Carey appointed first Negro chairman of President's Committee on Government Employment Policy, August 3.

Civil Rights Act of 1957 passed by Congress; first since 1875.

Federal Civil Rights Commission created.

Federal troops ordered to Little Rock, Ark., by President Eisenhower to prevent interference with school integration at Central High School, September 24.

Birmingham, Nashville, and other Southern cities are scenes of violence, mobs, and bombings as school integration is attempted.

Fair Housing Practice Law adopted in New York City, December 5.

1958 - Clifton Reginald Wharton named minister to Rumania, February 5.

Robert N. C. Nix elected to Congress from Philadelphia, May 20.

1959 - Lorraine Hansberry's *Raisin in the Sun* becomes first play written by a Negro woman to appear on Broadway; play was first to be directed by a Negro, Lloyd Richards, in over half a century; Sidney Poitier starred, March 11.

Brig. Gen. B. O. Davis, Jr., promoted to major general, May 22.

Public school system abandoned in Prince Edward County, Va., rather than integrate facilities, June 26.

1960 - Sit-in movement began at five-and-dime store in Greensboro, N.C., by four students from North Carolina A. & T. College, quickly spread to many Southern states.

Student Nonviolent Coordinating Committee (SNCC) organized April 15-17 at Shaw University, Raleigh, N.C.

Federal court ends restrictions against Negro voting in Fayette County, Tenn., April 25; first voting case under 1957 Civil Rights Act.

President Eisenhower signs Civil Rights Act of 1960, May 6.

Black nationalist leader, Elijah Muhammad, gains national attention by calling for the creation of a Negro state.

Andrew Hatcher named associate press secretary to President

Kennedy, November 10.

Death of Richard Wright, author of *Native Son,* November 28.

1961 - Adam Clayton Powell named chairman of Education and Labor Committee of House of Representatives.

Robert Weaver receives appointment to highest federal post held by an American Negro, Administrator of Housing and Home Finance Agency.

Clifton R. Wharton appointed Ambassador to Norway.

CORE begins Freedom Rides through South.

By May 24 more than 100 "Freedom Riders" had been jailed in Mississippi.

James B. Parsons, first Negro appointed to federal district court in continental U.S., August 9.

Thurgood Marshall nominated to U.S. Circuit Court of Appeals, September 23.

1962 - Continuation of demonstrations against discrimination in both North and South, resulting in many arrests and acts of violence against the demonstrators.

Citizens in large Northern cities begin suits claiming de facto segregation in Northern schools; parents in New York City, Chicago, Englewood, N.J., and Rochester present evidence to courts of racially segregated schools.

Lt. Cdr. Samuel L. Gravely assumes command of destroyer escort *USS Falgout,* January 31; first Negro to command a U.S. warship.

Two arrests of Rev. Martin Luther King and arrests of over 1,000 Negro demonstrators in Albany, Ga., lead to presidential suggestion of negotiation between city officials and local Negro leaders, August 1.

James H. Meredith, Negro Air Force veteran, with an escort of Federal marshals, finally registers and is admitted to U. of Mississippi after complete defiance of court orders by governor and lt. governor of the State of Mississippi, who were both found guilty of civil contempt.

1963 - Voter registration drives in Southern states.

Negro students enroll at U. of Alabama.

Medgar Evers, field secretary for NAACP in Mississippi, shot and killed, June 12.

W. E. B. Du Bois dies, August 27.

Four girls killed in church bombing in Birmingham, Ala., September 15.

225,000 students boycott Chicago schools in Freedom Day protest of segregation, October 22.

March on Washington for Jobs and Freedom. To help dramatize the Negro's 1963 revolution, over 210,000 whites and Negroes assemble from all parts of the nation and abroad to march from the Washington Monument to the Lincoln Memorial in well-behaved dignity to sing, pray, and hear speeches demanding the passage of Civil Rights legislation, integration of all public schools, a federal program to train and place all unemployed workers, and a federal Fair Employment Practices Act barring all job discrimination, August 28.

James Meredith first Negro graduated from U. of Mississippi, August 18.

1964 - Dick Gregory and 40 others participate in sit-in movement in Atlanta restaurants; several restaurants close rather than serve the demonstrators, January 1-10.

Bodies of three civil rights workers, Goodman, Scherner, Chaney, found in Philadelphia, Miss.; killed while working on voter registration, August 5.

Riots in Dixmoor, South Chicago, Philadelphia, and other northern cities, August 17-28.

Rev. Martin Luther King awarded Nobel Peace Prize, October 11.

Sidney Poitier becomes first Negro to receive an Oscar from the Motion Picture Arts and Science Academy for best actor, April 14.

Civil Rights Bill passed by Congress and signed by President Johnson, July 2; bill contains strong public accommodations and fair employment sections.

L. A. Penn, Negro school administrator from Washington, killed when returning from Army Reserve duty at Ft. Benning, Ga., July 11.

1965 - President Johnson issues order creating cabinet-level Council on Equal Opportunity, with Vice President Humphrey as chairman; council to coordinate the civil rights activities of all federal agencies, February 7.

First of several marches to Selma, Ala., courthouse with Rev. Martin Luther King as leader, March 7.

Rev. James Reeb killed in Selma.

King, Bunche, Abernathy, and 3,200 others begin 54-mile march from Selma to Montgomery, March 22.

Mrs. Viola Liuzzo shot and killed after Selma march, March 26.

Voting Rights Bill passed, August 8.

Thurgood Marshall named Solicitor General, August 10.

1966 - January 14, Dr. Robert C. Weaver appointed Secretary of Housing and Urban Development, first Negro Cabinet member.

January 25, Constance Baker Motley appointed first Negro woman federal judge.

v of 1778 declared, "divers evil-minded persons, intending to dis-
e public peace, did liberate and set free their slaves," and this
ed the courts of Perquimans and Pasquotank to order these
s captured and sold to the highest bidder. The act of 1778 ap-
this, but warned that no Negro who had gained his liberty by
l service in the Revolutionary Army was to be re-enslaved.
years later the North Carolina legislature passed another act on
estion because, despite the law of 1775, "divers persons from
s motives [mostly Quakers—ed.], in violation of the said law,
e to liberate their slaves, who are now going at large to the terror
eople of this State." This act of 1788 provided for the apprehen-
all such illegally manumitted Negroes, with 20 per cent of the
ice going to the informer. Something like a reign of terror
ded upon many free Negroes and quite a few fled the state. On
23, 1797, four of these Negroes, named Jacob Nicholson,
Nicholson, Joe Albert, and Thomas Pritchet, residing in Phila-
, petitioned Congress through Representative John Swanwick of
lvania for a redress of their grievances. On January 30, 1797, the
n as to whether or not to accept a petition from fugitive slaves
ated in Congress and rejected by a vote of 50 to 33. In the course
ebate, Representative William Smith of South Carolina declared:
ractice of a former time, in a similar case was that the petition
led up and sent back to the petitioners." This petition of 1797
s to be the first from Negroes to Congress, however, that is still
(pp. 39-44)

UIETING" NEGRO PETITION TO CONGRESS, 1800
cond day of the new century witnessed the presentation to Con-
y Representative Robert Waln of Pennsylvania, of a petition
d against the slave trade, the fugitive slave act of 1793, and the
ion of slavery itself. The petition came from the free Negroes of
lphia headed by the Reverend Absalom Jones. It precipitated a
and extended debate and was referred to a committee, where i
nly after the House expressed the opinion that portions of th
had "a tendency to create disquiet and jealousy." (p. 44)

ORGANIZED ANTI-SLAVERY WORK BY NEGROES, 1808-1809
the very earliest forms of organized anti-slavery activity was th
ted by Negroes themselves within and through their own soci
ree examples of this type of agitation were: first, an addre
d by the Reverend Peter Williams, Jr., in the New York Afric
on January 1, 1808, the day when the federal law barring t
slave trade went into effect; second, an address delivered t
ear by an anonymous member of the Boston African Socie

2. EARLY NEGRO PETITIONS AND PROTESTS

You cannot outlaw one part of the people without endanger-
ing the rights and liberties of all people. You cannot put a
chain on the ankle of the bondmen without finding the other
end of it about your own necks.

—Frederick Douglass

From *A Documentary History of the Negro People in the United States,*
edited by Herbert Aptheker. The reference and examples cited herein
are from actual documents demonstrating that Negro protests and struggles for rights against an enforced status date back to the earliest days of
U.S. history.

EARLY NEGRO PETITIONS FOR FREEDOM, 1661-1726
Individual Negroes quite frequently petitioned governmental bodies for
freedom prior to the American Revolution. Three examples of such
petitions had varying responses. The first, dated 1661, was in Dutch
and was addressed to the colony of New Netherlands (later New York).
Its prayer was granted. The second, dated 1675, was the work of a Virginia Negro and the decision that was made in regard to it does not appear. The third petition, dated 1726, was addressed to the North Carolina
General Court and was denied. (pp. 1-3)

STATEMENTS OF SLAVE REBELS, 1741
The history of American Negro slavery was marked by many conspiracies and revolts by Negroes. The colonial period was no exception to
this. The New York City slave plot of 1741, during which many build-
ings were destroyed by fire, was one of the major events of this character.
It provoked hysteria leading to exaggeration of the extent of the actual
conspiracy, but that one existed is clear. To obtain direct statements
from Negroes themselves concerning these events was not easy. So-

called "confessions" were made by two Negroes in New York City on the afternoon of May 30, 1741, while chained to stakes before a howling, impatient mob. Following these confessions, the slaves were burned alive. In addition, 29 other Negroes were executed as were four whites including, among the latter, two women. (pp. 4-5)

SLAVES PETITION FOR FREEDOM DURING THE REVOLUTION, 1773-1779
The ferment preceding and accompanying the Revolutionary War stimulated many Negro people, collectively and individually, to make public pleas against slavery and to point out to the less than two and a half million American white people the incongruity and the danger of shouting "Liberty or Death" while enslaving 750,000 human beings. Five examples of such statements covering the years 1773 through 1779 give dramatic evidence of the bitter opposition to slavery. (pp. 5-12)

NEGROES PROTEST AGAINST TAXATION WITHOUT REPRESENTATION, 1780
Seven Negroes of Dartmouth, Mass., including Paul Cuffee and his brother John, protested on February 10, 1780, in a petition to the revolutionary legislature of their state, against the fact that they were subjected to taxation without the right to vote. In 1783, by court decision, Negroes subject to taxation were declared to be entitled to the suffrage. Paul Cuffee became a successful ship captain and merchant, and in 1815 he pioneered in the actual colonization of West Africa by American Negroes, transporting at his own expense 38 Negroes for this purpose. (pp. 14-16)

A PIONEER NEGRO SOCIETY, 1787
A Negro society was formed in Philadelphia in 1787 as one of the first organized Negro groups. Shortly afterwards similar societies were formed elsewhere, as in Newport, Boston, and New York. These maintained a steady correspondence and members exchanged visits, thus serving as something of a link between centers of the Northern free Negro population of the post-Revolutionary generation. The insurance features of this Philadelphia society served, too, as the beginnings of a major modern Negro business—the Negro insurance companies. (pp. 17-19) The Boston African Society was established in 1796. The rules of this benevolent society were published by the group itself in 1802, at which time it listed 44 Negro men as its membership. (pp. 38-39)

BENJAMIN BANNEKER'S LETTERS, 1790-1791
One of the most remarkable figures of eighteenth-century America was the Maryland free Negro, Benjamin Banneker (1731-1806). Mechanical and mathematical aptitude combined to produce in this man a noteworthy American scientific pioneer. His *Almanacs* were widely used

throughout the United States in the 1790's three who planned and surveyed the site for ington. The depth of his brilliance is seen 1790, to a close friend, Major Andrew astronomical calculations, and another wri Jefferson, then Secretary of State, enclosing edition of his *Almanac*. The letter and ma and he sent the latter to Condorcet, Secret ences at Paris. (pp. 22-26)

SOUTH CAROLINA NEGROES DENOUNCE JIM CI
Until the end of the Civil War free Negro disabilities. Among the most onerous of throughout the South and in many Nort Negroes the privilege of testifying under oa them from instituting suit in any case wha against this was presented to the legisla Charleston free Negroes in January 1791. (pp. 26-28)

NEGROES PROTEST AGAINST POLL TAX, 179
In 1760 the first capitation or poll tax was South Carolina. In 1787 the poll tax law Negroes, female as well as male, from the required to pay nine shillings and four per already been subjected to other types of t was passed—to become effective in 1791— of any age or sex, to pay, in addition, a individual for the ensuing ten years. The very considerable economic burden to th free Negroes of South Carolina. Two peti legislature protested these laws. Both are u the legislature in December 1793, and the first was signed by 23 free Negro men an second by 34 Negro men and women of Ch accompanied by another, signed by many v able action. Neither won, although in 1809 to exclude Negroes physically incapable of 31)

THE EARLIEST EXTANT NEGRO PETITION TO
In 1775 the revolutionary state of North (ding the manumission of slaves, except judged and approved by a county court. N

to a la turb tl provol Negro proved faithfu

Ten this qu religio contin of the sion o sale p descen Januar Jupiter delphi Pennsy questi was de of the "The was se appear extant.

A "DISC The se gress, directe institut Philad heated died, petitio

EARLY Amon conduc ties. T delive Churcl Africa same

third, another delivered in New York City on January 2, 1809, the speaker being William Hamilton, a Negro pioneer abolitionist and an organizer of subsequent nation-wide Negro conventions. (pp. 51-53)

NEGROES ASK FOR EQUAL EDUCATIONAL FACILITIES, 1787
The Negro's effort to obtain equal educational rights has its beginnings in the eighteenth century. One of the first evidences of this comes from Boston and took the form of a petition to the State Legislature dated October 17, 1787, whose prayer was not granted. The leader behind this petition was Prince Hall, who was born in Barbados in 1748 and came to Massachusetts when 17 years old. He served in the Revolutionary Army and became a Methodist Minister in Cambridge after the war. He was the founder of the Negro Masonic Order in the United States (a charter was granted his lodge from London in 1787) and an early spokesman against the slave trade and slavery. At his home was established in 1798, a school for Negro children. The petition:

> To the Honorable the Senate and House of Representatives of the Commonwealth of Massachusetts Bay, in the General Court assembled.
>
> The petition of a great number of blacks, freemen of this Commonwealth, humbly sheweth, that your petitioners are held in common with other freemen of this town and Commonwealth and have never been backward in paying our proportionate part of the burdens under which they have, or may labor under; and as we are willing to pay our equal part of these burdens, we are of the humble opinion that we have the right to enjoy the privileges of free men. But that we do not will appear in many instances, and we beg leave to mention one out of many, and that is of the education of our children which now receive no benefit from the free schools in the town of Boston, which we think is a great grievance, as by woful experience we now feel the want of a common education. We, therefore, must fear for our rising offspring to see them in ignorance in a land of gospel light when there is provision made for them as well as others and yet can't enjoy them, and for not other reason can be given this they are black . . .
>
> We therefore pray your Honors that you would in your wisdom some provision may be made for the education of our dear children. And in duty bound shall ever pray. (pp. 19-20)

3. NEGROES IN UNITED STATES HISTORY

> It is a peculiar sensation, this double consciousness, this sense of always looking at one's self through the eyes of others . . . One feels his two-ness—an American, a Negro, two souls, two thoughts, two unreconciled strivings; two warring ideals in one dark body, whose dogged strength alone keeps it from being torn asunder.
>
> —W. E. B. Du Bois, *Souls of Black Folk*

Like all histories, this one is made by people. These people, likewise, have been systematically excluded from the history of their country. These names indicative of the fact that since early days in the U.S. there have been Negroes in virtually every sector of activity, making contributions no greater—but no less—than their fellow man, in spite of insurmountable obstacles and oppression. It was with a great deal of hesitation that any attempt was made to list names after World War I. The number of individuals who have made significant contributions in the fields of education, science, business, religion, culture, and government is virtually endless.

To 1915

Robert S. Abbott (1870-1940): Founder and editor of the *Chicago Defender,* one of the largest Negro newspapers in the United States.
Ira Aldridge (1807-1867): Famous Shakespearean actor acclaimed throughout the world.
Macon B. Allen: First Negro formally admitted to Bar, 1845.
Richard Allen (1760-1831): Born a slave; founder of African Methodist Movement and the A.M.E. Church.
Jo Anderson: Slave, trusted helper of Cyrus McCormick in the development of the reaping machine in the 1830's.
Osborne P. Anderson: One of John Brown's group that attacked Harper's Ferry, October 16, 1859; escaped and later served with distinction in Civil War.

C. C. Antoine: His father fought under Andrew Jackson at New Orleans in 1814; he raised a colored company for a Louisiana Union regiment and served as its captain; later served in the Louisiana State Senate and then as lt. governor.

Crispus Attucks (1723-1770): First person killed in Boston Massacre, March 5, 1770; generally recognized as first martyr of American Revolution. A statue in Boston Commons honors him.

John James Audubon (1785-1851): Artist, ornithologist; Audubon Society was named after him.

Dr. Alexander T. Augusta: Lt. Col. in the Union Army, highest rank achieved by a Negro during the Civil War; one of founders of National Medical Society in Washington, D.C.

Maria Louise Baldwin (b. 1856): Educator, lecturer, and poet.

Benjamin Banneker (1731-1805): Inventor, astronomer, mathematician, writer of first almanac; appointed by George Washington as one of the planners of the city of Washington.

Edwin M. Bannister (1828-1901): One of first distinguished artists; founder of Providence Art Club.

Ferdinand Lee Barnett: Lawyer and first Negro Assistant State's Attorney of Illinois; husband of Ida B. Wells.

Ida B. Wells Barnett (1862-1931): Negro leader who edited newspapers in Memphis and Chicago and initiated anti-lynching campaign of the 1890's.

Ebenezer Don Carlos Bassett (1833-1908): First Negro appointee in diplomatic service; minister to Haiti in 1869.

James Beckwourth (1798-1867): Fur trader, explorer; Beckwourth Pass on Pacific Coast named in his honor.

James Madison Bell (1826-1902): Anti-slavery lecturer and poet.

Thomas Green Bethune (1849-1908): Born a slave on plantation near Columbus, Ga.; became outstanding pianist (known as Blind Tom).

Jesse Binga (1865-1950): Chicago banker and financier.

Joshua Bishop: Pastor of First Baptist Church for whites, Portsmouth, Va., in 1792.

Henry Blair: First Negro to receive a patent for an invention, on a corn harvester, October 14, 1834.

James A. Bland (1854-1911): Composer of "Carry Me Back to Ole Virginny," official state song of Virginia; composed over 700 songs.

Andrew J. Board: Railroad worker who devised a coupling device for railroad cars known as the "Jenny Coupler"; in 1897 a New York railroad paid him $50,000 for this device.

Edward A. Bouchet: First Negro awarded Ph.D. by an American University—Yale, 1876.

Anthony Bower: Organized first Negro YMCA, Washington, D.C. 1853.

Charlotte Hawkins Brown (1882-1960): Founded Palmer Institute at Sedalia, N.C., in 1901.

Morris Brown: Minister in A.M.E. Church in Charleston, N.C.; fled to Philadelphia in 1823; in 1831 became bishop of A.M.E. Church, following Richard Allen's death.

William Wells Brown: Wrote and published *Clotel,* first novel by an American Negro (1853); also *Escape,* first play by an American Negro (1854). Runaway slave who became a famous lecturer on anti-slavery, women's rights, world peace, prison relief, etc.

Blanche Kelso Bruce (1841-1898): Born a slave; only Negro to serve full term in U.S. Senate, from Mississippi, 1875-1881.

Harry T. Burleigh (1866-1949): Singer, composer, arranger of Negro spirituals.

Anthony Burns: Escaped slave who became central figure in famous Boston trial in test of the Fugitive Slave Law, 1854.

Nannie H. Burroughs (1883-1961): Educator and one of the most dynamic church women; in 1909 founded the National Training School for Women, Washington, D.C.; active catalyst in Baptist Church from coast to coast.

Richard Harvey Cain (1825-1887); Served in Congress from South Carolina, 1873-1875 and 1877-1879; in 1880 became a Bishop of A.M.E. Church. Later president of Paul Quinn College in Waco, Tex.

Francis Louis Cardozo: Freeborn; attended University of Glasgow and then theological school in London; later Secretary of State, South Carolina (1868-1872), and then Treasurer (1872-1876).

William H. Carney: Negro sergeant; died a Civil War hero on July 18, 1863, and was awarded Congressional Medal of Honor.

George Washington Carver (1864-1943): Born a slave; became outstanding agricultural chemist; January 5 is "Carver Day" in New York State.

Lott Cary: Former slave; bought freedom for himself and family; in 1850 helped organize the Richmond African Baptist Missionary Society; was early missionary to Africa.

John Chavis: Educational product of a wager between two prominent gentlemen of North Carolina as to the capacity of a Negro for higher education. Was sent to Princeton; returned to North Carolina (1805); conducted preparatory school for sons of prominent gentlemen; also became Presbyterian clergyman.

Henry P. Cheatham: Elected congressman from North Carolina, 1889-1893.

Charles W. Chesnutt (1858-1932): Outstanding novelist and short story writer; also educator and attorney; among his outstanding books were *The House Behind the Cedars* (1900), *The Marrow of Tradition* (1901), *The Colonel's Dream* (1905).

Joseph Cinque: Son of Mendi Chief; sold in slavery 1839; leader of the Mutiny on the *Amistad* (1839); freed by U.S. Supreme Court in 1841; returned to Africa in 1842.

Alvin A. Coffey: Early California pioneer; made ox-team trip across the plains in 1849 as a slave; purchased own freedom and that of his family; settled and started long line of descendants prospering throughout the state.

Daniel Coker: A slave, fled to New York at early age; was a co-founder with Allen and Jones of A.M.E. Church; in 1814 was missionary to West Africa.

John Henry Conyers: Entered Annapolis September 21, 1872; later resigned.

John A. Copeland: One of John Brown's group that attacked Harper's Ferry October 16, 1859; later hanged with John Brown.

Samuel E. Cornish: Co-edited the *Journal of Freedom,* March 1827, first Negro newspaper in the United States; a trustee of schools for free Negroes in New York City; member of the executive committee of the Anti-Slavery Society; promoter of higher education for Negroes.

John W. Cromwell: Historian and secretary of the American Negro Academy for "the promotion of literature, science and art," founded in 1897.

Basil Croquere: Just prior to Civil War considered best swordsman in New Orleans; operated a fencing academy. Also interested in mathematics and philosophy.

Alexander Crummell (1819-1898): Episcopal clergyman; from 1853-1873 in Africa as a clergyman; political leader and agent of American Colonization Society. Also literary stylist, noted for contribution to ideologies of Negroes' prospects prior to Emancipation Proclamation.

Paul Cuffee (1759-1817): Seaman, philanthropist (Negro sea captain-colonizer in resettling Negroes in Africa).

Alexander K. Davis: Lt. Governor of Mississippi during Reconstruction.

Benjamin O. Davis, Sr. (b. 1877): First Negro general in U.S. Army.

Edmond Dede (1829-1903): Violinist and composer in New Orleans just prior to Civil War; later became director of an orchestra in Bordeaux, France.

John V. DeGrasse: Prominent physician; first Negro admitted to Massachusetts Medical Society August 24, 1854.

Major Martin R. Delany (1812-1885): Author, Civil War hero, Negro abolitionist, orator, and army officer.

George Washington Dennis: Early California pioneer; bought his freedom; extremely active in real estate investments. His son, Edward, was the first Negro policeman in San Francisco. Another son, George, was member of Democratic State Central Committee. Another son,

Carlisle, was first steward in mansion of Mark Hopkins, later secretary to Hopkins' widow. Daughter Margaret was first Negro girl to graduate from Girls High School, became language expert and taught in a Chinese school. Her husband, Capt. Benston, honored Civil War veteran, is buried with her in Presidio in San Francisco.

James Derham: Born a slave in Philadelphia in 1762: Generally recognized as first Negro physician in America.

Decatur Dorsey: Won Congressional Medal of Honor in the Civil War in 1864.

Frederick Douglass (1817-1895): Fugitive slave who became leading abolitionist, orator, and American statesman. Considered by many as the greatest Negro American of the 19th century. Appointed Secretary of the Commission to Santo Domingo, 1871; presidential elector, 1872; marshal for the District of Columbia, 1877; commissioner of deeds for the District of Columbia; Minister to Haiti, 1889.

William Edward Burghardt Du Bois (1868-1963): One of the greatest Negro scholars and leaders; first Negro to receive a Ph.D. from Harvard; author of many books. Leader of the Niagara Movement; one of the founders of NAACP; founder of Pan-African Movement; professor; leader in many civil rights and peace movements. Moved to Ghana to supervise *Encyclopedia Africana*. Listed in first *Who's Who* published in U.S. Died on eve of the March on Washington, 1963.

Paul Laurence Dunbar (1872-1906): First nationally known Negro poet in U.S.

Robert Duncanson (1821-1871): Pre-Civil War landscape artist.

Oscar J. Dunn: Ex-slave, lt. governor of Louisiana, 1868.

Jean Baptiste Pointe Du Sable (1745-1818): French-speaking Negro; first permanent settler of Chicago, 1790; considered founder of the city.

Robert B. Elliott (1842-1884): U.S. Congressman from South Carolina, 1871-1874.

Barney Ford: Runaway slave who came to Colorado in 1860; built the Inter-Ocean Hotel in Denver and was successful businessman and active in territorial politics.

Thomas T. Fortune: Negro journalist and supporter of Booker T. Washington; editor of the *New York Age*.

Estevanico (Little Stephen): Negro explorer; originally one of a party of 400 Spanish explorers who landed at Tampa Bay in 1528; led expedition from Mexico and discovered Arizona and New Mexico, 1538.

Henry O. Flipper (1856-1940): First Negro graduate from West Point.

James Forten (1776-1842): Inventor and pioneer abolitionist; provided financing for Garrison's paper, *The Liberator.*

Amos Fortune (1710-1801): African-born American slave; purchased his freedom.

Henry Highland Garnet (1815-1882): Born a slave; minister, abolitionist, and diplomat.

Richard H. Gleaves: Lt. governor in South Carolina during reconstruction.

Shields Green: One of John Brown's group that attacked Harper's Ferry October 16, 1859; later hanged with John Brown.

Richard T. Greener (1844-1922): First Negro graduate of Harvard; professor of metaphysics, University of South Carolina, 1873.

Elizabeth Taylor Greenfield (1809-1876): Born in slavery in Mississippi; concert singer; first Negro American musician to achieve both local and foreign distinction.

Sutton Griggs: Prominent Baptist minister and lecturer on race problems; wrote five novels from 1899 to 1908—*Imperium in Imperio* (1899), *Overshadowed* (1901), *Unfettered* (1902), *The Hindered Hand* (1905), *Pointing the Way* (1908).

Archibald H. Grimke (1849-1930): Author and crusader for Negro rights; graduate Harvard Law School; writer, editor; American consul to Santo Domingo, 1894-1898.

Prince Hall (1748-1807): Revolutionary War veteran; founder of Negro Masonic Order in America, 1787.

Jupiter Hammon (1720-1800): Slave on Long Island; probably first Negro poet in U.S. Published *Salvation by Christ with Penitential Cries* (1760); also, an *Address to Negroes in the State of New York* (1787).

Jeremiah Haralson: Elected to Congress from Alabama, 1875-1877.

Frances Ellen Watkins Harper (1825-1911): Associated with Underground Railroad; lecturer for Maine Anti-Slavery Society; writer of verse and fiction. Wrote *Iola Leroy* (1892).

Lemuel Haynes (1753-1833): Fought in Continental Army; Congregationalist; first regular Negro pastor to white congregations.

James Augustine Healy (1830-1900): First Negro Roman Catholic Bishop in America; son of Irish planter and Negro slave.

William Henry Heard (1850-1937): Active in South Carolina politics; appointed Minister to Liberia, 1895; also Bishop in A.M.E. Church.

Josiah Henson (1789-1883): Associated with Underground Railroad; Harriet Beecher Stowe's Uncle Tom based on Henson's life.

Matthew Alexander Henson (1866-1955): Co-discoverer of the North Pole with Robert E. Peary; a monument in his honor stands in Maryland.

A. F. Herndon (b. 1858): Leading businessman; developed real estate projects, banks, and insurance companies, namely Atlanta Standard

Life Insurance Co.

John Hope (1864-1936): President of Atlanta University; educator, leader in the Niagara Movement.

George Moses Horton (1797-1883): born a slave; self-taught poet.

Julien Hudson: Lived in New Orleans prior to Civil War; portrait painter who painted distinguished people of Louisiana.

John A. Hyman: Elected to Congress from North Carolina, 1875-1877.

Elijah Johnson: Colonizer; served in War of 1812; prepared for Baptist ministry; went to Africa as missionary and colonist in company of 100 Negroes; represented U.S. government and American Colonization Society.

Jack Johnson (1878-1946): First Negro heavyweight boxing champion, 1910.

James Weldon Johnson (1871-1938): Poet, composer, lawyer, writer; author of *The Autobiography of an Ex-Colored Man* (1912).

Joshua Johnston (1770-1830): Early portrait painter whose work hangs in Baltimore Museums.

Absalom Jones: Co-organizer of Philadelphia's Free African Society, 1787; first Negro minister ordained in America, 1794 (Episcopal).

John Jones (1816-1879); Chicago businessman and crusader; donated land for Jones Commercial School of Chicago; twice elected Cook County Commissioner.

Thomy Lafon (1810-1893): One of the richest men in New Orleans; large contributor to abolitionist cause and Underground Railroad.

Lucien and Sidney Lambert: Lived in New Orleans before Civil War; concert pianists; won recognition in Europe and South America.

Bishop Isaac Lane (1834-1937): Minister and Bishop; founder of Lane College, Jackson, Tenn.

Lunsford Lane: Born a slave; worked and bought his freedom; was leading tobacco dealer in Raleigh, N.C.; also anti-slavery agent and speaker.

John Mercer Langston (1829-1897): First American Negro to win an elective office—Brown Helm Township, Lorain, Ohio, 1885; U.S. Congressman from Virginia, 1890-1891; member Oberlin City Council.

Louis Latimer: Associate of Thomas Edison; drafted plans for first telephone; superintended installation of electric lights in New York City, Philadelphia, and London.

Sherrard Lewis Leary: One of John Brown's group, killed during attack on Harpers Ferry, October 16, 1859.

William Alexander Leidesdorff: Early California pioneer, 1841; launched first steamboat to sail on San Francisco Bay; built San Francisco's first hotel; Vice-Consul to Mexico, 1845; Leidesdorff Street in San Francisco was named in his honor.

Edmonia Lewis (1845-1890): Pioneer woman sculptor, 1850's.

James Lewis (1832-1897): Port of New Orleans tax collector.

Rev. J. W. Loguen (1813-1872): An escaped slave who became a minister in New York.

Jefferson Long (1836-1900): U.S. Congressman from Georgia, 1870-1871.

John R. Lynch (1847-1939): U.S. Congressman from Mississippi, 1873-1877, 1882-1883.

Elijah McCoy (1844-1928): Between 1872-1920 received over 57 patents for inventions on automatic lubricating appliances and other devices pertaining to telegraphy and electricity. The expression, "the real McCoy" came from these inventions; inventions for lubricating railroad cars were not considered complete unless they had the "McCoy" mark on them.

Mary Mahoney: First Negro graduate nurse in U.S., 1879.

Biddy Mason: Early California pioneer; came to West Coast as slave and acquired freedom; worked as practical nurse and bought property; owned good portion of area incorporated by City of Los Angeles.

Jan E. Matzeliger (1852-1887): Created first machine for attaching soles to shoes; his patent was bought by United Shoe Machinery Co. of Boston, 1883.

John Merrick (1859-1919): Founder of North Carolina Mutual Life Insurance Co.

Thomas E. Miller: Elected to Congress from South Carolina, 1890-1891.

Charles L. Mitchell: One of first two Negroes elected to American legislature—Massachusetts House of Representatives, 1866.

Garrett A. Morgan (1875-1963): Inventor of gas mask and the first electric stoplight signal.

Isaac Murphy (? - 1896): First jockey ever to ride three winners in the Kentucky Derby—1884, 1890, 1891.

George W. Murray: Elected Congressman from South Carolina, 1893-1897.

Charles Nash: Elected Congressman from Louisiana, 1875-1877.

William Cooper Nell (1816-1874): Organizer and speaker for abolitionist groups; in 1852 compiled *Services of Colored Americans in the Wars of 1776 and 1812;* in 1856, *Colored Patriots of the American Revolution.* In middle 1850's led a campaign that ended separate schools for Negroes in New York; in 1861 appointed by Postmaster of Boston as a clerk—first Negro to hold a post of this kind.

Dangerfield Newby: One of John Brown's group, killed during attack on Harpers Ferry.

James E. O'Hara: Elected Congressman from North Carolina, 1883-1887.

Anthony Overton (1864-1946): Newspaper publisher; cosmetic manufacturer; founder of Victory Mutual Life Insurance Co.; operated first Negro national bank in U.S.—Douglass National Bank, Chicago; recipient of Spingarn Award, 1929.

Rev. Daniel A. Payne (1811-1893): Negro abolitionist and A.M.E. leader.

Rev. James W. C. Pennington (1809-1870): Received Doctor of Divinity degree from University of Heidelberg; author of early history of the Negro; active in anti-slavery causes.

Bill Pickett (1860-1932): Negro cowboy; credited with inventing the art of bulldogging, or steer wrestling; member of famous 101 Ranch in Oklahoma.

P. B. S. Pinchback (1837-1920): Acting Governor of Louisiana, 1872; elected to U.S. Senate, 1873 (not seated).

Mary E. "Mammy" Pleasant: Early California pioneer, often referred to as "Mother of Civil Rights in California."

Salem Poor: Negro soldier; hero at battle of Bunker Hill, June 17, 1775.

Gabriel Prosser (1775-1800): Organized plan for major revolt of several thousand slaves in Richmond, Virginia, August 30, 1800; revolt was betrayed.

Robert Purvis (1810-1898): Leading Negro abolitionist.

Joseph H. Rainey (1832-1887): First Negro member of U.S. House of Representatives from South Carolina, 1871-1879.

Alonzo J. Ransier: Lt. governor of South Carolina, 1870; member of Congress, 1873-1875.

James T. Rapier: Congressman from Alabama, 1873-1875.

Charles Ray (1807-1886): Minister and abolitionist; published *The Colored American.*

Charlotte E. Ray: First Negro woman lawyer, graduated from Howard University Law School, February 27, 1872; also the first American woman to graduate from a university law school; admitted to practice April 23, 1872.

Charles L. Reason (1818-1898): Scholar, educator, and poet; headed Institute for Colored Youth in Philadelphia; professor of *belles lettres* and French at Central College, McGrawville, N.Y. "White" college had two other Negro professors, William G. Allen and George B. Vashon.

Patrick Reason: Portrait painter and engraver, 1850's.

Charles Lenox Remond (1810-1873): Negro abolitionist; born Salem, Mass.; first Negro lecturer employed by Anti-Slavery Society.

Hiram R. Revels (1822-1901): First Negro U.S. Senator—Mississippi, 1870; served with Union forces during Civil War.

Norbert Rillieux (1806–1894): New Orleans machinist and engineer;

invented and received a patent on a vacuum cup which revolution-
ized sugar refining methods.

Joseph Jenkins Roberts (1809-1876): Born in Virginia; first president
of Liberia, 1847.

John S. Rock: First Negro admitted to practice before U.S. Supreme
Court, February 1, 1865.

Daniel Rodgers: Early California pioneer, 1860's; journeyed to California as slave and purchased freedom; family settled in area of
Watsonville, with family descendants active in affairs of Sacramento.

Moses Rodgers: Early California pioneer; mining expert; statewide
reputation as a metallurgist; later moved to Stockton where he made
the city a gift of a public park.

David Ruggles (1810-1849): Negro abolitionist; published first Negro
magazine, *Mirror for Liberty,* New York City, 1838.

John B. Russwurm (1799-1851): First Negro college graduate—
Bowdoin, 1826; co-edited the *Journal of Freedom,* March, 1827, first
Negro newspaper in the United States; became first superintendent
of schools in Liberia.

Peter Salem (1750-1816): Negro soldier; hero at battle of Bunker Hill,
June 17, 1775; fired the shot that killed Major John Pitcairn of the
British Army.

J. B. Sanderson: Early California pioneer; promoted schools for Negro
youths in San Francisco, Sacramento, Oakland, and Stockton.

William S. Scarborough (1852-1926): First Negro classical scholar;
linguist; educator; president of Wilberforce U.

Victor Sejour (1821-1874): With other Negro poets he published a
volume of poetry called *Les Cenelles* (1846), first anthology of its
kind by Negro Americans; later went to France and became one of
the most popular playwrights in Paris in the time of Alexander
Dumas and Victor Hugo.

Benjamin "Pap" Singleton: Born Tennessee, 1810; leader in organizing mass migrations of Negroes from the South during 1870's.

Robert Smalls (1839-1915): Negro slave pilot; Civil War hero; sailed
armed Confederate steamer out of Charleston, S.C. harbor and presented it to U.S. Navy, May 13, 1862, as a prize of war; later became
a captain in Union Navy and a U.S. Congressman from South Carolina for three terms.

Dr. James McCune Smith (1813-1865): Graduate of University of
Glasgow; physician, scientist, orator, and writer on abolition; propri-
etor of drug stores in New York City before Civil War.

James W. Smith: First Negro student at West Point, 1870.

John H. Smythe (1844-1908): Artist, lawyer, U.S. Minister to Liberia.

William Still (1821-1902): Negro abolitionist leader, leading figure in
Underground Railroad, and author of a book, *Underground Railroad.*

Henry O. Tanner (1859-1937): Renowned artist.

George Edwin Taylor: Born free 1857, Little Rock, Ark.; presidential candidate, 1904, of National Liberty Party, an all Negro national political organization.

Lewis Temple: Born a slave, died May 18, 1854; inventor of Temple Toggle Harpoon.

Mary Church Terrell (1863-1954): Once president of National Association of Colored Women; life-long leader in anti-discrimination fights.

Camille Thierry (1814-1875): Poet of New Orleans prior to Civil War.

Augustus Tolton: First American Negro priest ordained in Rome, April 24, 1886.

William Monroe Trotter (1872-1934): Harvard graduate; founder of *Boston Guardian* newspaper, 1901; aided DuBois in organizing the Niagara Movement.

Sojourner Truth (1797-1883): Born a slave; first Negro woman anti-slavery lecturer; abolitionist; outstanding crusader for women's rights.

Harriet Tubman (1820-1913): Born a slave and escaped to freedom; known as the "Moses" of her people; most famous of the conductors on the Underground Railroad.

William Tucker: First Negro child born in America, 1624.

Benjamin S. Turner: Elected congressman from Alabama; served 1871-1873.

Dr. Charles Henry Turner (1867-1923): His studies of the social life of ants were an outstanding contribution to the scientific world.

Henry MacNeal Turner (1833-1915): A leader of the Reconstructed Negro Church; first Negro to be an Army Chaplain (of a Negro Civil War regiment); a bishop; legislator; recipient of an honorary degree from University of Pennsylvania.

Nat Turner (1800-1831): Leader of major slave revolt in Southampton County, Virginia, August 21-22, 1831.

James Varick: Born New York State around 1750; First Bishop of A.M.E.Z. Church, 1821.

George B. Vashon (1822-1878): Trained as lawyer; graduate of Oberlin; poet; one of three Negroes on faculty of white college established by abolitionists in McGrawville, N.Y.

Gustavus Vassa (1745-1801): Sold into slavery in U.S. at time of American Revolution; was a seaman who, when retired, worked for the suppression of the slave trade; his memoirs, *The Interesting Narrative of the Life of Oloudah Equiano, or Gustavus Vassa,* advocated the cause of the slave in the U.S. as part of the world problem of oppression.

Denmark Vesey (1767-1822): Negro freeman; organized one of the most elaborate slave conspiracies involving thousands of Negroes in Charleston, S.C., May 1822; it was betrayed and Vesey and 37 others were hanged.

David Walker (1785-1830): Negro abolitionist leader; born free 1785; author of *Appeal to the Colored Citizens of the World* (1829), a call to Negroes to struggle against slavery.

Edwin G. Walker: One of first two Negroes elected to American legislature—Massachusetts House of Representatives, 1866.

Sarah B. Walker (Madam C. J.) (1869-1919): Financial genius; founded oldest Negro cosmetic business.

Josiah T. Walls: Elected Congressman from Florida, 1871-1876.

Eugene and Daniel Warburg: Sculptors in New Orleans before the Civil War.

Samuel Ringgold Ward (1817-1866): Born a slave; became a minister, active abolitionist leader, and author.

Booker T. Washington (1856-1915): Born a slave; became advisor to Presidents of U.S.; famous educator in field of vocational education.

Isaiah T. Wears (1822-1900): Born free in Baltimore; prominent in abolitionist movement and a leader in the post-Civil War Philadelphia Negro community.

Phillis Wheatley (1753-1784): Slave child sold on docks of Boston in 1761; achieved international renown as a poet.

William Whipper (1805-1885); Anti-slavery leader; one of the founders of the American Moral Reform Society and editor of the *National Reformer*.

George H. White (1852-1918): Member of last post-Reconstruction Congress—term ended 1901.

Bert Williams (1878-1922): One of the first famous Negro stage personalities.

Dr. Daniel Hale Williams (1858-1941): Performed world's first successful heart operation at Provident Hospital, Chicago, July 9, 1893.

George Washington Williams (1849-1891): Foremost Negro historian of his generation; served in Union Army at age of 14; first Negro graduate of Newton Theological Seminary, 1874; admitted to Ohio bar; wrote two-volume *History of the Negro Race in America* and *History of the Negro Troops in the War of the Rebellion* (1877).

Robert H. Wood: Mayor of Natchez, Miss., 1870.

Granville T. Woods (1856-1910): Inventor of various industrial appliances and telephonic and telegraphic instruments.

Dr. Carter G. Woodson (1875-1950): Founded Association for the Study of Negro Life and History, 1915; publisher of the *Journal of Negro History;* author of many books on the Negro.

Jonathan Jasper Wright: Associate Justice of Supreme Court of South Carolina, 1870.

Charles Young (1864-1922): Son of ex-slave; third Negro admitted to West Point, graduated 1889; Major in Spanish-American War; at outbreak of World War I was highest ranking Negro officer—Lt. Colonel.

After 1915

Ralph D. Abernathy (b. 1926): Minister, treasurer of Southern Christian Leadership Conference, close associate of Martin Luther King; outstanding leader in civil rights struggle.

Archie A. Alexander (1888-1958): One of leading engineers in U.S.; designer of power plants, airports, sewage plants, freeways, etc.

Raymond P. Alexander (b. 1898): Outstanding Harvard Law School graduate appointed municipal judge in Philadelphia in 1958.

Sadie Tanner Mossell Alexander (b. 1898): First Negro woman admitted to Pennsylvania Bar; graduate of U. of Pennsylvania Law School; Ph.D. in economics.

Charles Alston (b. 1907): Well-known muralist and painter.

Charles W. Anderson (b. 1907): Elected to Kentucky House of Representatives, 1935, as first Negro Representative since Reconstruction.

Marian Anderson (b. 1908): Concert artist; first Negro to sing with the Metropolitan Opera in 1955; also delegate to U.N.

Louis (Satchmo) Armstrong (b. 1900): Outstanding jazz musician whose trumpet style influenced trumpeters during the twenties and thirties.

Arthur Ashe, Jr. (b. 1943): First Negro to be named to the American Davis Cup Squad, 1964.

William Attaway (b. 1912): Novelist; among his writings: *Let Me Breathe Thunder* (1939), *Blood on the Forge* (1941).

James Baldwin (b. 1924): Outstanding writer of novels, essays, plays; also active as lecturer and in civil rights movement; among his many works are: *Go Tell It on the Mountain* (1952), *Nobody Knows My Name* (1961), *Notes of a Native Son* (1955), *The Fire Next Time* (1962), *Another Country* (1964).

Claude A. Barnett (b. 1889): Founder and director of the Associated Negro Press; he and his wife, Etta Moten Barnett, former concert singer, are authorities on African art.

Richmond Barthe (b. 1901): Internationally known sculptor and painter.

Count Basie (b. 1904): In 1939 won The Most Popular-Band-Musician Award.

Charlotta Bass: Vice presidential candidate on Progressive party ticket in 1952; owner of the newspaper *California Eagle*.

Daisy Bates: NAACP executive in Arkansas active in integrating Central High in Little Rock.

Harry Belafonte (b. 1927): Singer, actor, civil rights leader.

Lerone Bennett, Jr. (b. 1928): Writer, historian, lecturer, senior editor of *Ebony;* among his works is *Before the Mayflower: A History of the Negro in America* (1962).

Mary McLeod Bethune (1875-1955): Educator, social worker, founder of Bethune-Cookman College.

Joseph Blair (b. 1904): Scientist; developer of early rockets for U.S. government.

Alden Bland (b. 1911): Writer; among his works: *Behold a Cry* (1947).

Jane M. Bolin (b. 1908): First Negro woman judge in U.S. (New York City).

Horace Mann Bond (b. 1904): Former president of Lincoln U. in Pennsylvania; dean of School of Education, Atlanta U.; writer of articles and books on history of the Negro and education.

Arna W. Bontemps (b. 1902): Outstanding writer of novels, plays, histories, and compiler of works on the Negro; also librarian of Fiske U.; among his many works are: *Story of the Negro; Golden Slippers: An Anthology of Negro Poetry* (1941); *American Negro Poetry,* ed. (1963); *Black Thunder* (1936); *Negro American Heritage* (1965).

William S. B. Braithwaite (1878-1962): Historian, critic, writer; former editor of poetry magazine.

Benjamin G. Brawley (1882-1939): Writer and educator; among his works: *A Social History of the American Negro; The Negro Genius; Early Negro American Writers.*

Andrew F. Brimmer (b. 1926): Economist; Assistant Secretary, U.S. Dept. of Commerce; appointed to Board of Governors of Federal Reserve Board, 1966.

Edward W. Brooke (b. 1919): Attorney General of Massachusetts; elected U.S. Senator from Massachusetts in 1966; first Negro U.S. Senator since Reconstruction.

Gwendolyn Brooks (b. 1917): Only Negro awarded Pulitzer Prize—for her collection of poems, *Annie Allen,* 1950.

Robert Brooks: First member of U.S. Armed Forces (tanks) to be killed in action in World War II; main parade ground at Fort Knox, Ky., named Brooks Field in his honor.

Anne Brown: Actress, concert singer; original Bess in *Porgy and Bess.*

Sterling A. Brown (b. 1901): Writer, poet, critic and authority on Negro literature; among his works are: *The Negro in American Fiction* (1937), *Negro Poetry and Drama* (1937), *The Negro Caravan* (1941).

William B. Bryant (b. 1911): Appointed to U.S. District Court for District of Columbia, 1965.

Ralph J. Bunche (b. 1904): Outstanding statesman, Under-Secretary of the U.N., highest-ranking American in U.N. Secretariat; awarded Nobel Peace Prize, 1950.

Margaret Goss Burroughs (b. 1917): Artist, founder and director of Museum of Negro History and Art, Chicago.

Ambrose Caliver (b. 1894): Member of President Roosevelt's "Black Cabinet," 1938; Chief of Adult Education in U.S. Office of Education, 1938.

E. Simms Campbell (b. 1908): First Negro cartoonist and commercial artist to appear in major magazines.

Archibald J. Carey, Jr. (b. 1908): Minister, lawyer, alderman, business executive; first Negro to head a committee on government employment policy.

Horace R. Cayton (b. 1903): Writer, sociologist; co-author of *Black Metropolis: A Study of Negro Life in a Northern City* (1945); grandson of first Negro U.S. Senator Hiram Revels.

Kenneth B. Clark (b. 1914): Educator, psychologist, author; active in projects concerned with Negro youth.

Cassius Clay (Muhammad Ali) (b. 1942): World heavyweight boxing champion.

Rufus Clement (b. 1900): President of Atlanta U.; elected to Atlanta Board of Education, 1953.

Montague W. Cobb (b. 1904): Anatomist, physical anthropologist, head of Department of Anatomy at Howard U.

Janet Collins: First Negro to appear as Premiere Danseuse at Metropolitan Opera, 1951, in *Aida*.

John Conyers, Jr. (b. 1929): Congressman elected in 1965 from 1st district of Michigan; re-elected 1966 with 85 per cent of the vote of his district.

Mercer Cook (b. 1903): Ambassador to Nigeria, Director of African Affairs with Congress of Cultural Freedom.

Will Marion Cook (1869-1944): Born Washington, D. C.; studied composition with Anton Dvorak; trained choruses for Broadway shows and toured Europe with his own orchestra.

James D. Corrothers: Writer; wrote primarily during 1916-1930.

Countee Cullen (1903-1946): Outstanding poet; among his works: *Caroling Dusk* (1927) and *On These I Stand* (1927).

Ulysses Grant Dailey (1885-1961): One of the most distinguished surgeons in the United States.

Allison Davis (b. 1902): Professor of Education, U. of Chicago.

Benjamin J. Davis Jr. (1903-1964): Member of the National Committee of the Communist party; elected to New York City Council in 1943.

Benjamin O. Davis, Jr. (b. 1912): First Negro Air Force General; first Negro to command an airbase.

Dr. Elizabeth Bishop Davis: Psychoanalyst, in charge of Department of Psychiatry of Harlem Hospital, New York City.

Ossie Davis (b. 1917): Actor and playwright; lead in *Purlie Victorious;* active in civil rights movement.

Sammy Davis, Jr. (b. 1925): Outstanding entertainer and actor.

William L. Dawson (b. 1886): Congressman from Illinois; first Negro Congressman to head a congressional committee.

William L. Dawson (b. 1898): Composer, arranger; Composed Negro Folk Symphony No. 1; director of Tuskegee Choir.

Ruby Dee: Actress; female lead in *Purlie Victorious.*

Hubert T. Delany (b. 1902): Judge of New York City Domestic Relations Court.

Oscar DePriest (1871-1951): First Negro elected to Congress since 1900; three-term Congressman (1928-1934); first Negro in Chicago City Council.

R. Nathaniel Dett (1882-1943): American Negro composer.

Earl B. Dickerson (b. 1891): President of Supreme Life Insurance Co.; member of Roosevelt's FEPC; active in civic affairs of Chicago; first Negro to take a law degree at U. of Chicago.

Charles C. Diggs, Jr. (b. 1922): Congressman from Detroit, Mich.

Dean Dixon (b. 1915): Internationally known conductor of symphony orchestras.

Mattwilda Dobbs (b. 1925): Opera singer.

Owen Dodson (b. 1914): Writer; among his works: *Boy at the Window* (1951).

Aaron Douglas (b. 1899): Leading painter and educator.

St. Clair Drake (b. 1911): Sociologist and anthropologist; professor of African Affairs; co-author of *Black Metropolis: A Study of Negro Life in a Northern City* (1945).

Dr. Charles R. Drew (1904-1950): Developer of blood plasma.

Edward R. Dudley (b. 1911): Lawyer, judge; president of Borough of Manhattan, 1962; Minister to Liberia, 1948-1953.

Todd Duncan (b. 1904): Concert singer; 1935 to 1943 male lead in *Porgy and Bess.*

Katherine Dunham (b. 1910): Anthropologist and outstanding choreographer.

Edward "Duke" Ellington (b. 1899): Orchestra leader and composer of national and international fame.

Ralph Ellison (b. 1914): Outstanding writer; author of *Invisible Man,* widely acclaimed by critics and winner of National Book Award, 1952.

Medgar Evers (1926-1963): Field secretary, Mississippi NAACP; killed by segregationist.

James L. Farmer (b. 1920): National director of Congress of Racial Equality (CORE) until 1965; author of *Freedom—When?*

Jessie Fauset: Writer; among her works: *There is Confusion* (1924),

Plum Bun (1928), *The Chinaberry Tree* (1931), *Comedy American Style* (1933).

Dorothy Boulding Ferebee: Medical director of Howard U.

Angela Ferguson (b. 1925): Heads Research Section of Pediatrics at Howard U. College of Medicine.

Rudolph Fisher (b. 1897): Writer; among his works: *The Walls of Jericho* (1928); practiced medicine in order to support his career as a writer.

James Forman (b. 1929): Executive director of Student Nonviolent Coordinating Committee (SNCC).

John Hope Franklin (b. 1915): Historian, educator, Ph.D from Harvard, former head of History Department, Brooklyn College, Professor of History, U. of Chicago; among his works: *From Slavery to Freedom: A History of American Negroes; Reconstruction After the Civil War; The Militant South.*

E. Franklin Frazier (1894-1962): Outstanding scholar in field of sociology pertaining to the Negro; among his works: *The Negro in the United States; The Negro Family in the United States; Black Bourgeoisie.*

Meta Warrich Fuller (b. 1877): Outstanding woman sculptor.

S. B. Fuller (b. 1905): Publisher of *Pittsburgh Courier;* businessman.

Marcus A. Garvey (1887-1940): Nationalist who organized Universal Negro Improvement Association advocating a "back to Africa" movement for Negroes.

Arthur G. Gaston (b. 1892): Self-made millionaire—banker, insurance executive, real estate, motels, funeral homes.

Zelma Watson George: Served as alternate delegate to U.N.

Althea Gibson (b. 1927): Famous woman athlete (tennis).

Truman K. Gibson, Sr. (b. 1882): Established Supreme Life Insurance Co. in Chicago; leading business and civic leader.

Charles Gilpin (1878-1930): Actor, famous for his role in *Emperor Jones.*

Shirley Graham (b. 1907): Writer; recipient of Anisfield-Wolf Award; among her works: *Jean Baptiste du Sable* (1953), *The Story of Phillis Wheatley* (1949), *Dr. George Washington Carver* (1944); first editor of *Freedomways.*

Lester Blackwell Granger (b. 1896): For many years executive secretary of the National Urban League.

Dick Gregory (b. 1932): Outstanding comedian; active leader in civil rights movement.

Lloyd Hall (b. 1894): Industrial chemist: holds numerous patents and author of many monographs.

William C. Handy (1873-1958): Negro composer and arranger, known as "Father of the Blues."

Lorraine Hansberry (1930-1965): First Negro woman playwright to have play presented on Broadway—*Raisin in the Sun.*

Leonard Harmon (1916-1942): Navy hero; *USS Harmon* named for him.

Abram L. Harris (1899-1963): Professor of Economics at U. of Chicago.

Mrs. Patricia R. Harris: First Negro woman named to ambassadorial post abroad (Luxembourg), 1965.

Richard B. Harrison (1864-1935): Actor; famous for role of "De Lawd" in *Green Pastures.*

William H. Hastie (b. 1904): Appointed U.S. district judge, Virgin Islands, 1937; first Negro appointed to Federal bench; appointed Governor of Virgin Islands, 1944; judge of U.S. Circuit Court of Appeals, 1949.

Andrew Hatcher (b. 1923): Associate press secretary in White House during Kennedy administration.

Augustus Hawkins (b. 1907): Congressman from California; chairman of House Rules Committee.

Palmer Hayden (b. 1893): Artist; won Harmon Award in 1920's for his painting.

Roland Hayes (b. 1887): Concert artist; broke the color bar in concert halls for Negro classical singers.

George E. C. Haynes (b. 1912): Founder of the Urban League; race relations expert for U.S. Department of Labor.

Irene Dorothy Height (b. 1912): National president of National Council of Negro Women.

George Wylie Henderson (b. 1904): Writer; among his works: *Ollie Miss* (1935), *Jule* (1946).

A. Leon Higginbotham, Jr. (b. 1928): U.S. district judge, Pennsylvania; first Negro to be member of Federal Trade Commission.

Chester B. Himes (b. 1909): Writer; among his works: *If He Hollers Let Him Go* (1945), *Lonely Crusade* (1947), *Cast the First Stone* (1952).

William A. Hinton (1883–1959): Bacteriologist; developer of Hinton test for syphilis.

Lena Horne (b. 1917): Singer, actress, author (with R. Schickel) of *Lena.*

Charles H. Houston (1895–1950): Considered one of the greatest constitutional lawyers; Phi Beta Kappa, Amherst; distinguished law school graduate.

Norman O. Houston (b. 1893): President and Co-Founder of Golden State Mutual Life Insurance Company.

Langston Hughes (1902-1967): Poet, writer, playwright, historian—prolific author; among his many works: *A Pictorial History of the*

Negro in America; the *Simple* books; *First Book of Jazz* (1955); *Famous American Negroes* (1954).

Richard Hunt (b. 1935): Metal sculptor.

Zora Neale Hurston (1903-1960): Authority on Negro folklore and anthropology; among her works: *Jonah's Gourd Vine* (1934), *Their Eyes Were Watching God* (1937), *Seraph on the Suwannee* (1948).

Elmer Imes: Physicist, authority on spectroscopy.

William Lloyd Imes (b. 1889): Religious leader (Presbyterian); Negro rights champion; officer of NAACP.

Hulan Jack (b. 1906): First Negro elected president of the Borough of Manhattan, 1953.

Dr. Joseph A. Jackson: President of National Baptist Convention of United States— approximately 5,000,000 members.

Mahalia Jackson (b. 1912): Leading gospel singer in U.S.

Charles S. Johnson (1893-1956): Eminent sociologist; studied Negro life and problems; first Negro president of Fisk U.

Sgt. Henry Johnson: First American soldier in World War I to receive the French Croix de Guerre.

John H. Johnson (b. 1918): Editor and publisher, Johnson Publishing Co., includes books and *Ebony, Negro Digest, Jet.*

Leroy R. Johnson: Negro senator in Georgia State Legislature, 1962.

Malvin Gray Johnson (1896-1934): Artist.

Mordecai W. Johnson (b. 1890): Minister; first Negro president of Howard U. (1926-1960); Established school as leading training center for Negro doctors and lawyers.

Rafer Johnson (b. 1934): Outstanding athlete at U. of California; established new world record in Olympic decathlon.

Violette A. Johnson (b. 1882): First Negro woman admitted to practice before the U.S. Supreme Court.

Eugene K. Jones (1885-1951): Organizer and one of first executive officers of Urban League.

LeRoi Jones (b. 1934): Playwright, "Beat."

Percy Julian (b. 1898): Famous Negro scientist; renowned for his work in production, research, and development of steroids.

Ernest E. Just (1884-1940): Internationally famous scientist-biologist in field of fertilization and cycloplasm of cells.

Phillip B. Kaye: Writer, author of *Taffy* (1950).

William J. Kennedy, Jr. (b. 1922): Founder and president of North Carolina Mutual Insurance Co., 1958, largest Negro life insurance company in U.S.

John O. Killens (b. 1916): Writer; among his works: *Youngblood, And Then We Heard the Thunder;* screenplay, *Odds Against Tomorrow.*

Martin Luther King (b. 1929): President of Southern Christian Leadership Conference; major leader of civil rights movement; awarded Nobel Peace Prize, 1964.

Eartha Kitt (b. 1928): Outstanding actress, singer, and night club entertainer.

Clinton E. Knox (b. 1908): U.S. foreign service officer.

Samuel L. Kountz: Researcher in transplanting of human kidneys; "Outstanding Young Investigator of 1964" from American College of Cardiology.

Gerald A. Lamb: State treasurer of Connecticut, 1962.

Nella Larsen: Writer; among her works: *Quicksand* (1928), *Passing* (1929).

Louis R. Lautier: First Negro correspondent admitted to congressional press gallery.

Theodore K. Lawless (b. 1894): Internationally known dermatologist; research in treatment of leprosy and syphilis.

Jacob Lawrence (b. 1917): Important artist; considered outstanding Negro painter in America.

Marjorie Lawson (b. 1912): Appointed associate judge, Juvenile Court, Washington, D.C., on October 15, 1962; U.S. Representative to UNESCO. U.S. Representative to the U.N. Economic and Social Council's Social Commission.

Warner Lawson: Dean of Music and Choral Director, Howard U.

Canada Lee (1907-1951): Actor; took role of Richard Wright's "Bigger Thomas."

John Lewis (b. 1940): President of Student Nonviolent Coordinating Committee (SNCC).

Julian Lewis (b. 1891): Scientist, physician, pathologist.

Malcolm Little (Malcolm X) (b. 1925): Leader of the Black Muslims; founder of Organization for Afro-American Unity; author, *Autobiography of Malcolm X* (1965). Assassinated in 1965.

Alain L. Locke (1886-1954): Scholar, philosopher, historian, educator; literary and art critic; first Negro to receive a Rhodes Scholarship; among his works: *The Negro and His Music* (1936), *The Negro in Art* (1940), *Negro Art: Past and Present* (1936).

Dr. Myra Logan: Heart specialist and surgeon.

Rayford W. Logan (b. 1895): Former head of Howard U. Department of History; among his works: *The Betrayal of the Negro* (rev. ed. of *The Negroes in American Life and Thought*), *The Negro in the United States.*

Louis E. Lomax (b. 1922): Journalist, writer, teacher, lecturer, civil rights spokesman.

Joe Louis (b. 1914): Heavyweight boxing champion.

Curtis Lucas (b. 1914): Writer; *Third Ward Newark* (1946).

Autherine Lucy: U. of Alabama's first Negro student.

Lutie A. Lytle: Pioneer Negro woman lawyer.

Peter Murray Marshall: First Negro to head unit of American Medical Association, president of New York County Medical Society, 1954.

Thurgood Marshall (b. 1908): NAACP civil rights lawyer; U.S. circuit judge; as lawyer handled major cases before Supreme Court as regards rights of Negroes, including *Brown vs. Board of Education* (1954); appointed Solicitor General of U.S. in 1965.

Maceo C. Martin (b. 1897): President of National Bankers Association.

Dorothy Maynor (b. 1910): Internationally famous soprano.

Benjamin E. Mays (b. 1895): Minister, famous orator, president of Morehouse College.

Mary Holloway McCoo: Specialist in anesthesiology at University Hospital in Los Angeles, Calif.

Wade H. McCree, Jr. (b. 1920): U.S. Circuit Court judge, Detroit.

Claude McKay (1889-1948): Gifted writer of poetry and prose; among his works: *Home to Harlem* (1928), *Banjo* (1929), *Banana Bottom* (1933).

James H. Meredith (b. 1933): Student involved in integration struggle at U. of Mississippi; first Negro graduate, 1963.

Ralph Metcalfe (b. 1910): Famous athlete in 1932 and 1936 Olympics.

Oscar Micheaux (b. 1884): Writer; among his works: *The Conquest* (1930), *The Forged Note* (1915), *The Case of Mrs. Wingate* (1945).

Dorie Miller (1919-1943): Hero at Pearl Harbor on the *Arizona;* received Navy Cross.

Kelly Miller (1863-1939): Noted educator, mathematician, and author; dean of College of Arts and Science, Howard U.; wrote famous World War I polemic, *The Disgrace of Democracy.*

Loren Miller (b. 1903): Judge, Los Angeles Municipal Court.

William Ming (b. 1911): Lawyer, former chairman of American Veteran's Committee.

Arthur Mitchell (b. 1886): First Negro Democrat elected to Congress, 1935-1943.

Fred Moore: First Negro sentry to guard the Tomb of the Unknown Soldier in Arlington National Cemetery, March 1961.

Frederic E. Morrow (b. 1909): Administrative aide to President Eisenhower; author of *Black Man in the White House.*

Constance Baker Motley (b. 1921): President of the Borough of Manhattan, New York City; highest paid Negro woman in municipal government; first Negro woman federal judge.

Willard Motley (1912-1965): Novelist; author of *Knock on Any Door* and *We Fished All Night.*

R. R. Moton (1867-1940): President of Tuskegee Institute.

Elijah Muhammed (b. 1897): Leader of Black Muslim Movement; advocates a separate Negro state.

Hugh Mulzac (b. 1886): First Negro to receive a Master's License in 1918; first captain of the ship *Booker T. Washington,* 1942.

Carl Murphy (b. 1889): President and editor of the *Afro-American* newspapers.

James M. Nabrit (b. 1900): President of Howard U.; appointed to U.N.

William Nickerson, Jr. (1879-1945): Founder and first president of Golden State Mutual Life Insurance Co.

Robert N. C. Nix, Sr. (b. 1905): First Negro congressman from Pennsylvania; elected 1959.

Joseph "King" Oliver (1885-1938): One of great jazz pioneers.

Roi Ottley (1906-1960): Journalist, writer; among his works: *New World A-Coming* (1943), *Black Odyssey* (1948), *Lonely Warrior: Life of Robert S. Abbott* (1955).

Jesse Owens (b. 1913): Outstanding athlete; broke records in 1936 Olympics.

Gordon Parks (b. 1912): Award-winning photographer, composer of a piano concerto and piano sonatas, and author.

Rosa Parks (b. 1909): Seamstress of Montgomery, Ala., who sparked the famous Montgomery bus boycott by refusing to take a back seat in a bus.

James B. Parsons (b. 1911): First Negro appointed as a judge of a United States District Court in the continental U.S.

Frederick D. Patterson (b. 1901): President of Tuskegee Institute.

William Patterson (b. 1892): Veteran Civil Rights leader and attorney.

Marion Perkins (1908-1961): Award-winning sculptor, art teacher.

Ann Petry (b. 1911): Writer, journalist, and social worker; among her works: *The Street* (1946), *Country Place* (1947), *Harriet Tubman* (1955).

Horace Pippin (1888-1946): Oustanding Negro primitive painter.

Willa Beatrice Player (b. 1909): President, Bennett College.

Hildrus A. Poindexter: Graduate of Lincoln U. Harvard U. and Columbia U.; has contributed to medical journals and served the U.S. Public Health Service and the federal government in health assignments in foreign countries.

Sidney Poitier (b. 1927): Stage and screen actor; first Negro to receive an "Oscar" for *Lilies of the Field;* recipient of Silver Bear Award at Berlin Film Festival, New York Film Critics Award.

Cecil F. Poole (b. 1907): First Negro to be U.S. attorney; former Assistant District Attorney, San Francisco.

Adam Clayton Powell, Sr. (1865-1953): Founder of America's largest Negro congregation, the Abyssinian Baptist Church, New York; a force in Harlem politics in the thirties and forties.

Adam Clayton Powell, Jr. (b. 1908): U.S. Congressman from New York; chairman of Labor and Education Committee; minister of largest Baptist congregation in the United States.

Leontyne Price (b. 1927): Concert and opera singer; has appeared in opera houses all over the world; received the Order of Merit of the Italian Republic.

Pearl Primus (b. 1921): Internationally famous American dancer and anthropologist.

Benjamin Quarles (b. 1904): Professor, historian, author; among his works: *The Negro in the Making of America* (1964), *The Negro in the American Revolution* (1961), *Lincoln and the Negro* (1962), *The Negro in the Civil War* (1953).

Gertrude "Ma" Rainey (1886-1936): Pioneer blues singer.

Asa Philip Randolph (b. 1889): Vice president of AFL-CIO; one of organizers of March on Washington in 1941 that led to the formation of FECP; organized and first president of Brotherhood of Sleeping Car Porters.

L. D. Reddick (b. 1910): Writer, educator, author of *Crusader Without Violence: Biography of Martin Luther King* (1959).

J. Saunders Redding (b. 1906): Educator, writer; among his works: *Stranger and Alone* (1950), *On Being Negro in America* (1951), *The Lonesome Road* (1958).

Paul Robeson (b. 1898): Actor, singer, athlete, Phi Beta Kappa, lawyer; leader in civil rights struggles of Negro people.

Bernard W. Robinson: First Negro commissioned in U.S. Navy (1942).

Bill "Bojangles" Robinson (1878-1949): Dancer; in 1930's made over 14 movies in Hollywood.

Jackie Robinson (b. 1919): First Negro to enter major league baseball; Most Valuable Player, 1949; television commentator.

Spottswood W. Robinson, III (b. 1916): First Negro to be a federal district court judge in the District of Columbia.

Charlemae Rollins (b. 1897): Librarian, writer, lecturer; among her works: *Famous American Negro Poets* (1965), *They Showed the Way* (1964).

Carl T. Rowan (b. 1925): Writer, journalist, former Deputy Assistant Secretary of State; Ambassador to Finland; U.N. alternate delegate; director of U.S. Information Agency.

Wilma Rudolph (b. 1940): World's fastest woman runner; won three gold medals in the Olympic games, 1960.

Bayard Rustin (b. 1910): Civil rights leader; planner of March on Washington in 1963; organized first Freedom Ride in 1947.

Edith Sampson (b. 1901): Alternate U.N. delegate, first Negro woman to be elected judge of a municipal court.

Doris Saunders (b. 1921): Editor of book publishing company.

Augusta Savage (b. 1900): Woman sculptor.

Willard Savoy (b. 1916): Author of *Alien Land* (1949).

Gale Sayers (b. 1943): Halfback, Chicago Bears; established new professional football record for total touchdowns in one season (22); tied all-time record for total touchdowns in one game (6).

George Schuyler (b. 1895): Journalist-writer, author of *Black No More* (1931), *Slaves Today* (1931).

Phillipa Schuyler (1932-1967): Child prodigy, concert pianist.

William E. Scott (1884–1964): Portrait artist.

John H. Sengstacke (b. 1912): Publisher and editor of the *Chicago Defender*.

Rev. Fred L. Shuttlesworth: Outstanding leader in civil rights movement; president, Alabama Christian Movement; president Southern Conference Educational Fund; secretary, Southern Christian Leadership Conference.

Frank Silvera (b. 1914): Actor.

Georginia Rosa Simpson: Professor of German; in 1921 became the first Negro woman to receive a Ph.D. degree in the U.S.

Noble Sissle (b. 1889): Leading jazz band leader and pioneer in influencing the jazz idiom.

Bessie Smith (1900-1937): One of the first blues and jazz singers to win popular acclaim and attention; style and voice timbre set pattern for many singers after her time.

Otis M. Smith (b. 1922): Auditor general of State of Michigan, 1962.

William Gardner Smith (b. 1926): Author of *Last of the Conquerors* (1948), *Anger at Innocence* (1950).

Frank M. Snowden (b. 1911): Negro educator; dean of college at Howard U.; American cultural attaché in Rome.

Asa T. Spaulding (b. 1902): President of one of the largest Negro businesses in the U.S., the North Carolina Mutual Life Insurance Co.

Charles C. Spaulding (1874-1952): President and developer of North Carolina Mutual Life Insurance Co.

William Grant Still (b. 1895): Composer and conductor; first Negro to lead a symphony orchestra, the Los Angeles Philharmonic.

Judge Juanita K. Stout (b. 1919): First Negro woman appointed as a judge in Pennsylvania.

Dr. Hilda G. Straker: World famous dermatologist.

Merze Tate: Authority on international relations.

Art Tatum (1910-1956): Jazz pianist with unique technique that established a new school of piano soloists.

Hobart Taylor, Jr. (b. 1920): Executive vice chairman of Equal Employment and Opportunity Committee.

Lawrence Taylor: Modern sculptor.

Will Thomas (b. 1905): Author of *God Is for White Folks* (1947).

Era Bell Thompson: Magazine editor, author, Negro woman editor of nationally circulated magazine.

Wallace Thurman (1902-1934): Author and playwright, co-author of Broadway play *Harlem* (1929), Novels: *The Blacker The Berry* (1929) and *Infants of the Spring* (1932).

Channing Tobias (b. 1902): chairman of the board of directors, NAACP.

Eddie Tolan (d. 1967): Olympic star at Berlin Olympic games (1936), Los Angeles Olympic games (1932).

Jean Toomer (b. 1894): Writer and poet: *Cane* (1923).

Willard Townsend (1895-1957): Head of "Redcaps" and behind-the-scenes labor statesman who brought the Negroes into the CIO; vice president of AFL-CIO.

Lorenzo Turner (b. 1895): Expert on language and literature.

Robert L. Vann (1887–1940): Founder and publisher of the *Pittsburgh Courier;* political figure; Minister to Liberia.

Clinton A. Walker: Modern sculptor.

Maggie L. Walker (1867–1934): Woman banker, insurance executive, civic worker.

Margaret Walker (b. 1915): Writer and Negro educator.

Wyatt T. Walker (b. 1929): Southern Christian Leadership Conference; editor of *Negro Heritage.*

William Warfield (b. 1920): Actor, contemporary singer.

Ethel Waters (b. 1900): Actress, singer.

George L-P. Weaver (b. 1912): Assistant Secretary, U.S. Department of Labor; director of AFL-CIO.

Robert C. Weaver (b. 1907): Economist; administrator of the federal Housing and Home Finance Agency; first Negro appointed to a President's cabinet (1966).

Charles H. Wesley (b. 1892): Orator, minister, former president of Central State College; executive director of Association for the Study of Negro Life and History; wrote many works on Negro history: *Negro Labor in the United States: 1850-1925,* co-authored *The Negro in Our History, Negro Makers of History, The Story of the Negro Retold.*

Dorothy West (b. 1905): Author of *The Living is Easy* (1948).

Clifton Wharton (b. 1899): Diplomat, U.S. Minister to Rumania; Ambassador to Norway.

John H. Wheeler: President of Farmers and Mechanics Bank of Durham, N.C.

Charles White (b. 1918): Outstanding modern painter.

Clarence Cameron White (1880-1960): Noted violinist-composer.

Walter F. White (1893-1955): Executive secretary of NAACP for 24 years; outstanding leader in the fight for Negro rights.

J. Ernest Wilkins, Sr. (1894-1959): Appointed Assistant Secretary of Labor by President Eisenhower, 1954.

J. Ernest Wilkins, Jr. (b. 1923): Mathematician, Phi Beta Kappa, Ph.D. in mathematics U. of Chicago at 19 years of age.

Roy Wilkins (b. 1901): Executive Secretary of NAACP; former editor of *Crisis* magazine.

Robert Shaw Wilkinson: Educator.

Paul R. Williams (b. 1894): Noted architect; City Architect of Los Angeles; has designed and erected many famous hotels, homes, places of business in southern California.

Hale Woodruff (b. 1900): Art instructor at New York U., famous painter in his own right.

Beulah Woodward (1895-1955): Painter and sculptress, known for her African types and masks.

Alonzo Wright: Came to Cleveland with six cents; built a string of gas stations; became one of many Negro millionaires.

Dr. Jane Wright (b. 1919): Noted surgeon and director of cancer research at the New York U. Medical Center.

Richard Wright (1908-1960): Famous author; *Native Son,* his most famous work of fiction, was both a Broadway play and a motion picture

Richard Robert Wright, Jr. (b. 1878): Leading A.M.E. bishop and editor; co-founder and later president of a bank in Philadelphia.

Stephen J. Wright (b. 1910): President of Fisk U.

Frank Yerby (b. 1916): Writer of romantic historical fiction; several of his works have been adapted to motion pictures; among his works: *The Foxes of Harrow* (1946) became major Hollywood film from book by Negro; *The Vixens* (1947); *The Golden Hawk* (1948); *Pride's Castle* (1949); *A Woman Called Fancy* (1951); *The Saracen Blade* (1952).

Max Yergan: YMCA official; worked with African students.

Whitney M. Young, Jr. (b. 1921): Social work administrator; executive director of the National Urban League.

Paul B. Zuber (b. 1927): Civil rights lawyer; active in de facto segregation school suits.

4. NEGROES IN CONGRESS, 1870–1966

> No state shall make or enforce any law which shall abridge the privileges or immunities of citizens of the United States, nor shall any State deprive any person of life, liberty, or property without due process of law, nor deny to any person within its jurisdiction the equal protection of the laws.
>
> —Fourteenth Amendment to the Constitution, ratified in 1868

Between 1870 and the turn of the century, there were 22 Negro members of the U.S. Congress—two Senators, twenty Representatives. There is virtually no mention of these Congressmen in our history books. Twenty-nine years passed before another Negro was elected to Congress.

NAME	STATE	YEAR
Senate:		
1. Hiram R. Revels	Mississippi	1870–1871
2. B. K. Bruce	Mississippi	1875–1881
3. Edward W. Brooke	Massachusetts	1967–
House of Representatives:		
4. Jefferson F. Long	Georgia	1870–1871
5. Robert C. DeLarge	South Carolina	1871–1873
6. Josiah T. Walls	Florida	1871–1876
7. Benjamin S. Turner	Alabama	1871–1873
8. Joseph S. Rainey	South Carolina	1870–1879
9. Robert B. Elliott	South Carolina	1871–1874
10. James T. Rapier	Alabama	1873–1875
11. Alonzo J. Ransier	South Carolina	1873–1875
12. Richard H. Cain	South Carolina	1873–1875, 1877–1879
13. John R. Lynch	Mississippi	1873–1877, 1882–1883
14. John A. Hyman	North Carolina	1875–1877

NAME	STATE	YEAR
15. Jeremiah Haralson	Alabama	1875–1877
16. Robert Smalls	South Carolina	1875–1879, 1882–1883, 1885–1887
17. Charles Nash	Louisiana	1875–1877
18. James E. O'Hara	North Carolina	1883–1887
19. Henry P. Cheatham	North Carolina	1889–1893
20. John M. Langston	Virginia	1890–1891
21. Thomas E. Miller	South Carolina	1890–1891
22. George W. Murray	South Carolina	1893–1897
23. George H. White	North Carolina	1897–1901

(29 years passed before election of another Negro Congressman)

NAME	STATE	YEAR	
24. Oscar S. DePriest	Illinois	1929–1935	
25. Arthur W. Mitchell	Illinois	1935–1943	
26. William L. Dawson	Illinois	1943–	*
27. Adam Clayton Powell, Jr.	New York	1945–	*
28. Charles C. Diggs, Jr.	Michigan	1955–	*
29. Robert N. C. Nix, Sr.	Pennsylvania	1959–	*
30. Augustus Hawkins	California	1961–	*
31. John Conyers, Jr.	Michigan	1965–	

*Re-elected in 1966 for another term in the House.

5. NEGROES IN AMERICAN WARS

"Our Fight for Freedom begins when we get to San Francisco."
—A Negro returning from Okinawa in 1945

The American Negro has participated valiantly and given of himself as a soldier in every war of his country.

THE AMERICAN REVOLUTION
March 5, 1770—The Boston Massacre. Crispus Attucks (a Negro) died with Samuel Gray, James Caldwell, Patrick Carr, and Samuel Maverick. Their death rallied the colonies to fight for independence and freedom. There were Negro soldiers in the Revolutionary Army from every one of the original thirteen colonies. The 5,000 or more Negroes who participated in the Revolutionary War fought in integrated units and participated in all of the major battles of the war. Among them were such men as Peter Salem, Salem Poor, Titus Coburn, Cato Howe, Alexander Ames, Seymour Burr, Pomp Fiske, and Prince Hall, founder of the Negro Masonic Order.

WAR OF 1812
Fifty Negroes served with Captain Perry when he defeated the British man-o'-war in the battle of Lake Erie. Two battalions of 500 free Negroes fought with Andrew Jackson to break the hold of the British on New Orleans.

CIVIL WAR
Negroes in the Union Navy: About one out of every four Union sailors was a Negro. At least four Negro sailors won Congressional Medals of Honor.

Negroes in the Union Army: The approximately 200,000 Negro soldiers in the Union Army were organized into 166 all-Negro regiments (145 infantry, 7 cavalry, 12 heavy artillery, 1 light artillery, 1 engineer). In addition, there were Negro soldiers in so-called "white" regiments. The largest number of Negro soldiers came from Louisiana (24,052), followed by Kentucky (23,703) and Tennessee (20,133). Pennsylvania contributed more Negro soldiers than any other Northern state (8,612). Negro soldiers participated in 449 battles, 39 of them major engagements. Sixteen Negro soldiers received Congressional Medals of Honor for gallantry in action. Some 37,638 Negro soldiers lost their lives during the war.

SPANISH AMERICAN WAR
The third Negro graduate from West Point, Colonel Charles Young, was an outstanding hero of the Spanish American War. Volunteer Negro troops were raised in Alabama, Illinois, Kansas, Ohio, and Virginia to fight in this war.

WORLD WAR I
At the beginning of this war there were 10,000 Negroes in the Regular Army and 10,000 in the National Guard.

Between June 5, 1917, and September 12, 1918, 2,290,529 Negro men registered for service with the United States Army.

Two hundred thousand Negro men went to France: 42,000 served as combat troops.

One hundred and ninety-four Negro officers and men received decorations, among them the Congressional Medal of Honor, the Distinguished Service Cross, the Croix de Guerre, and the Legion of Honor. Two Negro soldiers (Henry Johnson and Needham Roberts) were the first American soldiers to receive the French Croix de Guerre for wiping out a German raiding party of 20 men. These two men were the very first American soldiers decorated in World War I.

A Negro regiment (the 15th Regiment of New York) was under fire for 91 days.

WORLD WAR II
3,000,000 Negro men registered for service.
  701,678 Negro men served in the Army.
  165,000 Negro men served in the Navy.
    5,000 Negro men served in the Coast Guard.
   17,000 Negro men served in the Marine Corps.
    4,000 Negro women served as WAVES and WACS.
Five hundred thousand Negro men and women served overseas.

Colonel Benjamin O. Davis, Sr., became the first Negro Brigadier General. His son, Lieutenant Colonel Benjamin O. Davis, Jr., was a member of the Negro Air Combat Unit.

In December 1944 2,500 Negroes served in army units fighting in the Battle of the Bulge.

Dorie Miller, messman aboard *USS Arizona*, shot down four enemy planes during Pearl Harbor attack; he later received the Navy Cross.

Leonard Roy Harmon, who lost his life in the Battle of Guadalcanal in 1942, received the Navy Cross for extraordinary heroism in that engagement. The first naval vessel named for a Negro was named in his honor when the *USS Harmon* was launched July 25, 1943. Thirteen Liberty Ships built by the United States Government for service in the Merchant Marine were named in honor of Negroes. Among them was the *S.S. George Washington Carver*, the *S.S. Frederick Douglass*, the *S.S. James Weldon Johnson*, the *S.S. Paul Lawrence Dunbar*, and the *S.S. Harriet Tubman*.

KOREAN WAR

In this war the armed forces of the United States were completely integrated. Negroes served together with whites in all branches of the armed forces. Dr. John A. Hannah, president of Michigan State University, then the Assistant Secretary of Defense, stated: "The obligation to defend our country and our beliefs are borne equally by all citizens without regard to race or color or religion. It should be a real gratification to all thinking Americans to know that our Armed Forces are leading the way in demonstrating both at home and abroad that America provides opportunities for all of her people."

Congressional Medal of Honor, 1863–1966

ARMY

1863 Sgt. William Harvey Carney, Co. C., 54th Mass. Vols.
1864 Sgt. Maj. Christian A. Fleetwood, 4th U.S.C.T.
1864 Sgt. Alfred B. Hilton, Co. H, 4th U.S.C.T.
1864 Cpl. Charles Veal, Co. D, 4th U.S.C.T.
1864 Sgt. Milton M. Holland, Co. C, 5th U.S.C.T.
1864 1st Sgt. James E. Bronson, Co. D, 5th U.S.C.T.
1864 1st Sgt. Powhatan Beatty, Co. G, 5th U.S.C.T.
1864 1st Sgt. Robert A. Pinn, Co. I, 5th U.S.C.T.
1864 Sgt. Maj. Thomas R. Hawkins, 6th U.S.C.T.
1864 Sgt. Alexander Kelly, Co. F, 6th U.S.C.T.
1864 Cpl. Miles James, Co. B, 36th U.S.C.T.
1864 Pvt. James Gardiner, Co. I, 36th U.S.C.T.
1864 1st Sgt. Edward Ratcliffe, Co. C, 38th U.S.C.T.
1864 Sgt. James H. Harris, Co. B, 38th U.S.C.T.

1864   Pvt. William H. Barnes, Co. C. 38th U.S.C.T.
1864   Sgt. Decatur Dorsey, Co. B, 39th U.S.C.T.
1870   Sgt. Emanuel Stance, Troop F, 9th U.S. Cav.
1877   Cpl. Clinton Greaves, Troop C, 9th U.S. Cav.
1879   Sgt. Thomas Boyne, Troop C, 9th U.S. Cav.
1879   Sgt. John Denny, 9th U.S. Cav.
1879   Sgt. Henry Johnson, Troop D, 9th U.S. Cav.
1880   Sgt. George Jordan, Troop K, 9th U.S. Cav.
1881   Sgt. Thomas Shaw, Troop K, 9th U.S. Cav.
1881   Sgt. George Jordan, Troop K, 9th U.S. Cav.
1881   1st Sgt. Moses Williams, Troop I, 9th U.S. Cav.
1881   Sgt. Brent Woods, Troop B, 9th U.S. Cav.
1881   Pvt. Augustus Walley, Troop I, 9th U.S. Cav.
1887   Cpl. Clinton Greaves, Troop C, 9th U.S. Cav.
1890   Cpl. William O. Wilson, Troop I, 9th U.S. Cav.
1890   Sgt. William McBryar, Troop K, 10th U.S. Cav.
1898   Pvt. Dennis Bell, Troop H, 10th U.S. Cav.
1898   Pvt. William H. Thompkins, Troop M, 10th U.S. Cav.
1898   Pvt. Fitz Lee, Troop M, 10th U.S. Cav.
1898   Pvt. George H. Wanton, 10th U.S. Cav.
1898   Sgt. Edward L. Baker, 10th U.S. Cav.
1951   P.F.C. William Thompson, 24th Infantry, Korea*
1952   Sgt. Cornelius H. Charlton, 24th Infantry, Korea*
1966   Pvt. Milton L. Olive, III, 503rd Infantry, Viet Nam*
* Awarded posthumously.

NAVY
1863   Robert Blake, Contraband, U.S.S. *Marblehead*
1864   Joachim Pease, Seaman, U.S.S. *Kearsarge*
1864   John H. Lawson, Landsman, U.S.S. *Hartford*
1864   Clement Dees, Seaman, U.S.S. *Pontoosuc*
1865   Aaron Anderson, Landsman, U.S.S. *Wyandank*
1872   Joseph B. Noil, Seaman, U.S.S. *Powhatan*
1898   Daniel Atkins, Ship's Cook, U.S.S. *Cushing*
1898   Robert Penn, Fireman, U.S.S. *Iowa*

Negro Graduates of the Service Academies

GRADUATES OF THE U.S. MILITARY ACADEMY
*Flipper, Henry O., 1877 Infantry
*Alexander, John H., 1887 Infantry
*Young, Charles D., 1889 Cavalry
Davis, Benjamin O., Jr., 1936 USAF
Fowler, James D., 1941 Infantry
*Tresville, Robert B., Jr., 1943 USAF

Davenport, Clarence M., 1943 Artillery
****Francis, Henry M., 1944 Artillery
Davis, Ernest J., Jr., 1945 USAF
****Rivers, Mark E., Jr., 1945 USAF
*McCoy, Andrew A., Jr., 1946 USAF
Howard, Edward B., 1949 Signal Corps
Smith, Charles L., 1949 Signal Corps
**Carlisle, David K, 1950 CE
**Green, Robert W., 1950 CE
*Brown, Norman J., 1951 Armor
Wainer, Douglas F., 1951 Signal Corps
Robinson, Roscoe, Jr., 1951 Infantry
**Woodson, William B., 1951 Artillery
Young, James R., Jr., 1951 USAF
Corprew, Gerald, 1953 Signal Corps
Hughes, Bernard C., 1953 CE
Worthy, Clifford, 1953 Artillery
Lee, Ronald B., 1954 Signal Corps
**Turner, Leroy, 1954 Infantry
Robinson, Hugh G., 1954 CE
Hamilton, John M., Jr., 1955 Infantry
Olive, Lewis C., Jr., 1955 USAF
Cassells, Cyrus, 1955 USAF
Batchman, G. R., 1955 Infantry
Brown, John, 1955 Infantry
Blunt, Roger, 1956 CE
Bradley, Martin G., 1957 USAF
McCollum, Cornell, Jr., 1957 Signal Corps
Brunner, Ronald S., 1958 Artillery
Baugh, Raymond C., 1959 Signal Corps
Kelley, Welbourne A., III, 1959 CE
Dorsey, Ira, 1960 Artillery
Brown, Reginald J., 1961 Infantry
Quinn, Kenneth L., 1961 Signal Corps
Gorden, Fred A., 1962 Artillery
Handcox, Robert C., 1963 Infantry
Banks, Edgar, 1963 Artillery
Ivy, William L., 1963 USAF
Jackson, David S., 1963 Artillery
Miller, Warren F., Jr., 1964 Artillery
Ramsay, David L., 1964 USAF
Anderson, Joseph B., 1965 Infantry
Conley, James S., 1965 Artillery
Hester, Arthur C., 1965 Armor
Jenkins, Harold A., Jr., 1965 Infantry

Cox, Robert R. E., 1966 Unknown
Davis, Thomas B., III, 1966 Unknown
Ramsay, Robert B., 1966 Unknown

GRADUATES OF THE U.S. NAVAL ACADEMY
Brown, Wesley A., 1949 USN
Chambers, Lawrence, 1952 USN
Taylor, Reeves, 1953 USN
***Raiford, John, 1954
**Gregg, Lucius P., Jr., 1955 USAF
Sechrest, Edward, 1956 USN
Bauduit, Harold S., 1956 USAF
Jamison, Vencin, 1957 USN
*Slaughter, Kent W., 1957 USAF
*Fennell, George M., 1958 USN
Bruce, Malvin D., 1959 USN
Bush, William S., III, 1959 USN
Clark, Maurice E., 1959 USN
Powell, William E., Jr., 1959 USN
Byrd, Willie C., 1961 USN
Johnson, Mack, Jr., 1961 USN
Shelton, John A., 1961 USN
Jackson, John T., 1962 USAF
McCray, Donald, 1962 USN
Newton, Robert C., 1963 USN
Jones, W. C., 1964 US Marine Corps
McDonald, James E., 1964 US Marine Corps
Prout, Patrick M., 1964 US Marine Corps
Thomas, Benjamin F., 1964 USN
Carter, Stanley J., Jr., 1965 USN
Grayson, Floyd F., Jr., 1965 USN
Reason, Joseph Paul, 1965 USN

GRADUATES OF THE U.S. AIR FORCE ACADEMY
Bush, Charles Vernon, 1963 USAF
Payne, Isaac S., IV, 1963 USAF
Sims, Roger, 1963 USAF
Gregory, Frederick, 1964 USAF
Beamon, Arthur, 1965 USAF
Thomas, Charles, 1965 USAF
Plummer, Bentley V., 1965 USAF
Wiley, Fletcher H., 1965 USAF
* *Deceased.*
** *Resigned.*
*** *Graduated but not commissioned.*
**** *Retired.*

6. EARLY NEGRO INVENTORS

> Men are not superior by reason of accidents of race or color.
> They are superior who have the best heart—the best brain.
>
> —Ralph Ingersoll

There is no attempt here to list inventions after 1900—but only to show the existence of these many contributions in the earlier years.

From D. W. Culp, *Twentieth Century Negro Literature.* Atlanta, J. L. Nichols, 1902, pp. 405-413.

LIST OF COLORED INVENTORS IN THE UNITED STATES AS FURNISHED FOR THE PARIS EXPOSITION, 1900. Virtually all of these inventions are patented with the U.S. Patent Office, issued at the dates indicated.

Inventor	*Invention*	*Date*
Abrams, W. B.	Hame Attachment	Apr. 14, 1891
Allen, C. W.	Self-Leveling Table	Nov. 1, 1898
Allen, J. B.	Clothes Line Support	Dec. 10, 1895
Ashbourne, A. P.	Process for Preparing Coconut for Domestic Use	June 1, 1875
Ashbourne, A. P.	Biscuit Cutter	Nov. 30, 1875
Ashbourne, A. P.	Refining Coconut Oil	July 27, 1880
Ashbourne, A. P.	Process of Treating Coconut	Aug. 21, 1877
Bailes, Wm.	Ladder Scaffold Support	Aug. 5, 1879
Bailey, L. C.	Combined Truss and Bandage	Sept. 25, 1883
Bailey, L. C.	Folding Bed	July 18, 1899
Bailiff, C. O.	Shampoo Headrest	Oct. 11, 1898
Ballow, W. J.	Combined Hatrack and Table	Mar. 29, 1898
Barnes, G. A. E.	Design for Sign	Aug. 19, 1898
Beard, A. J.	Rotary Engine	July 5, 1892
Beard, A. J.	Car-coupler	Nov. 23, 1897
Becket, G. E.	Letter Box	Oct. 4, 1892

Inventor	Invention	Date
Bell, L.	Locomotive Smoke Stack	May 23, 1871
Bell, L.	Dough Kneader	Dec. 10, 1872
Benjamin, L. W.	Broom Moisteners and Bridles	May 16, 1893
Benjamin, Miss M. E.	Gong and Signal Chairs for Hotels	July 17, 1888
Binga, M. W.	Street Sprinkling Apparatus	July 22, 1879
Blackburn, A. B.	Railway Signal	Jan. 10, 1888
Blackburn, A. B.	Spring Seat for Chairs	Apr. 3, 1888
Blackburn, A. B.	Cash Carrier	Oct. 23, 1888
Blair, H.	Corn Planter	Oct. 14, 1834
Blair, Henry	Cotton Planter	Aug. 31, 1836
Blue, L.	Hand Corn Shelling Device	May 20, 1884
Booker, L. F.	Design Rubber Scraping Knife	Mar. 28, 1899
Boone, Sarah	Ironing Board	Apr. 26, 1892
Bowman, H. A.	Making Flags	Feb. 23, 1892
Brooks, C. B.	Punch	Oct. 31, 1893
Brooks, C. B.	Street-Sweepers	Mar. 17, 1896
Brooks, C. B.	Street-Sweepers	May 12, 1896
Brooks, Hallstead and Page	Street-Sweepers	Apr. 21, 1896
Brown, Henry	Receptacle for Storing and Preserving Papers	Nov. 2, 1886
Brown, L. F.	Bridle Bit	Oct. 25, 1892
Brown, O. E.	Horseshoe	Aug. 23, 1892
Brown & Latimer	Water Closets for Railway Cars	Feb. 10, 1874
Burkins, Eugene	Rapid-Fire Gun	
Burr, J. A.	Lawn Mower	May 9, 1899
Burr, W. F.	Switching Device for Railways	Oct. 31, 1899
Burwell, W.	Boot or Shoe	Nov. 28, 1899
Butler, R. A.	Train Alarm	June 15, 1897
Butts, J. W.	Luggage Carrier	Oct. 10, 1899
Byrd, T. J.	Improvement in Holders for Reins for Horses	Feb. 6, 1872
Byrd, T. J.	Apparatus for Detaching Horses from Carriages	Mar. 19, 1872
Byrd, T. J.	Improvement in Neck Yokes for Wagons	Apr. 30, 1872
Byrd, T. J.	Improvement in Car-Couplings	Dec. 1, 1874
Campbell, W. S.	Self-Setting Animal Trap	Aug. 30, 1881
Cargill, B. F.	Invalid Cot	July 25, 1899
Carrington, T.A .	Range	July 25, 1876
Carter, W. C.	Umbrella Stand	Aug. 4, 1885
Certain, J. M.	Parcel Carrier for Bicycles	Dec. 26, 1899

Inventor	Invention	Date
Cherry, M. A.	Velocipede	May 8, 1888
Cherry, M. A.	Street Car Fender	Jan. 1, 1895
Church, T. S.	Carpet Beating Machine	July 29, 1884
Clare, O. B.	Trestle	Oct. 9, 1888
Coates, R.	Overboot for Horses	Apr. 19, 1892
Cook, G.	Automatic Fishing Device	May 30, 1899
Coolidge, J. S.	Harness Attachment	Nov. 13, 1888
Cooper, A. R.	Shoemaker's Jack	Aug. 22, 1899
Cooper, J.	Shutter and Fastening	May 1, 1883
Cooper, J.	Elevator Device	Apr. 2, 1895
Cooper, J.	Elevator Device	Sept. 21, 1897
Cornwell, P. W.	Draft Regulator	Oct. 2, 1888
Cornwell, P. W.	Draft Regulator	Feb. 7, 1893
Cralle, A. L.	Ice-Cream Mold	Feb. 2, 1897
Creamer, H.	Steam Feed Water Trap	Mar. 17, 1885
Creamer, H.	Steam Traps	Mar. 8, 1887
Creamer, H.	Steam Traps	Jan. 17, 1888
Creamer, H.	Steam Trap Feeder	Dec. 11, 1888
Creamer, H.	Steam Trap	May 28, 1889
Creamer, H.	Steam Trap	Aug. 18, 1891
Creamer, H.	Steam Trap	Nov. 21, 1893
Cosgrove, W. F.	Automatic Stop Plug for Gas Oil Pipes	Mar. 17, 1885
Darkins, J. T.	Ventilation	Feb. 19, 1895
Davis, I. D.	Tonic	Nov. 2, 1886
Davis, W. D.	Riding Saddles	Oct. 6, 1896
Davis, W. R., Jr.	Library Table	Sept. 24, 1878
Deitz, W. A.	Shoe	Apr. 30, 1867
Dickinson, J. H.	Pianola	Detroit, Mich., 1899
Dorsey, O.	Door-Holding Device	Dec. 10, 1878
Dorticus, C. J.	Device for Applying Coloring Liquids to Sides of Soles or Heels of Shoes	Mar. 19, 1895
Dorticus, C. J.	Machine for Embossing Photo	Apr. 16, 1895
Dorticus, C. J.	Photographic Print Wash	Apr. 23, 1895
Dorticus, C. J.	Hose Leak Stop	July 18, 1899
Downing, P. B.	Electric Switch for Railroad	June 17, 1890
Downing, P. B.	Letter Box	Oct. 27, 1891
Downing, P. B.	Street Letter Box	Oct. 27, 1891
Dunnington, J. H.	Horse Detachers	Mar. 16, 1897
Edmonds, T. H.	Separating Screens	July 20, 1897

Inventor	Invention	Date
Elkins, T.	Dining, Ironing Table and Quilting Frame Combined	Feb. 22, 1870
Elkins, T.	Chamber Commode	Jan. 9, 1872
Elkins, T.	Refrigerating Apparatus	Nov. 4, 1879
Evans, J. H.	Convertible Settees	Oct. 5, 1897
Faulkner, H.	Ventilated Shoe	Apr. 29, 1890
Ferrell, F. J.	Steam Trap	Feb. 11, 1890
Ferrell, F. J.	Apparatus for Melting Snow	May 27, 1890
Ferrell, F. J.	Valve	May 27, 1890
Ferrell, F. J.	Valve	Apr. 14, 1891
Ferrell, F. J.	Valve	Nov. 10, 1891
Ferrell, F. J.	Valve	Jan. 26, 1892
Ferrell, F. J.	Valve	Feb. 2, 1892
Ferrell, F. J.	Valve	Feb. 9, 1892
Ferrell, F. J.	Valve	Jan. 17, 1893
Ferrell, F. J.	Valve	July 18, 1893
Fisher, D. A.	Joiners' Clamp	Apr. 20, 1875
Fisher, D. A.	Furniture Castor	Mar. 14, 1876
Flemming, R. F., Jr.	Guitar	Mar. 3, 1886
Goode, Sarah E.	Folding Cabinet Bed	July 14, 1885
Grant, G. F.	Golf-Tee	Dec. 12, 1899
Grant, W. S.	Curtain Rod Support	Aug. 4, 1896
Gray, R. H.	Bailing Press	Aug. 28, 1894
Gray, R. H.	Cistern Cleaners	Apr. 9, 1895
Gregory, J.	Motor	Apr. 26, 1887
Grenon, H.	Razor Stropping Device	Feb. 18, 1896
Griffin, F. W.	Pool Table Attachment	June 13, 1899
Gunn, S. W.	Boot or Shoe	Jan. 16, 1900
Haines, J. H.	Portable Basin	Sept. 28, 1897
Hammonds, J. F.	Apparatus for Holding Yarn Skeins	Dec. 15, 1896
Harding, F. H.	Extension Banquet Table	Nov. 22, 1898
Hawkins, J.	Gridiron	Mar. 26, 1845
Hawkins, R.	Harness Attachment	Oct. 4, 1887
Headen, M.	Foot Power Hammer	Oct. 5, 1886
Hearness, R.	Sealing Attachment for Bottles	Feb. 15, 1898
Hearness, R.	Detachable Car Fender	July 4, 1899
Hilyer, A. F.	Water Evaporator Attachment for Hot Air Registers	Aug. 26, 1890
Hilyer, A. F.	Registers	Oct. 14, 1890
Holmes, E. H.	Gage	Nov. 12, 1895

Inventor	*Invention*	*Date*
Hunter, J. H.	Portable Weighing Scales	Nov. 3, 1896
Hyde, R. N.	Composition for Cleaning and Preserving Carpets	Nov. 6, 1888
Jackson, B. F.	Heating Apparatus	Mar. 1, 1898
Jackson, B. F.	Matrix Drying Apparatus	May 10, 1898
Jackson, B. F.	Gas Burner	Apr. 4, 1899
Jackson, H. A.	Kitchen Table	Oct. 6, 1896
Jackson, W. H.	Railway Switch	Mar. 9, 1897
Jackson, W. H.	Railway Switch	Mar. 16, 1897
Jackson, W. H.	Automatic Locking Switch	Aug. 23, 1898
Johnson, D.	Rotary Dining Table	Jan. 15, 1888
Johnson, D.	Lawn Mower Attachment	Sept. 10, 1889
Johnson, D.	Grass Receivers for Lawn Mowers	June 10, 1890
Johnson, I. R.	Bicycle Frame	Oct. 10, 1899
Johnson, P.	Swinging Chairs	Nov. 15, 1881
Johnson, P.	Eye Protector	Nov. 2, 1880
Johnson, W.	Egg Beater	Feb. 5, 1884
Johnson, W.	Velocipede	June 20, 1899
Johnson, W. A.	Paint Vehicle	Dec. 4, 1888
Johnson, W. H.	Overcoming Dead Centers	Feb. 4, 1896
Johnson, W. H.	Overcoming Dead Centers	Oct. 11, 1898
Jones & Long	Caps for Bottles	Sept. 13, 1898
Joyce, J. A.	Ore Bucket	Apr. 26, 1898
Latimer, L. H.	Manufacturing Carbons	June 17, 1882
Latimer, L. H.	Apparatus for Cooling and Disinfecting	Jan. 12, 1886
Latimer, L. H.	Locking Racks for Hats, Coats and Umbrellas	Mar. 24, 1896
Lavalette, W. A.	Printing Press	Sept. 17, 1878
Lee, H.	Animal Trap	Feb. 12, 1867
Lee, J.	Kneading Machine	Aug. 7, 1894
Lee, J.	Bread Crumbing Machine	June 4, 1895
Leslie, F. W.	Envelope Seal	Sept. 21, 1897
Lewis, A. L.	Window Cleaner	Sept. 27, 1892
Lewis, E. R.	Spring Gun	May 3, 1887
Linden, H.	Piano Truck	Sept. 8, 1891
Little, E.	Bridle-Bit	Mar. 7, 1882
Loudin, F. J.	Sash Fastener	Dec. 12, 1892
Loudin, F. J.	Key Fastener	Jan. 9, 1894
Love, J. L.	Plasterers' Hawk	July 9, 1895
Love, J. L.	Pencil Sharpener	Nov. 23, 1897
Marshall, T. J.	Fire Extinguisher	May 26, 1872

Inventor	Invention	Date
Marshall, W.	Grain Binder	May 11, 1886
Martin, W. A.	Lock	July 23, 1889
Martin, W. A.	Lock	Dec. 30, 1890
Matzeliger, J. E.	Mechanism for Distributing Tacks	Nov. 26, 1899
Matzeliger, J. E.	Nailing Machine	Feb. 25, 1896
Matzeliger, J. E.	Tack Separating Mechanism	Mar. 25, 1890
Matzeliger, J. E.	Lasting Machine	Sept. 22, 1891
McCoy, E.	Lubricator for Steam Engines	July 2, 1872
McCoy, E.	Lubricator for Steam Engines	Aug. 6, 1872
McCoy, E.	Lubricator	May 27, 1873
McCoy, E.	Steam Lubricator	Jan. 20, 1874
McCoy, E.	Ironing Table	May 12, 1874
McCoy, E.	Steam Cylinder Lubricator	Feb. 1, 1876
McCoy, E.	Steam Cylinder Lubricator	July 4, 1876
McCoy, E.	Lubricator	Mar. 28, 1882
McCoy, E.	Lubricator	July 18, 1882
McCoy, E.	Lubricator	Jan. 9, 1883
McCoy, E.	Lawn Sprinkler Design	Sept. 26, 1899
McCoy, E.	Steam Dome	June 16, 1885
McCoy, E.	Lubricator	June 16, 1885
McCoy, E.	Lubricator	Feb. 8, 1887
McCoy, E.	Lubricator Attachment	Apr. 19, 1887
McCoy, E.	Lubricator for Safety Valves	May 24, 1887
McCoy, E.	Lubricator	May 29, 1888
McCoy, E.	Lubricator	May 29, 1888
McCoy, E.	Dope Cup	Sept. 29, 1891
McCoy, E.	Lubricator	Dec. 29, 1891
McCoy, E.	Lubricator	Mar. 1, 1892
McCoy, E.	Lubricator	Apr. 5, 1892
McCoy, E.	Lubricator	June 6, 1893
McCoy, E.	Lubricator	Sept. 13, 1898
McCoy, E.	Lubricator	Oct. 4, 1898
McCoy, E.	Lubricator	Nov. 15, 1898
McCoy, E.	Lubricator	June 27, 1899
McCoy & Hodges	Lubricator	Dec. 24, 1889
McCree, D.	Portable Fire Escape	Nov. 11, 1890
Mendenhall, A.	Holder for Driving Reins	Nov. 28, 1899
Miles, A.	Elevator	Oct. 11, 1887
Mitchell, C. L.	Phoneterisin	Jan. 1, 1884
Mitchell, J. M.	Cheek Row Corn Planter	Jan. 16, 1900
Moody, W. U.	Game Board Design	May 11, 1897
Morehead, K.	Reel Carrier	Oct. 6, 1896

Inventor	*Invention*	*Date*
Murray, G. W.	Combined Furrow Opener and Stalk-knocker	Apr. 10, 1894
Murray, G. W.	Cultivator and Marker	Apr. 10, 1894
Murray, G. W.	Planter	June 5, 1894
Murray, G. W.	Cotton Chopper	June 5, 1894
Murray, G. W.	Fertilizer Distributer	June 5, 1894
Murray, G. W.	Planter	June 5, 1894
Murray, G. W.	Combined Cotton Seed	June 5, 1894
Murray, G. W.	Planter and Fertilizer Distributer Reaper	June 5, 1894
Murray, W.	Attachment for Bicycles	Jan. 27, 1891
Nance, L.	Game Apparatus	Dec. 1, 1891
Nash, H. H.	Life Preserving Stool	Oct. 5, 1875
Newman, Miss L. D.	Brush	Nov. 15, 1898
Newson, S.	Oil Heater or Cooker	May 22, 1894
Nichols & Latimer	Electric Lamp	Sept. 13, 1881
Nickerson, W. J.	Mandolin and Guitar Attachment for Pianos	June 27, 1899
O'Conner & Turner	Alarm for Boilers	Aug. 25, 1896
O'Conner & Turner	Steam Gage	Aug. 25, 1896
O'Conner & Turner	Alarm for Coasts Containing Vessels	Feb. 8, 1898
Outlaw, J. W.	Horseshoes	Nov. 15, 1898
Perryman, F. R.	Caterers' Tray Table	Feb. 2, 1892
Peterson, H.	Attachment for Lawn Mowers	Apr. 30, 1889
Phelps, W. H.	Apparatus for Washing Vehicles	Mar. 23, 1897
Pickering, J. F.	Air Ship	Feb. 20, 1900
Pickett, H.	Scaffold	June 30, 1874
Pinn, T. B.	File Holder	Aug. 17, 1880
Polk, A. J.	Bicycle Support	Apr. 14, 1896
Pugsley, A.	Blind Stop	July 29, 1890
Purdy, W.	Device for Sharpening Edged Tools	Oct. 27, 1896
Purdy, W.	Device for Sharpening Edged Tools	Aug. 16, 1898
Purdy, W.	Device for Sharpening Edged Tools	Aug. 1, 1899
Purdy & Peters	Design for Spoons	Apr. 23, 1895
Purdy & Sadgwar	Folding Chair	June 11, 1889
Purvis, W. B.	Bag Fastener	Apr. 25, 1882

Inventor	Invention	Date
Purvis, W. B.	Hand Stamp	Feb. 27, 1883
Purvis, W. B.	Paper Bag Machine	Feb. 12, 1884
Purvis, W. B.	Fountain Pen	Jan. 7, 1890
Purvis, W. B.	Paper Bag Machine	Jan. 28, 1890
Purvis, W. B.	Paper Bag Machine	June 24, 1890
Purvis, W. B.	Paper Bag Machine	Aug. 19, 1890
Purvis, W. B.	Paper Bag Machine	Sept. 2, 1890
Purvis, W. B.	Paper Bag Machine	Sept. 22, 1891
Purvis, W. B.	Electric Railway	May 1, 1894
Purvis, W. B.	Paper Bag Machine	May 8, 1894
Purvis, W. B.	Paper Bag Machine	May 8, 1894
Purvis, W. B.	Paper Bag Machine	Dec. 11, 1894
Purvis, W. B.	Magnetic Car Balancing Device	May 21, 1895
Purvis, W. B.	Paper Bag Machine	Mar. 9, 1897
Purvis, W. B.	Electric Railway Switch	Aug. 17, 1897
Queen, W.	Guard for Companion Ways and Hatches	Aug. 18, 1891
Ray, E. P.	Chair Supporting Device	Feb. 21, 1899
Ray, L. P.	Dust Pan	Aug. 3, 1897
Reed, J. W.	Dough Kneader and Roller	Sept. 23, 1884
Reynolds, R. R.	Non-Refillable Bottle	May 2, 1899
Reynolds, H. H.	Window Ventilator for R. R. Cars	Apr. 3, 1883
Reynolds, H. H.	Safety Gate for Bridges	Oct. 7, 1890
Rhodes, J. B.	Water Closets	Dec. 19, 1899
Richardson, A. C.	Hame Fastener	Mar. 14, 1882
Richardson, A. C.	Churn	Feb. 17, 1891
Richardson, A. C.	Casket Lowering Device	Nov. 13, 1894
Richardson, A. C.	Insect Destroyer	Feb. 28, 1899
Richardson, A. C.	Bottle	Dec. 12, 1899
Richardson, W. H.	Cotton Chopper	June 1, 1886
Richardson, W. H.	Child's Carriage	June 18, 1889
Richardson, W. H.	Child's Carriage	June 18, 1889
Richey, C. V.	Car Coupling	June 15, 1897
Richey, C. V.	Railroad Switch	Aug. 3, 1897
Richey, C. V.	Railroad Switch	Oct. 26, 1897
Richey, C. V.	Fire Escape Bracket	Dec. 28, 1897
Richey, C. V.	Combined Hammock and Stretcher	Dec. 13, 1898
Rickman, A. L.	Overshoe	Feb. 8, 1898
Ricks, J.	Horseshoe	Mar. 30, 1886
Ricks, J.	Overshoe for Horses	June 6, 1899
Robinson, E. R.	Electric Railway Trolley	Sept. 19, 1893

Inventor	Invention	Date
Robinson, E. R.	Casting Composite	Nov. 23, 1897
Robinson, J.	Dinner Pails	Feb. 1, 1887
Robinson, J. H.	Life Saving Guards for Locomotives	Mar. 14, 1899
Robinson, J. H.	Life Saving Guards for Street Cars	Apr. 25, 1899
Romain, A.	Passenger Register	Apr. 23, 1889
Ross, A. L.	Runner for Stops	Aug. 4, 1896
Ross, A. L.	Bag Closure	June 7, 1898
Ross, J.	Bailing Press	Sept. 5, 1899
Ross, A. L.	Trousers Support	Nov. 28, 1899
Roster, D. N.	Feather Curler	Mar. 10, 1896
Ruffin, S.	Vessels for Liquids and Manner of Sealing	Nov. 20, 1899
Russell, L. A.	Guard Attachment for Beds	Aug. 13, 1895
Sampson, G. T.	Sled Propeller	Feb. 17, 1885
Sampson, G. T.	Clothes Drier	June 7, 1892
Scottron, S. R.	Adjustable Window Cornice	Feb. 17, 1880
Scottron, S. R.	Cornice	Jan. 16, 1883
Scottron, S. R.	Pole Tip	Sept. 21, 1886
Scottron, S. R.	Curtain Rod	Aug. 30, 1892
Scottron, S. R.	Supporting Bracket	Sept. 12, 1893
Shanks, S. C.	Sleeping Car Berth Register	July 21, 1897
Shewcraft, Frank	Letter Box	Detroit, Mich.
Shorter, D. W.	Feed Rack	May 17, 1887
Smith, J. W.	Improvement in Games	Apr. 17, 1900
Smith, J. W.	Lawn Sprinkler	May 4, 1897
Smith, J. W.	Lawn Sprinkler	Mar. 22, 1898
Smith, P. D.	Potato Digger	Jan. 21, 1891
Smith, P. D.	Grain Binder	Feb. 23, 1892
Snow & Johns	Liniment	Oct. 7, 1890
Spears, H.	Portable Shield for Infantry	Dec. 27, 1870
Standard, J.	Oil Stove	Oct. 29, 1889
Standard, J.	Refrigerator	July 14, 1891
Stewart, E. W.	Punching Machine	May 3, 1887
Stewart, E. W.	Machine for Forming Vehicle Seat Bars	Mar. 22, 1887
Stewart, T. W.	Mop	June 13, 1893
Stewart, T. W.	Station Indicator	June 20, 1893
Stewart & Johnson	Metal Bending Machine	Dec. 27, 1887
Sutton, E. H.	Cotton Cultivator	Apr. 7, 1874
Sweeting, J. A.	Device for Rolling Cigarettes	Nov. 30, 1897

Inventor	Invention	Date
Sweeting, J. A.	Combined Knife and Scoop	June 7, 1898
Taylor, B. H.	Rotary Engine	Apr. 23, 1878
Taylor, B. H.	Slide Valve	July 6, 1897
Thomas, S. E.	Waste Trap	Oct. 16, 1883
Thomas, S. E.	Waste Trap for Basins, Closets, etc.	Oct. 4, 1887
Thomas, S. E.	Casting	July 31, 1888
Thomas, S. E.	Pipe Connection	Oct. 9, 1888
Toliver, George	Propeller for Vessels	Apr. 28, 1891
Tregoning & Latimer	Globe Supporter for Electric Lamps	Mar. 21, 1882
Walker, Peter	Machine for Cleaning Seed Cotton	Feb. 16, 1897
Walker, Peter	Bait Holder	Mar. 8, 1898
Waller, J. N.	Shoemaker's Cabinet or Bench	Feb. 3, 1880
Washington, Wade	Corn Husking Machine	Aug. 14, 1883
Watkins, Isaac	Scrubbing Frame	Oct. 7, 1890
Watts, J. R.	Bracket for Miners' Lamp	Mar. 7, 1893
West, E. H.	Weather Shield	Sept. 5, 1899
West, J. W.	Wagon	Oct. 18, 1870
White, D. L.	Extension Steps for Cars	Jan. 12, 1897
White, J. T.	Lemon Squeezer	Dec. 8, 1896
Williams, Carter	Canopy Frame	Feb. 2, 1892
Williams, J. P.	Pillow Sham Holder	Oct. 10, 1899
Williams, P. B.	Electro-Magnetic Electrical Railway Track Switch	Apr. 24, 1900
Williams, P. B.	Electrically Controlled and Operated Railway Switch	Jan. 15, 1901
Winn, Frank	Direct Acting Steam Engine	Dec. 4, 1888
Winters, J. R.	Fire Escape Ladder	May 7, 1878
Winters, J. R.	Fire Escape Ladder	Apr. 8, 1879
Woods, G. T.	Steam Boiler Furnace	June 3, 1884
Woods, G. T.	Telephone Transmitter	Dec. 2, 1884
Woods, G. T.	Apparatus for Transmission of Messages by Electricity	Apr. 7, 1885
Woods, G. T.	Relay Instrument	June 7, 1887
Woods, G. T.	Polarized Relay	July 5, 1887
Woods, G. T.	Electro Mechanical Brake	Aug. 16, 1887
Woods, G. T.	Telephone System and Apparatus	Oct. 11, 1887
Woods, G. T.	Electro-Magnetic Brake Apparatus	Oct. 18, 1887
Woods, G. T.	Railway Telegraphy	Nov. 15, 1887

Inventor	*Invention*	*Date*
Woods, G. T.	Induction Telegraph System	Nov. 29, 1887
Woods, G. T.	Overhead Conducting System for Electric Railway	May 29, 1888
Woods, G. T.	Electro-Motive Railway System	June 26, 1888
Woods, G. T.	Tunnel Construction for Electric Railway	July 17, 1888
Woods, G. T.	Galvanic Battery	Aug. 14, 1888
Woods, G. T.	Railway Telegraphy	Aug. 28, 1888
Woods, G. T.	Automatic Safety Cut-out for Electric Circuits	Jan. 1, 1889
Woods, G. T.	Automatic Safety Cut-out for Electric Circuits	Oct. 14, 1889
Woods, G. T.	Electric Railway System	Nov. 10, 1891
Woods, G. T.	Electric Railway Supply System	Oct. 31, 1893
Woods, G. T.	Electric Railway Conduit	Nov. 21, 1893
Woods, G. T.	System of Electrical Distribution	Oct. 13, 1896
Woods, G. T.	Amusement Apparatus	Dec. 19, 1899
Wormley, James	Life Saving Apparatus	May 24, 1881

7. POPULATION CENSUS FIGURES

Year	U.S. Population	Negro Population	Percentage
1790	3,929,214	757,208	19.3
1800	5,308,483	1,002,037	18.9
1810	7,239,881	1,377,808	19.0
1820	9,638,453	1,771,656	18.4
1830	12,866,020	2,328,642	18.1
1840	17,069,453	2,874,000	16.8
1850	23,191,876	3,638,808	15.7
1860	31,443,790	4,441,830	14.1
1870	39,818,449	4,880,009	12.7
1880	50,155,783	6,580,793	13.1
1890	62,947,714	7,488,676	11.9
1900	75,994,575	8,833,994	11.6
1910	93,402,151	9,827,763	10.7
1920	105,710,620	10,463,131	9.9
1930	122,775,046	11,891,143	9.7
1940	131,669,275	12,865,518	9.8
1950	150,697,361	15,042,286	10.0
1960	179,323,175	18,171,831	10.5
1966	196,173,000	21,508,000	10.1

Part Two: Bibliographies

You degrade us and then ask why we are degraded—you
shut our mouths, and then ask why we don't speak—you
close your colleges and seminaries against us, and then ask
why we don't know more.

—Frederick Douglass

8. A SUGGESTED BASIC LIBRARY
OF NEGRO HISTORY

> In the context of the Negro problem neither whites nor
> blacks, for excellent reasons of their own, have the faintest
> desire to look back; but I think that the past is all that
> makes the present coherent, and further, that the past will
> remain horrible for exactly as long as we refuse to assess it
> honestly.
>
> —James Baldwin, *Notes of a Native Son*

I have been presumptuous enough to set forth a suggested list of basic
books. The selected bibliography is not intended to be exhaustive nor
necessarily the most definitive works in the field. It is but an opinion—a
suggestion for a beginning. It is an attempt to set forth a representative,
readily accessible list of books, some in paperback and therefore not too
expensive, that can be the base of a library on the history of the Negro
in the United States on an adult level, for individuals, schools, churches,
lay groups, and others. To this selected bibliography can be added books
from the young adult and children's list.

Russell L. Adams, *Great Negroes, Past and Present.* Chicago, Afro-Am,
  1963. 182 pp.
*Adventures in Negro History, Vol. I: Adventures in Negro History; Vol.
  II: The Frederick Douglass Years: 1817-1895.* Record albums pro-
  duced by Pepsi-Cola Company, New York, N.Y.
American Oil Company, *American Traveler's Guide to Negro History.*
  Chicago, American Oil Co., 1963. 36 pp. *Paperback.*
Herbert Aptheker, *A Documentary History of the Negro People in the
  United States.* Vol. 1: *From Colonial Times Through The Civil War.*
  New York, Citadel, 1951. Vol. II: *From The Reconstruction Era to
  1910.* 942 pp. *Also in paperback.*
_____,*The Negro in the Abolitionist Movement.* New York, Inter-
  national, 1941. 48 pp. *Paperback.*

————, *The Negro in the American Revolution.* New York, International, 1940. 47 pp. *Paperback.*

————, *The Negro in the Civil War.* New York, International, 1938. 48 pp. *Paperback.*

————, *Negro Slave Revolts in the United States, 1526-1860.* New York, International, 1939. 72 pp. *Paperback.*

Helen A. Archibald, ed., *Negro History and Culture: Selected Material For Use With Children,* Chicago, Chicago City Missionary Society, 1965. *Paperback.*

Richard Bardolph, *The Negro Vanguard.* New York, Rinehart, 1959. 388 pp. *Also in paperback.* Traces the achievements of outstanding American Negroes from 1770 to the present.

Ruth Benedict, *Race: Science and Politics.* New York, Modern Age, 1940. 274 pp. *Also in paperback.*

Lerone Bennett, Jr., *Before the Mayflower: A History of the Negro in America, 1619–1962.* Chicago, Johnson, 1962. 404 pp. Rev. ed. 1966 (*1619–1966*). *Also in paperback.*

Robert A. Bone, *The Negro Novel in America,* rev. ed. New Haven, Yale U. Press, 1965. *Also in paperback.*

Arna Wendell Bontemps, *Story of the Negro,* New York, Knopf, 1962. 243 pp.

————, ed., *American Negro Poetry.* New York, Hill and Wang, 1963. 197 pp. *Also in paperback.*

————, ed., *Negro American Heritage.* San Francisco, Century Schoolbook Press, 1965. 136 pp.

B. A. Botkin, ed., *Lay My Burden Down: A Folk History of Slavery.* Chicago, U. of Chicago Press, 1945. 285 pp. *Also in paperback.*

Sarah Bradford, *Scenes in the Life of Harriet Tubman.* Auburn, N.Y., W. J. Moses, 1869. 132 pp. *Available in paperback as Hariet Tubman: The Moses of Her People.*

Sterling A. Brown, ed., *The Negro Caravan.* New York, Dryden, 1941. 1,082 pp. Selections from novels, poetry, folk literature, spirituals, ballads, blues, and protest songs.

Henrietta Buckmaster, *Let My People Go.* New York, Harper, 1941. 398 pp. The story of the Underground Railroad and the growth of the abolition movement.

Margaret Just Butcher, *The Negro in American Culture.* New York, Knopf, 1956. 294 pp.

David M. Chalmers, *Hooded Americanism: The First Century of the Ku Klux Klan, 1865-1965.* New York, Doubleday, 1965. 420 pp.

Kenneth B. Clark, *Prejudice and Your Child.* Boston, Beacon, 1963. 247 pp. *Also in paperback.*

Sylvia G. Dannett, ed., *Profiles of Negro Womanhood: 1619-1900.* Yonkers, Educational Heritage, 1964.

John P. Davis, ed., *The American Negro Reference Book.* Englewood

Cliffs, Prentice-Hall, 1966. 969 pp. One-volume encyclopedia of the American Negro.

Lavinia Dobler and Edgar A. Toppin, *Pioneers and Patriots: The Lives of Six Negroes of the Revolutionary Era*. Garden City, Doubleday Zenith, 1965. 118 pp. *Also in paperback*. Biographical sketches of Peter Salem, Jean Baptiste Pointe du Sable, Phillis Wheatley, Benjamin Banneker, Paul Cuffee, and John Chavis.

Frederick Douglass, *Life and Times of Frederick Douglass*. Hartford, Park, 1881. 516 pp. *Also in paperback*.

_____, *Narrative of the Life of Frederick Douglass, An American Slave*. Boston, Anti-Slavery Office, 1845. 125 pp. *Also in paperback*.

W. E. B. Du Bois, *Black Reconstruction*. New York, Harcourt, 1935. 746 pp. *Also in paperback*.

_____, *The Souls of Black Folk*. Chicago, McClurg, 1903. 264 pp. *Also in paperback*.

Eugene Feldman, ed., *Figures in Negro History*. Chicago, Museum of Negro History and Art, 1964. 98 pp. *Paperback*.

Miles Mark Fisher, *Negro Slave Songs in the United States*. New York, Citadel, 1963. 223 pp. *Also in paperback*.

Philip S. Foner, *Frederick Douglass*. New York, Citadel, 1964. 444 pp. *Also in paperback*.

John Hope Franklin, *From Slavery to Freedom: A History of American Negroes*. New York, Knopf, 1956. 639 pp.

_____, *Reconstruction After the Civil War*. Chicago, U. of Chicago Press, 1961. 258 pp. *Also in paperback*.

_____, *The Emancipation Proclamation*. New York, Doubleday, 1963. 181 pp. *Also in paperback*.

E. Franklin Frazier, *Black Bourgeoisie*. New York, Collier, 1962. 222 pp. *Paperback*.

_____, *The Negro in the United States*, rev. ed. New York, Macmillan, 1957. 769 pp.

Freedomways, Freedomway Associates, Inc., 799 Broadway, New York, N.Y. Quarterly periodical.

L. H. Giles and L. F. Holmes, *Color Me Brown*. Chicago, Johnson, 1963, 1965. Includes poems and pictures to color of famous Negroes in American history.

Ralph Ginzburg, ed., *100 Years of Lynchings*. New York, Lancer, 1962. 270 pp. *Paperback*.

Mary Ellen Goodman, *Race Awareness in Young Children*. Cambridge, Addison-Wesley, 1952. 280 pp. *Also in paperback*.

Jean Gould, *That Dunbar Boy: The Story of America's Famous Negro Poet*. New York, Dodd, 1958. 245 pp.

Shirley Graham, *Booker T. Washington*. New York, Messner, 1955. 192 pp.

—————, *Jean Baptiste Pointe de Sable.* New York, Messner, 1953. 180 pp.

—————, *The Story of Phillis Wheatley.* New York, Messner, 1949. 176 pp.

—————, *There Once Was a Slave: The Heroic Story of Frederick Douglass.* New York, Messner, 1947. 310 pp.

—————, *Your Most Humble Servant: The Story of Benjamin Banneker.* New York, Messner, 1949. 235 pp.

————— and George D. Lipscomb, *Dr. George Washington Carver, Scientist.* New York, Messner, 1944. 248 pp.

Josiah Henson, *Father Henson's Story of His Own Life.* Boston, J. P. Jewett, 1858. 212 pp. *Also in paperback.* The autobiography of an escaped Negro slave in pre-Civil War Days, whose life served as an inspiration for Harriet Beecher Stowe's *Uncle Tom's Cabin.*

Melville J. Herskovits, *The Myth of the Negro Past.* New York, Harper, 1941. 374 pp. *Also in paperback.*

Thomas Wentworth Higginson, *Army Life in a Black Regiment.* Boston, Fields, Osgood, 1870. 296 pp. *Also in paperback.*

Langston Hughes, *Famous Negro Music Makers.* New York, Dodd, 1955. 179 pp.

————— and Arna Wendell Bontemps, eds., *The Poetry of the Negro: 1746-1949.* Garden City, Doubleday, 1949. 429 pp. Contains the selected poems of 66 American Negro poets, plus tributary poems by non-Negroes and poems by native poets of the Caribbean, British Guiana, British Honduras, Barbados, Trinidad, Haiti, Martinique, French Guiana, Cuba, and Africa; with a brief biographical sketch of each poet.

————— and Milton Meltzer, *A Pictorial History of the Negro in America,* rev. ed. New York, Crown, 1963. 337 pp.

Journal of Negro History, Assn. for the Study of Negro Life and History, 1538 9th St., N.W., Washington, D.C. Quarterly periodical.

Robert T. Kerlin, *Negro Poets and Their Poems.* rev. ed. Washington, Associated, 1935. 342 pp.

Leon F. Litwack, *North of Slavery: The Negro in the Free States, 1790-1860.* Chicago, U. of Chicago Press, 1961. *Also in paperback.*

Rayford W. Logan, *The Negro in the United States.* Princeton, Van Nostrand, 1957. 191 pp. *Paperback.*

—————, *The Betrayal of the Negro.* New York, Collier, 1965. *Also in paperback.*

D. P. Mannix and Malcolm Cowley, *Black Cargoes: History of the Atlantic Slave Trade, 1518-1865.* New York, Viking, 1962. 306 pp. *Also in paperback.*

Lloyd Marcus, *The Treatment of Minorities in Secondary School Textbooks.* New York, Anti-Defamation League, 1961. 63 pp.

Milton Meltzer, ed., *In Their Own Words: A History of the American Negro.* Vol. I, *1691–1865.* New York, Crowell, 1964. 195 pp. Vol. II, *1865–1916.* Crowell, 1965. *Vol. III, 1916–1966.* Crowell, 1967, 213 pp.

Gustavus Myers, *History of Bigotry in the United States.* New York, Putnam, 1960. 474 pp. *Also in paperback.*

Gunnar Myrdal, *An American Dilemma.* New York, Harper, 1944 (2 vols.). *Also in paperback.*

Negro History Bulletin, Assn. for the Study of Negro Life and History, 1538 9th St., N.W., Washington, D.C. Monthly periodical.

J. W. Nordholt-Schulte, Sr., *The People that Walk in Darkness.* New York, Ballantine, 1956. *Paperback.* A history of the Negro in America.

Benjamin Quarles, *The Negro in the American Revolution.* Chapel Hill, U. of North Carolina Press, 1961. 231 pp. *Also in paperback.*

————, *The Negro in the Civil War.* Boston, Little, Brown, 1953. 379 pp.

————, *The Negro in the Making of America.* New York. Collier, 1964. 288 pp. *Paperback.*

J. Saunders Redding, *The Lonesome Road.* Garden City, Doubleday, 1958. 335 pp. The American Negro's dfficult struggle for freedom and equality is traced through the lives of 13 outstanding Negroes: Robert S. Abbott, Frederick Douglass, W. E. B. Du Bois, Marcus Garvey, Joe Louis, Thurgood Marshall, Isaiah Montgomery, Daniel Payne, A. Philip Randolph, Paul Robeson, Sojourner Truth, Booker T. Washington, and Daniel Hale Williams.

Louis Ruchames, ed., *A John Brown Reader.* New York, Abelard-Schuman, 1960. 431 pp.

————, *The Abolitionists.* New York, Putnam, 1963. 259 pp. *Also in paperback.* A collection of the writings of outstanding Abolitionists.

Kenneth M. Stampp, *The Peculiar Institution.* New York, Knopf, 1956. 435 pp. *Also in paperback.* An account of American Negro slavery.

Marion L. Starkey, *Striving to Make It My Home: The Story of Americans from Africa.* New York, 1964. 256 pp.

David Walker, *One Continual Cry. David Walker's Appeal to the Colored Citizens of the World, 1829-1830: Its Setting and Its Meaning.* Ed. by Herbert Aptheker. New York, Marzani and Munsell, 1965. *Also in paperback.*

Booker T. Washington, *Up from Slavery.* New York, Doubleday, 1901. 330 pp. *Also in paperback.* Autobiography.

Erwin K. Welsch, *The Negro in the United States: A Research Guide.* Bloomington, Indiana U. Press, 1965.

Carter G. Woodson, *The Story of the Negro Retold,* 4th ed. Washington, Associated, 1959. 472 pp.

Carter G. Woodson and Charles H. Wesley, *The Negro in Our History,*

10th ed., rev. & enlarged. Washington, Associated, 1962. 833 pp.
————, *Negro Makers of History,* 5th ed. Washington, Associated, 1958. 406 pp.
C. Vann Woodward, *The Strange Career of Jim Crow.* New York, Oxford, 1955. 155 pp. *Also in paperback.* 2nd rev. ed. 1966, 205 pp.
The Race Question in the Modern Science Series. Separate booklets available on all aspects of the race question. UNESCO, 317 E. 34th St., New York, N.Y. 10016.
The Negro in American History: A Curriculum Resource Bulletin for Secondary Schools. Department of History, Public Schools of the District of Columbia.
The Negro in American History: Curriculum Bulletin, 1964-65, Series #4. Board of Education, City of New York, 1964. 110 Livingston St., Brooklyn, N.Y. 11210.
A Guide for the Study of Negro History in the Churches. Commission on Religion and Race, Presbytery of Chicago, 29 E. Madison St., Chicago, Ill.; and Rev. Edward A. White, Director, City Church Project, United Presbyterian Church, Room S, 746 W. Fullerton Ave., Chicago, Ill.

9. BOOKS ON THE GENERAL HISTORY OF THE NEGRO IN THE UNITED STATES

We hold these truths to be self-evident, that all men are created equal, that they are endowed by their Creator with certain unalienable rights, that among these are life, liberty, and the pursuit of happiness. That to secure these rights, governments are instituted among men, deriving their just powers from the consent of the governed.

—The Declaration of Independence

The general history section lists books that cover the history of the Negro in the United States from the earliest times, not restricted to any specific period or area of interest.

Russell L. Adams, *Great Negroes, Past and Present*. Chicago, Afro-Am, 1963. 182 pp.

American Oil Company, *American Traveler's Guide to Negro History*. Chicago, American Oil Company, 1965. 57 pp. *Paperback*.

Herbert Aptheker, *A Documentary History of the Negro People in the United States*. New York, Citadel, reprinted 1962, 1964. 942 pp. in 2 vol. Vol. I: *From Colonial Times Through the Civil War*. Vol. II: *From the Reconstruction Era to 1910. Paperback*.

_____, *Toward Negro Freedom*. New York, New Century, 1956. 191 pp. Historic highlights in the lives and struggles of the American Negro people from colonial days to the present. *Paperback*.

_____, *To Be Free: Studies in American Negro History*. New York, International, 1948. 256 pp.

_____, *Essays in the History of the American Negro*. New York, International, 1945, 1960, 1964. 216 pp. *Also in paperback*.

Richard Bardolph, *The Negro Vanguard*. New York, Rinehart, 1959. 388 pp. *Also in paperback*. Traces the achievements of hundreds of notable Negroes from 1770 to the present; with extensive bibliographic notes.

Lerone J. Bennett, *Before the Mayflower: A History of the Negro in*

America, 1619–1962. Chicago, Johnson, 1962. 404 pp. Rev. ed. 1966 (*1619–1966*). *Also in paperback.*

Jesse Bernard, *Marriage and Family Among Negroes.* Englewood Cliffs, N.J.. Prentice-Hall, 1966. *Also in paperback.*

Arna W. Bontemps, *Story of the Negro,* 3rd ed. rev. New York, Knopf, 1962. 243 pp. A history of the American Negro for young people; contains a chronology of important events in Negro history from 300 to 1955 A.D.

Benjamin Brawley, *A Short History of the American Negro.* New York, Macmillan, 1939. 288 pp.

Ina Corrine Brown, *The Story of the American Negro,* 2nd rev. ed. New York, Friendship, 1957. 212 pp. *Paperback.*

William W. Brown, *The Rising Sun, or the History of the Colored Race.* Boston, Brown, 1874. 552 pp.

Alfred E. Cain, ed., *The Winding Road to Freedom: A Documentary Study.* Yonkers, N.Y., Educational Heritage, 1965. From the earliest anti-slavery resolutions of the Germantown Quakers in 1688 to the Civil Rights Bill of 1964, here are the documentary milestones in three centuries of struggle.

Arthur B. Caldwell, ed., *History of the American Negro.* Atlanta, published by the author, 1919 (3 vols.).

John W. Caughey, John Hope Franklin, and Ernest R. May, *Land of the Free — A History of the United States.* New York, Benziger Brothers, 1966. 658 pp. New integrated textbook for 8th grade.

Earl Conrad, *The Invention of the Negro.* New York, Paul S. Eriksson, Inc., Hill and Wang, 1966.

Bishop L. J. Coppin, *Unwritten History.* Philadelphia, A.M.E., 1919. 375 pp.

John W. Cromwell, *The Negro in American History.* Washington, American Negro Academy, 1914. 284 pp.

Marion Cuthbert, *We Sing America.* New York, Friendship, 1936. 117 pp. Presents the importance of Negro contributions to the history of the United States.

Maurice Rea Davie, *Negroes in American Society.* New York, Whittlesey House, 1949. 542 pp. Negro history from slavery to the present.

John P. Davis, ed., *The American Negro Reference Book.* Englewood Cliffs, Prentice-Hall, 1966. One-volume encyclopedia of the American Negro.

Carl N. Degler, *Out of Our Past.* New York, Harper, 1959. 484 pp. *Also in paperback.*

Merle R. Eppse and A. P. Foster, *Elementary History of America, Including the Contributions of the Negro Race.* Nashville, National, 1939. 312 pp.

Merle R. Eppse, *The Contribution of the Negro to American Life.* Nashville, National Educational Publishing, 1937.

_____, *The Negro, Too, in American History*. Nashville, National Educational Publishing, 1939. 544 pp. Appendices contain important dates in Negro history, a bibliography, historical facts about Negro churches and schools, a list of Negro towns in the United States, and other extremely useful information not readily available elsewhere in any one volume.

Eugene P. R. Feldman, ed., *Figures in Negro History*. Chicago, Museum of Negro History and Art, 1964. 98 pp. *Paperback*. Biographical sketches of Negro personalities.

William Z. Foster, *The Negro People in American History*. New York, International, 1954. 608 pp.

John Hope Franklin, *From Slavery to Freedom: A History of American Negroes*, 2nd ed. rev. New York, Knopf, 1956. 639 pp.

E. Franklin Frazier, *The Negro in the United States,* rev. ed. New York, Macmillan, 1957. 769 pp. Contains bibliographical footnotes, a 43-page "classified" bibliography, and a two-page "supplementary" bibliography.

T. O. Fuller, *Pictorial History of the American Negro*. Memphis, Pictorial, 1933. 375 pp.

J. W. Gibson and W. H. Crogman, *The Colored American from Slavery to Honorable Citizenship*. Atlanta, Nichols, 1902. 732 pp.

Thos. S. Gossett, *Race: The History of an Idea in America*. Dallas, Southern Methodist U. Press, 1943. 512 pp.

Langston Hughes and Milton Meltzer, *A Pictorial History of the Negro in America,* rev. ed. New York, Crown, 1963. 337 pp.

Edward A. Johnson, *A School History of the Negro Race in America*. New York, Goldman Co., 1911. 111 pp.

Rayford W. Logan, *The Negro in the United States*. Princeton, Van Nostrand, 1957. 191 pp. *Paperback*.

Norman McRae and Jerry Blocker, *The American Negro: A History in Biography and Pictures* (includes Teacher's Manual). Chicago, Rand McNally, 1966.

August Meier and Elliott M. Rudwick, *From Plantation to Ghetto: An Interpretive History of American Negroes*. New York, Hill and Wang, 1966. 288 pp.

Thomas Patrick Melody, *The Revolution of Color*. New York, Hawthorn Books, 1966.

Milton Meltzer, ed., *In Their Own Words: A History of the American Negro*. Vol. I, *1619-1865*. New York, Crowell, 1964. 195 pp. Vol. II, *1865-1916*. Crowell, 1965. *Vol. III, 1916-1966*. Crowell, 1967, 213 pp. Excerpts from letters, diaries, speeches, newspapers, pamphlets; presented as records of past happenings and reactions to past happenings.

_____ and Dr. Angus Meier, *Time of Trial, Time of Hope*, Garden City, N.Y., Zenith, 1966. 128 pp. (History of the Negro during World Wars I and II.) *Also in paperback*.

J. W. Nordholt-Schulte, *The People That Walk in Darkness*. New York, Ballantine, 1956. *Paperback*. A history of the Negro in America.

Roi Ottley, *Black Odyssey*. New York, Scribner's, 1948. 340 pp. An American Negro history, 1619-1945.

Talcott Parsons and Kenneth B. Clark, eds., *The Negro American*. Boston, Houghton Mifflin, 1966.

Samuel D. Proctor, *The Young Negro in America, 1960–1980*. New York, Association Press, 1966.

Benjamin Quarles, *The Negro in the Making of America*. New York, Collier, 1964. 288 pp. *Paperback*.

Frank A. Ross and Louise V. Kennedy, *A Bibliography of Negro Migrations*. New York, Columbia U. Press, 1934.

Irving J. Sloan, *The American Negro: A Chronology and Fact Book*. Dobbs Ferry, N.Y., Oceana, 1965. 84 pp. Reference book on the Negro, covering significant phases of his life in America from the Spanish explorers through the award of the Nobel Peace Prize to Dr. Martin Luther King, Jr.

Southern Regional Council, *America's Tenth Man: A Brief Survey of the Negro's Part in American History*. Atlanta, 1944.

Marion L. Starkey, *Striving to Make It My Home: The Story of Americans from Africa*. New York, Norton, 1964. 256 pp.

Earl E. Thorpe, *The Mind of the Negro: An Intellectual History of Afro-Americans, 1619–1960*. Baton Rouge, Ortlieb, 1961. 562 pp.

Richard C. Wade, *The Negro in American Life*. Part One, From Slavery to Citizenship: 1619–1900; Part Two, Toward Full Equality: Since 1900. New York. Houghton Mifflin, 1966. *Also in paperback*.

Willis D. Weatherford, *The Negro from Africa to America*. New York, Doran, 1924. 487 pp.

Erwin K. Welsch, *The Negro in the United States: A Research Guide*. Bloomington, Indiana U. Press, 1965. *Also in paperback*.

Charles H. Wesley, *Neglected History: Essays in Negro History*. Wilberforce, Ohio, Central State College Press, 1965. 24 pp.

George W. Williams, *History of the Negro Race in America, 1619-1880*. New York, Putnam, 1883 (2 vols.).

Carter G. Woodson and Charles H. Wesley, *The Negro in Our History*, 10th ed. rev. Washington, Associated, 1962. 833 pp.

Richard Wright, *12 Million Black Voices: A Folk History of the Negro in the United States*. New York, Viking, 1941. 152 pp.

A Guide for the Study of Negro History in the Churches. Commission on Religion and Race, Presbytery of Chicago; Rev. Edward A. White, Director, City Church Project, United Presbyterian Church, Chicago, Ill.

The Annals of the American Academy of Political and Social Science. Philadelphia, November 1928. 859 pp. Entire volume devoted to "The American Negro," ed. by Donald Young.

The Negro Handbook. Chicago, Johnson Publishing, 1966. 535 pp. (Compiled by the editors of *Ebony.*)

The Negro in American History: A Curriculum Resource Bulletin for Secondary Schools. Washington, Public Schools of the District of Columbia.

The Negro in American History: Curriculum Bulletin, 1964–65, Series #4. City of New York, Board of Education, July 1964. 158 pp.

10. THE COLONIAL PERIOD AND THE AMERICAN REVOLUTION, 1492-1789

The following sections contain selective rather than complete lists, from among the many titles available, of books on the political, social, and economic history of the Negro people.

Lorenzo J. Greene, *The Negro in Colonial New England: 1620–1776.* New York, Columbia U., 1942. 404 pp.

Frank J. Klingberg, *An Appraisal of the Negro in Colonial South Carolina.* Washington, Associated, 1941. 180 pp.

Walter H. Mazyck, *George Washington and the Negro.* Washington, Associated, 1932. 180 pp.

John H. Russell, *The Free Negro in Virginia, 1619–1865.* Baltimore, Johns Hopkins Press, 1913. 194 pp.

O. A. Sherrard, *Freedom from Fear.* New York, St. Martin's, 1959. 200 pp. Slavery during ancient times and up to the English colonies, and the steps that led to the emancipation of the slaves in America.

Bernard C. Steiner, *History of Slavery in Connecticut.* Baltimore, Johns Hopkins Press, 1893. 84 pp.

Edward Raymond Turner, *The Negro in Pennsylvania: Slavery, Servitude, Freedom, 1639–1861.* Washington, American Historical Assn., 1911. 314 pp.

James Martin Wright, *The Free Negro in Maryland, 1634–1860.* New York, Columbia U. Press, 1921. 362 pp.

11. PRE-CIVIL WAR AMERICA: SLAVERY AND ABOLITION, 1789–1860

Osborne P. Anderson, *A Voice from Harper's Ferry*. Boston, by author, 1861. 24 pp. Written by the only Negro survivor of the men who fought with John Brown at Harper's Ferry.

Annual Reports of The American Colonization Society. Washington, 1818–60.

Herbert Aptheker, *The Negro in the Abolitionist Movement*. New York, International, 1941. 48 pp. *Paperback.*

————, *The Labor Movement in the South During Slavery*. New York, International, 1954. 24 pp. *Paperback.*

————, *One Continual Cry: David Walker's "Appeal to the Colored Citizens of the World, 1829."* New York, Humanities, 1965. *Also in paperback.*

Wilson Armistead, *A Tribute for the Negro*. New York, Manchester, Irwin, 1848. 564 pp.

A Statistical Inquiry into the Condition of the People of Colour of the City of Philadelphia. Philadelphia, 1849.

Charles Ball, *Fifty Years in Chains; or The Life of an American Slave*. New York, Dayton, 1859. 430 pp.

Frederic Bancroft, *Slave Trading in the Old South*. New York, Ungar, 1959. 415 pp.

————, "The Colonization of American Negroes, 1801–65," in Jacob E. Cooke, *Frederic Bancroft*. Norman, U. of Oklahoma Press, 1957. 282 pp.

Gilbert H. Barnes, *The Antislavery Impulse*. New York, Appleton-Century, 1933. 298 pp. *Also in paperback.*

Austin Bearse, *Reminiscences of Fugitive-Slave Law Days in Boston*. Boston, Richardson, 1880. 41 pp.

B. A. Botkin, ed., *Lay My Burden Down: A Folk History of Slavery*. Chicago, U. of Chicago Press, 1945. 297 pp. *Also in paperback.*

James H. Boykin, *The Negro in North Carolina Prior to 1861*. New York, Pageant, 1958. 84 pp.

Sarah E. Bradford, *Scenes in the Life of Harriet Tubman*. Auburn, N.Y., Moses, 1869, 132 pp. *Also in paperback.*

William Breyfogle, *Make Free*. Philadelphia, Lippincott, 1958. 287 pp. Story of the Underground Railroad.

William Wells Brown, *The American Fugitive in Europe*. Boston, Jewett, 1855. 315 pp.

————, *The Black Man: His Antecedents, His Genius, and His Achievements*. New York, Hamilton, 1863. 288 pp.

Henrietta Buckmaster, *Let My People Go*. New York, Harper, 1941. 398 pp. Story of the Underground Railroad and growth of the abolitionist movement. *Also in paperback*.

George W. Cable, *Creoles and Cajuns: Stories of Old Louisiana*, ed. by Arlin Turner. New York, Doubleday, 1959. 432 pp.

————, *The Grandissimes*. New York, Scribner's, 1899. 491 pp. *Also in paperback*.

————, *Old Creole Days*. New York, New American Library, 1961. 215 pp. *Also in paperback*.

————, *Strange True Tales of Louisiana*. New York, Scribner's, 1889. 350 pp.

Helen H. Catterall, ed., *Judicial Cases Concerning American Slavery and the Negro*. Washington, Carnegie Inst., 1926–37 (5 vols.).

John W. Cromwell, *The Early Negro Convention Movement; Occasional Papers, No. 9*. Washington, American Negro Academy, 1904. 23 pp.

Richard O. Curry, ed., *The Abolitionists—Reformers or Fanatics?* New York, Holt, 1965. 122 pp. *Paperback*.

Clara K. Curtis, *Fighters for Freedom*. Rochester, published by the author, 1933. 168 pp. Conditions leading to the antislavery movement.

Basil Davidson, *Black Mother: The Years of the African Slave Trade*. Boston, Little, Brown, 1961. 311 pp.

Martin R. Delany, *The Condition, Elevation, Emigration, and Destiny of the Colored People of the United States*. Philadelphia, 1852.

Elizabeth Donnan, ed., *Documents Illustrative of the History of the Slave Trade to America*. Washington, Carnegie Inst., 1930–35 (4 vols.), reprinted New York, Octagon, 1965.

Martin Duberman, ed., *The Antislavery Vanguard: New Essays on the Abolitionists*, Princeton, Princeton U. Press, 1965. 508 pp.

W. E. B. DuBois, *The Suppression of the African Slave Trade to the United States of America*. New York, Longmans, 1896. 335 pp.

Dwight L. Dumond, *Antislavery Origins of the Civil War in the United States*. Ann Arbor, U. of Michigan Press, 1961. 143 pp. *Also in paperback*.

————, *Anti-Slavery: The Crusade for Freedom in America*. Ann Arbor, U. of Michigan Press, 1961. 422 pp.

Hosea Easton, *A Treatise on the Intellectual Character, and Civil and Political Conditions of the Colored People of the United States; and the Prejudice Exercised Towards Them*. Boston, Knapp, 1837. 54 pp.

Louis Filler, *The Crusade Against Slavery:* 1830–1860. New York, Harper, 1960. 318 pp. *Also in paperback.*

George Fitzhugh and Hinton R. Helper, *Ante-Bellum: Three Classic Writings on Slavery in the Old South,* ed. by Harvey Wish. New York, Putnam, 1960. 256 pp. *Also in paperback.*

Philip Foner, ed., *Frederick Douglass: Selections from His Writings.* New York, International, 1945. 95 pp. *Paperback.*

————, *The Life and Writings of Frederick Douglass.* New York, International, 1950 (4 vols.).

Charlotte L. Forten, *A Free Negro in the Slave Era,* ed. by Roy Billington. New York, Collier, 1961. 286 pp. *Also in paperback.* Diary of a Negro woman during the time of slavery.

Early Lee Fox, *The American Colonization Society, 1817–40.* Baltimore, Johns Hopkins Press, 1919. 231 pp.

John Hope Franklin, *The Militant South, 1800–1861.* Cambridge, Harvard U. Press, 1956. 317 pp. *Also in paperback.*

————, *The Free Negro in North Carolina, 1790–1860.* Chapel Hill, U. of North Carolina Press, 1943. 271 pp.

E. Franklin Frazier, *The Free Negro Family: A Study of Family Origins Before the Civil War.* Nashville, Fisk U. Press, 1932. 75 pp.

J. C. Furnas, *The Road to Harper's Ferry.* New York, Sloane, 1959. 477 pp. Story of the John Brown raid and the men and forces behind it; surveys the history of slavery in the New World—how it began, how it worked, rebellions, etc.

Larry Gara, *The Liberty Line: The Legend of the Underground Railroad.* Lexington, U. of Kentucky Press, 1961. 201 pp.

Henry Highland Garnet, *Walker's Appeal, With a Brief Sketch of His Life.* New York, 1848.

Joshua R. Giddings, *The Exiles of Florida.* Columbus, Ohio, Follett, Foster, 1858. 338 pp.

Bella Gross, *Clarion Call: The History and Development of the Negro People's Convention Movement in the United States from 1817–1840.* New York, published by the author, 1947. 57 pp. *Paperback.*

Charles T. Hickok, *The Negro in Ohio, 1802–1870.* Cleveland, Williams, 1896. 182 pp.

Richard J. Hinton, *John Brown and His Men.* New York, Funk & Wagnalls, 1894. 752 pp.

Luther P. Jackson, *Free Negro Labor and Property Holding in Virginia, 1830–1860.* New York, Appleton-Century, 1942. 270 pp.

William Jay, *On the Conditions of the Free People of Colour in the United States.* New York, 1839.

Elizabeth Lawson, *Lincoln's Third Party.* New York, International, 1948. 48 pp. *Paperback.*

Leon P. Litwack, *North of Slavery.* Chicago, U. of Chicago Press, 1961. 318 pp. *Also in paperback.* An examination of the social, political, educational, economic, and religious status of the Negro in the free states from 1790 to 1860; includes a bibliographical essay.

Bernard Mandel, *Labor: Free and Slave; Workingmen and the Anti-Slavery Movement in the U.S.* New York, Associated Authors, 1955. 256 pp.

D. P. Mannix and Malcolm Cowley, *Black Cargoes: History of the Atlantic Slave Trade, 1518–1865.* New York, Viking, 1962. 306 pp. *Also in paperback.*

Truman Nelson, *The Sin of the Prophet.* Boston; Little, Brown, 1952. 450 pp. A novel about Anthony Burns, the last runaway slave returned from Boston under the Fugitive Slave Act.

Emil Olbrich, *The Development of Sentiment on Negro Suffrage to 1806.* Madison, U. of Wisconsin Press, 1912. 135 pp.

Frederick Law Olmsted, *The Slave States,* ed. by Harvey Wish. New York, Putnam, 1959. 255 pp. *Also in paperback.*

Jane and William Pease, *The Antislavery Argument.* Indianapolis, Bobbs-Merrill, 1965.

Ulrich B. Phillips, *American Negro Slavery: A Survey of the Supply, Employment and Control of Negro Labor as Determined by the Plantation Regime.* New York, Appleton, 1918. 529 pp.

J. Saunders Redding, *They Came in Chains.* Philadelphia, Lippincott, 1950. 320 pp.

Eugene C. Rozwenc, ed., *Slavery as a Cause of the Civil War.* Boston, Heath, 1963. 120 pp. *Paperback.*

————, and Wayne A. Frederick, eds., *Slavery and the Breakdown of the American Consensus.* New York, Heath, 1964. 79 pp. *Paperback.*

Louis Ruchames, ed., *A John Brown Reader.* New York, Abelard-Schuman, 1959. 431 pp.

————, *The Abolitionists.* New York, Putnam, 1963. 259 pp. *Also in paperback.* A collection of their writings.

John H. Russell, *The Free Negro in Virginia, 1619–1865.* Baltimore, Johns Hopkins Press, 1913. 194 pp.

O. A. Sherrard, *Freedom from Fear.* New York, St. Martin's, 1959. 200 pp. Slavery during ancient times and up to the English colonies, and the steps that led to the emancipation of the slaves in America.

Joseph Sidney, *An Oration, Commemorative of the Abolition of the Slave Trade in the United States: Delivered before the Wilberforce Philanthropic Association, in the City of New York, on the Second of January, 1809.* New York, 1809

Wilbur Henry Siebert, *The Mysteries of Ohio's Underground Railroad.* Columbus, Long's College Book Co., 1951. 330 pp.

————, *The Underground Railroad from Slavery to Freedom.* New York, Macmillan, 1898. 478 pp.

————, *The Underground Railroad in Massachusetts.* Worcester, Mass., American Antiquarian Society (Proceedings), 1935, 76 pp.

————, *Vermont's Anti-Slavery and Underground Railroad Record.* Columbus, Spahr and Glenn, 1937. 113 pp.

Samuel Sillen, *Women against Slavery.* New York, Masses & Mainstream, 1955. 102 pp. *Paperback.*

Robert C. Smedley, *History of the Underground Railroad in Chester, Pennsylvania.* Lancaster, Office of *The Journal,* 1883, 407 pp.

Kenneth M. Stampp, *The Peculiar Institution.* New York, Knopf, 1956. 435 pp. *Also in paperback.* An account of American Negro slavery.

William Still, *The Underground Railroad.* Philadelphia, Porter and Coates, 1872. 780 pp.

Horatio T. Strother, *The Underground Railroad in Connecticut.* Middletown, Wesleyan U. Press, 1962. 262 pp.

Frank Tannenbaum, *Slave and Citizen: The Negro in the Americas.* New York, Knopf, 1947. 128 pp. *Also in paperback.*

Edward Raymond Taylor, *The Negro in Pennsylvania: 1639–1861.* Philadelphia, 1899.

Orville W. Taylor, *Negro Slavery in Arkansas.* Durham, N.C., Duke U. Press, 1959.

Rosser H. Taylor, *The Free Negro in North Carolina.* Chapel Hill, North Carolina Historical Society, 1920. 26 pp. *Paperback.*

Jacobus Ten Broek, *Equal under Law.* New York, Collier, 1965. 347 pp. *Also in paperback.* Originally published as *The Anti-Slavery Origins of the 14th Amendment.* Berkeley, U. of California Press, 1951. 232 pp. This is a new enlarged edition.

John L. Thomas, ed., *Slavery Attacked: The Abolitionist Crusade.* Englewood Cliffs, Prentice-Hall, 1965. 178 pp. *Paperback.*

Edward Raymond Turner, *The Negro in Pennsylvania: Slavery, Servitude, Freedom, 1639–1861.* Washington, American Historical Assn., 1911. 314 pp.

Lorenzo Turner, *Anti-Slavery Sentiment in American Literature.* Washington, Assn. for the Study of Negro Life and History, 1929. 188 pp.

David Walker, *One Continual Cry; David Walker's Appeal to the Colored Citizens of the World, 1829–1830: Its Setting and Its Meaning,* by Herbert Aptheker. New York, Hill and Wang, 1965. *Also in paperback.*

————, *David Walker's Appeal to the Coloured Citizens of the World.* New York, Hill and Wang, 1965. 78 pp. *Also in paperback.*

————, *Walker's Appeal, in four Articles together with a Preamble.* Boston, David Walker, 1830. 88 pp.

Eric Williams, *Capitalism and Slavery.* Chapel Hill, U. of North Carolina Press, 1944. 285 pp. *Also in paperback.*

Harvey Wish, ed., *Slavery in the South.* New York, Farrar, Straus, 1964. 290 pp. *Also in paperback.*

Carter G. Woodson, *The Education of the Negro Prior to 1861*. New York, Putnam, 1915. 454 pp.

————, *Free Negro Heads of Families in the United States in 1830*. Washington, Assn. for the Study of Negro Life and History, 1925. 296 pp. Account of the approximately 500,000 American Negroes who were free before emancipation.

————, *Free Negro Owners of Slaves in the United States in 1830*. Washington, Assn. for the Study of Negro Life and History, 1924. 78 pp.

————, ed., *The Mind of the Negro as Reflected in Letters Written During the Crisis, 1800–1860*. Washington, Assn. for the Study of Negro Life and History, 1926. 672 pp.

James Martin Wright, *The Free Negro in Maryland, 1634–1860*. New York, Columbia U. Press, 1921. 362 pp.

William Yates, *Rights of Colored Men to Suffrage, Citizenship and Trial by Jury*. Philadelphia, Merrihew and Gunn, 1838. 104 pp.

Negro Slave Revolts

> If there is no struggle, there is no progress. Those who profess to favor freedom, and yet deprecate agitation, are men who want crops without plowing up the ground. They want rain without thunder and lightning. They want the ocean without the awful roar of its many waters. Power concedes nothing without a demand.
>
> —Frederick Douglass (on the West India Emancipation, 1857)

Not docile or childlike, the Negro, like all other oppressed people in bondage, has struggled for his independence and freedom. This reflects a basic desire in all men. But this phase of his history, like others, has been systematically excluded from our history books. This censorship by omission was necessary in order to create the myth and maintain the stereotype of a backward people. By eliminating the chapters on struggle and contributions, one negates the human picture and makes discrimination more palatable and digestible This is a partial listing to show the history of these struggles and is a guide to further investigation of the subject.

✓Herbert Aptheker, *Nat Turner's Revolt: The Environment, the Event, the Effects.* New York, Humanities, 1966. Contains full text of the so-called "Confessions" of Turner made soon after his capture late in 1831. *Also in paperback.*

————, *American Negro Slave Revolts.* New York, International, 1964. *Also in paperback.*

————, "American Negro Slave Revolts," *Science and Society,* 1937.

————, "Maroons Within the Present Limits of the United States," *Journal of Negro History,* April, 1939.

————, *Negro Slave Revolts in the United States, 1526-1860.* New York, International, 1939. 72 pp. *Paperback.*

————, *To Be Free: Studies in American Negro History.* New York, International, 1948. 256 pp.

Raymond and Alice Bauer, "Day to Day Resistance to Slavery," ✓*Journal of Negro History,* October, 1942.

✓Arna W. Bontemps, *Black Thunder.* New York, Macmillan, 1936. 298 pp. A novel recreating Gabriel's Conspiracy in Virginia in 1800. *Also in paperback.*

Joseph C. Carroll, *Slave Insurrections in the United States, 1800-1865.* Boston, Chapman & Grimes, 1938. 229 pp.

Joshua Coffin, *An Account of Some of the Principal Slave Insurrections.* New York, American Anti-Slavery Society, 1860. 36 pp.

R. C. Dallas, *The History of the Maroons,* 2 Vols. London, T. N. Longman and O. Rees, 1803.

W. S. Drewry, *Slave Insurrections in Virginia, 1830-1865.* Washington, Neale Co., 1900. 201 pp.

Nicholas Halasz, *The Rattling Chains: Slave Unrest and Revolt in the Antebellum South.* New York, McKay, 1966. 266 pp.

James Hamilton, *Negro Plot.* Boston, Ingraham, 1822. An account of Denmark Vesey's Conspiracy and its betrayal.

✓C. L. R. James, *A History of Negro Revolt,* London, Fact, 1938. 97 pp.

✓F. Roy Johnson, *The Nat Turner Slave Insurrection.* Murfreesboro, N.C., Johnson Pub., 1966. 248 pp.

Lionel Kennedy and Thomas Parker, *An Official Report of the Trials of Sundry Negroes Charged with an Attempt to Raise an Insurrection in the State of South Carolina.* Charleston, Lionel Kennedy and Thomas Parker, 1822. Prepared and published at the request of the Court.

Marion Kilson, "Towards Freedom: An Analysis of Slave Revolts in the United States," *Phylon,* 1964.

John Lofton, *Insurrection in South Carolina: The Turbulent World of Denmark Vesey.* Yellow Springs, Ohio, Antioch Press, 1964. 294 pp. About the Charleston slave rebellion of 1822 led by Denmark Vesey.

John M. Lofton, Jr., "Denmark Vesey's Call to Arms," *Journal of Negro History*, October, 1948.

William A. Owens, *Slave Mutiny*. New York, John Day, 1953. 312 pp. The incredible story of a shipload of Negro slaves who mutinied on the schooner *Amistad* and took control of the ship, bringing it to a U.S. port and eventually being freed by the U.S. Supreme Court.

Nat Turner, *The Confessions of Nat Turner*, ed. by T. R. Gray. Richmond, T. R. Gray, 1832. 24 pp.

Harvey Wish, "American Slave Insurrections before 1861," *Journal of Negro History*, July, 1937.

————, "Slave Disloyalty Under the Confederacy," *Journal of Negro History*, October, 1938.

————, "The Slave Insurrection Panic of 1856," *Journal of Negro History*, 1939.

12. CIVIL WAR, EMANCIPATION, RECONSTRUCTION, 1860–1876

James S. Allen, *Reconstruction: The Battle for Democracy (1865–1876)*. New York, International, 1937. 256 pp. *Also in paperback.*

George R. Bentley, *A History of the Freedman's Bureau*. Philadelphia, U. of Pennsylvania Press, 1955. 298 pp.

J. Mason Brewer, *Negro Legislators of Texas and Their Descendants*. Dallas, Mathis, 1935. 134 pp.

Phillip A. Bruce, *The Plantation Negro as a Freeman*. New York, G. P. Putnam's Sons, 1889. 262 pp.

Paul H. Buck, *The Road to Reunion, 1865–1900*. Boston, Little, Brown, 1937. 320 pp. *Also in paperback.*

Henrietta Buckmaster, *Freedom Bound: The Real Story of the Reconstruction, 1868–1875*. New York, Macmillan, 1965. 155 pp.

Hodding Carter, *The Angry Scar: The Story of Reconstruction*. Garden City, Doubleday, 1959. 425 pp.

Lydia M. Child, *The Freedmen's Book*. Boston, Ticknor & Fields, 1865. 277 pp.

LaWanda and John Cox, *Politics, Principle and Prejudice, 1865–1866: The Dilemma of Reconstruction America*. New York, Free Press, 1963. 294 pp.

Richard Current, ed., *Reconstruction, 1865–1877*. Englewood Cliffs, Prentice-Hall, 1965. 183 pp. *Paperback.*

Henderson H. Donald, *The Negro Freedman: Life Conditions of the American Negro in the Early Years after Emancipation*. New York, Schuman, 1952. 270 pp.

William O. Douglas, *Mr. Lincoln and the Negroes: The Long Road to Equality*. New York, Atheneum, 1963. 237 pp.

W. E. B. DuBois, *Black Reconstruction in America*. Cleveland, Meridian, 1964. 746 pp. *Also in paperback.* Part which black folk played in the attempt to reconstruct democracy in America, 1860–1880.

Howard Fast, *Freedom Road*. New York, Duell, 1944. 263 pp. *Also in paperback.* An historical novel set in the Reconstruction period in the South, when Negroes and whites worked together in harmony.

Walter L. Fleming, *The Freedman's Savings Bank*. Chapel Hill, U. of North Carolina Press, 1927. 170 pp.

Philip Foner, ed., *Frederick Douglass: Selections from His Writings.* New York, International, 1945. 95 pp. *Paperback.*

————, *The Life and Writings of Frederick Douglass.* New York, International, 1950 (4 vols.).

√John Hope Franklin, *The Emancipation Proclamation.* New York, Doubleday, 1963. 181 pp. *Also in paperback.*

————, *Reconstruction After the Civil War.* Chicago, U. of Chicago Press, 1961. 258 pp. *Also in paperback.*

Robert F. Ivanov, *The Struggles of Negroes for Land and Freedom in the Southern U.S.A., 1865–1877.* Moscow, Publishing House of the Academy of Science of the U.S.S.R., 1958. 321 pp.

Luther P. Jackson, *Negro Office-Holders in Virginia, 1865–1895.* Norfolk, Va., Guide Quality Press, 1945. 88 pp.

Johns Hopkins University Studies in Historical and Political Science: Reconstruction Period: The Negro in Maryland, etc. Boston, Johns Hopkins U.

Lewis Wade Jones, *Cold Rebellion: The South's Oligarchy in Revolt.* London, MacGibbon and Kee, 1962. 203 pp. Negro subordination in the South since Reconstruction.

Elizabeth Keckley, *Behind the Scenes.* New York, Carleton, 1868. 371 pp. Written by an ex-slave-modiste, friend of Mrs. Abraham Lincoln.

John R. Lynch, *The Facts of Reconstruction.* New York, Neale, 1913. 325 pp. Negro congressmen of the Reconstruction era.

Grady McWhiney, ed., *Reconstruction and the Freedmen.* Chicago, Rand McNally, 1963. 54 pp. *Paperback.*

Paul S. Pierce, *The Freedman's Bureau.* Iowa City, U. of Iowa Press, 1904.

Hugh D. Price, *The Negro and Southern Politics: A Chapter of Florida History.* New York, New York U. Press, 1957. 133 pp.

Benjamin Quarles, *Lincoln and the Negro.* New York, Oxford, 1962. 275 pp.

Willie Lee Rose, *Rehearsal for Reconstruction: The Port Royal Experiment.* Indianapolis, Bobbs-Merrill, 1964. 442 pp.

√Eugene C. Rozwenc, ed., *Slavery as a Cause of the Civil War.* Boston, Heath, 1963. 120 pp. *Paperback.*

William Sinclair, *The Aftermath of Slavery.* Boston, Small, Maynard, 1905. 358 pp. Writer is an ex-slave who became a doctor-missionary.

Samuel D. Smith, *The Negro in Congress, 1870–1901.* Chapel Hill, U. of North Carolina Press, 1940. 160 pp.

Kenneth M. Stampp, *The Era of Reconstruction.* New York, Knopf, 1965. 228 pp.

Alrutheus A. Taylor, *The Negro in South Carolina during Reconstruction.* Washington, Assn. for the Study of Negro Life and History, 1924. 341 pp.

————, *The Negro in Tennessee from 1865 to 1880*. Washington, Associated, 1941. 306 pp.

————, *The Negro in the Reconstruction of Virginia*. Washington, Assn. for the Study of Negro Life and History, 1926. 300 pp.

Jacobus Ten Broek, *Equal under Law*. New York, Collier, 1965. 347 pp. *Also in paperback*. Originally published as *The Anti-Slavery Origins of the 14th Amendment*. Berkeley, U. of California Press, 1951. 232 pp. This is a new enlarged edition.

C. L. Wagandt, *The Mighty Revolution: Negro Emancipation in Maryland*. Baltimore, Johns Hopkins Press, 1965.

John E. Washington, *They Knew Lincoln*. New York, Dutton, 1942. 244 pp.

Vernon L. Wharton, *The Negro in Mississippi, 1865–1890*. Chapel Hill, U. of North Carolina Press, 1947. 298 pp. *Also in paperback*.

Bell I. Wiley, *Southern Negroes: 1861–1865*. New Haven, Yale U. Press, 1938. 366 pp. *Also in paperback*.

Joel Williamson, *After Slavery: The Negro in South Carolina During Reconstruction, 1861–1877*. Chapel Hill, U. of North Carolina Press, 1965. 442 pp.

C. Vann Woodward, *Reunion and Reaction*. New York, Doubleday, 1956. 297 pp. *Also in paperback*.

13. THE TRIUMPH OF WHITE SUPREMACY, 1876–1900

George W. Cable, *The Negro Question,* ed. by Arlin Turner. New York, Doubleday, 1958. 257 pp. *Also in paperback.*

———, *The Silent South.* New York, Scribner's, 1885. 180 pp.

James E. Cutler, *Lynch Laws: An Investigation into the History of Lynching in the United States.* New York, Longmans, 1905. 287 pp.

Ben Haas, *KKK.* Evanston, Regency, 1963. 158 pp. *Paperback.* History of the Klan from the Civil War to the present.

Hugh Hawkins, ed., *Booker T. Washington and His Critics: The Problem of Negro Leadership.* Boston, Heath, 1962. 113 pp. *Paperback.*

Stanley P. Hirshson, *Farewell to the Bloody Shirt: Northern Republicans and the Southern Negro, 1877–1893.* Bloomington, Indiana U. Press, 1962. 334 pp.

Luther P. Jackson, *Negro Office-Holders in Virginia, 1865–1895.* Norfolk, Va., Guide Quality Press, 1945. 88 pp.

Lewis Wade Jones, *Cold Rebellion: The South's Oligarchy in Revolt.* London, MacGibbon and Kee, 1962. 203 pp. Negro subordination in the South since Reconstruction.

Frenise A. Logan, *The Negro in North Carolina, 1876–1894.* Chapel Hill, U. of North Carolina Press, 1964. 244 pp.

Rayford W. Logan, *The Betrayal of the Negro.* New York, Collier, 1965. (Originally *The Negro in American Life and Thought.*) *Paperback.*

William A. Mabry, *The Negro in North Carolina Politics Since Reconstruction.* Durham, Duke U. Press, 1940. 87 pp.

A. D. Mayo, *Southern Women in the Recent Educational Movement in the South.* Washington, USGPO, 1892. 300 pp.

August Meier, *Negro Thought in America, 1880–1915: Racial Ideologies in the Age of Booker T. Washington.* Ann Arbor, U. of Michigan Press, 1963. 336 pp. *Also in paperback.*

I. Garland Penn, *The Afro-American Press and Its Editors.* Springfield, Mass., Willey, 1891, 565 pp.

William J. Simmons, *Men of Mark: Eminent, Progressive and Rising.* Cleveland, Rewell, 1887. 1,138 pp.

Samuel D. Smith, *The Negro in Congress, 1870–1901.* Chapel Hill, U. of North Carolina Press, 1940. 160 pp.

Samuel R. Spencer, Jr., *Booker T. Washington and the Negro's Place in American Life.* Boston; Little, Brown, 1955.

William H. Thomas, *The American Negro.* New York, Macmillan, 1901. 440 pp.

George B. Tindall, *South Carolina Negroes, 1877–1900.* Columbia, U. of South Carolina Press, 1952. 336 pp.

E. D. Washington, ed., *Selected Speeches of Booker T. Washington.* New York, Doubleday, 1932. 283 pp.

C. Vann Woodward, *Origins of the New South, 1877–1913.* Baton Rouge, Louisiana State U. Press, 1951. 542 pp.

————, *Reunion and Reaction.* New York, Doubleday, 1956. 297 pp. *Also in paperback.*

————, *The Strange Career of Jim Crow,* new and rev. ed. New York, Oxford, 1957. 183 pp. 2nd rev. ed. 1966, 205 pp. *Also in paperback.* The development of American racial segregation by law; includes three pages of books for "suggested reading."

————, ed., *Southern Prophecy: The Prosperity of the South Dependent on the Elevation of the Negro* (1889), by Lewis H. Blair. Boston, Little, Brown, 1964. 201 pp.

14. THE TWENTIETH CENTURY

Ray S. Baker, *Following the Color Line: American Negro Citizenship in the Progressive Era*, ed. by Dewey W. Grantham, Jr. New York, Harper, 1964. 311 pp. *Also in paperback.*

Brailsford R. Brazeal, *The Brotherhood of Sleeping Car Porters*. New York, Harper, 1946. 258 pp.

Fred L. Brownlee, *New Day Ascending*. Boston, Pilgrim, 1946. 310 pp.

W. Haywood Burns, *The Voices of Negro Protest in America*. New York, Oxford, 1963. 88 pp. *Paperback.*

Horace R. Cayton and George S. Mitchell, *Black Workers and the New Unions*. Chapel Hill, U. of North Carolina Press, 1939. 473 pp.

Allan K. Chalmers, *They Shall Be Free*. Garden City, Doubleday, 1951. 255 pp. Story of the Scottsboro Case.

Carol Drisko and Dr. Edgar A. Toppin, *The Unfinished March: The Negro in the United States, Reconstruction to World War I*. Garden City, N.Y., Zenith, 1967. 128 pp. *Also in paperback.*

W. E. B. Du Bois, *Color and Democracy*. New York, Harcourt, 1945. 143 pp.

—————, *The Souls of Black Folk*. Chicago, McClurg, 1903. 264 pp. *Also in paperback.*

—————, *The World and Africa*. New York, Viking, 1947. 276 pp. *Also in paperback.*

—————, *An ABC of Color*. Berlin, Seven Seas, 1964. 211 pp. *Paperback.* Selections from over a half century of the writings of W. E. B. Du Bois.

Edwin R. Embree and Julia Waxman, *Investment in People: The Story of the Julius Rosenwald Fund*. New York, Harper, 1949. 291 pp.

E. U. Essien-Udom, *Black Nationalism: A Search for an Identity*. Chicago, U. of Chicago Press, 1962. 367 pp. *Also in paperback.* History and appraisal of the Black Muslim movement, with a chapter on the historical development of Black Nationalism.

E. Franklin Frazier, *Black Bourgeoisie*. New York, Collier, 1962. 222 pp. *Also in paperback.* The rise of a new middle class.

Amy Jaques Garvey, ed., *Philosophy and Opinions of Marcus Garvey*. New York, Universal Publishing House, 1923.

J. R. Gay, *Progress and Achievements of the Colored People*. Jenkins, 1913.

J. W. Gibson and W. H. Crogman, *Progress of a Race*. Naperville, Ill., Nichols, 1929. 480 pp.

Lorraine Hansberry, *The Movement*. New York, Simon and Schuster, 1964. 127 pp. *Also in paperback*. Photos depicting Negro struggles —poverty, ghetto life, lynching, Jim Crow, riots—and how these struggles led to the current protest movement.

William H. Holtzclaw, *The Black Man's Burden*. New York, Neale, 1915. 232 pp. Student's account of life at Tuskegee Institute.

Howard University Graduate School, *The New Negro Thirty Years Afterward*. Washington, Howard U. Press, 1955.

Langston Hughes, *Fight for Freedom: The Story of the NAACP*. New York, Norton, 1962. 224 pp. *Also in paperback*.

Harold R. Isaacs, *The New World of Negro Americans*. New York, Viking, 1963. 366 pp. *Also in paperback*.

Alain Locke, ed., *The New Negro*. New York, Boni, 1925. 446 pp.

Rayford W. Logan, *The Negro in the Postwar World: A Primer*. Washington, Minorities, 1945. 95 pp.

Louis Lomax, *The Negro Revolt*. New York, Harper, 1962. 271 pp. *Also in paperback*. A report on the civil rights movement of the 1950's and 1960's.

Walter Lord, *Peary to the Pole*. New York, Harper, 1963. 141 pp. Includes a picture of Matthew Henson as well as information concerning Henson's role in the expedition.

Donald R. Matthews and James W. Prothro, *Negroes and the New Southern Politics*. New York, Harcourt, 1966. 551 pp.

August Meier, *Negro Protest Thought in the Twentieth Century*. Indianapolis, Bobbs-Merrill, 1965.

George S. Merriam, *The Negro and the Nation,* New York, Holt, 1906. 436 pp.

Glenford E. Mitchell and William H. Peace, III, eds., *Angry Black South*. New York, Corinth, 1962. 159 pp. *Paperback*. Southern Negroes tell their own story.

Henry Lee Moon, *Balance of Power: The Negro Vote*. Garden City, Doubleday, 1948. 256 pp.

Florence Murray, ed., *The Negro Handbook*. New York, Current Books, 1946–47. 2 vols.

Gunnar Myrdal, *An American Dilemma*. New York, Harper, 1962. 1,483 pp. *Also in paperback*.

William F. Nowlin, *The Negro in American National Politics (1868–1930)*. Boston, Stratford, 1931. 148 pp.

Mary W. Ovington, *The Walls Came Tumbling Down*. New York, Harcourt, 1947. 307 pp. One of the founders of the NAACP chronicles forty years of Negro progress.

Haywood Patterson and Earl Conrad, *Scottsboro Boy*. Garden City, Doubleday, 1950. 309 pp. One of the central figures in the Alabama Scottsboro trial.

William L. Patterson, ed., *We Charge Genocide*. New York, Civil Rights Congress, 1951. *Paperback*. A petition to the U.N. charging government crimes against the Negro people.

Adam Clayton Powell, Sr., *Against the Tide*. New York, Smith, 1938. 327 pp.

Adam Clayton Powell, Jr., *Marching Blacks*. New York, Dial Press, 1945. 218 pp.

J. Saunders Redding, *On Being Negro in America*. Indianapolis, Bobbs-Merrill, 1951. 156 pp. *Also in paperback*.

G. F. Richings, *Evidences of Progress Among Colored People*. Philadelphia, Ferguson, 1905. 595 pp.

John H. Rohrer and Munro S. Edmonson, eds., *The Eighth Generation*. New York, Harper, 1960. 346 pp. *Also in paperback*.

Arnold Rose, ed., *Assuring Freedom to the Free*. Detroit, Wayne State U. Press, 1964. 306 pp.

Carl Rowan, *South of Freedom*. New York, Knopf, 1952. 270 pp.

————, *Go South to Sorrow*. New York, Random House, 1957. 246 pp.

Tracy Sugarman, *Stranger at the Gates: A Summer in Mississippi*. New York, Hill and Wang, 1966. 256 pp.

Booker T. Washington and others, *A New Negro for a New Century*. Chicago, American Publishing House, 1900. Includes description of Negro soldiers in battle in Spanish-American War.

Booker T. Washington and W. E. B. Du Bois, *The Negro in the South*. Philadelphia, Jacobs, 1907. 222 pp.

Booker T. Washington et al., *The Negro Problem*. New York, 1903.

Arthur I. Waskow, *From Race Riot to Sit-In: 1919 and the 1960's*. New York, Doubleday, 1966. 380 pp.

15. NEGROES IN WARS

PRIOR TO WORLD WAR I

Randolph G. Adams, "New Light on the Boston Massacre," American Antiquarian Society *Proceedings,* 1937.

M. P. Allen, *Battle Lanterns.* New York, Longmans, 1949. 278 pp. A historical novel of the Revolutionary War which shows the contributions of Negroes in the fight for independence.

Herbert Aptheker, *The Negro in the American Revolution.* New York, International, 1940. 47 pp. *Paperback.*

_____, "Negro Casualties in the Civil War," *Journal of Negro history,* January 1947.

_____, "The Negro in the Union Navy," *Journal of Negro History,* April 1947.

_____, *The Negro in the Civil War.* New York, International, 1938. 48 pp. *Paperback.*

Henry Carey Baird, ed., *Washington and Jackson on Negro Soldiers.* Philadelphia, by author, 1863. 8 pp.

Martha M. Bigelow, "The Significance of Milliken's Bend in the Civil War," *Journal of Negro History,* July 1960.

Frederick M. Binder, "Pennsylvania Negro Regiments in the Civil War," *Journal of Negro History,* October 1952.

William Wells Brown, *The Negro in the American Rebellion.* Boston, Lee and Shepard, 1867. 380 pp.

Peter Burchard, *One Gallant Rush.* New York, St. Martin's, 1965. 168 pp. Story of the 54th Regiment of Massachusetts Volunteers— first U.S. Army regiment of free Negroes, and its commander, Col. Robert G. Shaw.

Herschel V. Cashin and others, *Under Fire with the Tenth U.S. Cavalry.* New York, Neeley, 1899. Review of the Negro's participation in the wars up to and including the Cuban War of 1899. 361 pp.

Dudley Taylor Cornish, *The Sable Arm: Negro Troops in the Union Army.* New York, Longmans, 1956. 337 pp. Includes critical bibliography.

W. E. B. Du Bois, "The Negro and the American Civil War: A Communication," *Science and Society,* December 1961.

Luis F. Emilio, *History of the Fifty-Fourth Regiment of Massachusetts Volunteer Infantry, 1863-1865*. Boston, Boston Book, 1894. 452 pp.

Edward L. Glass, *A History of the Tenth Cavalry, 1866-1921*. Tucson, Acme Printing Co., 1921. 141 pp.

Corporal W. T. Goode, *The Eighth Illinois*. Chicago, Blakely Printing Co., 1899. 32 pp. Journal of the Eighth Illinois Volunteer Regiment from its formation in 1871 until 1899.

Shirley Graham, "Negroes in the American Revolution," *Freedomways*, Summer 1961.

Lorenzo J. Greene, "Some Observations on the Black Regiment of Rhode Island in the American Revolution," *Journal of Negro History*, April 1952.

Samuel A. Greene, "The Boston Massacre," American Antiquarian Society *Proceedings,* October 1900.

Chaplain James M. Guthrie, *Campfires of the Afro-American*. Philadelphia, Afro-American, 1899. 710 pp.

W. B. Hartgrove, "The Negro Soldier in the American Revolution," *Journal of Negro History*, April 1916.

Thomas Wentworth Higginson, *Army Life in a Black Regiment*. Boston, Fields, Osgood, 1870. 296 pp. *Also in paperback.*

Edith H. Ingraham, *Negroes in Military Service*. Washington, Assn. for the Study of Negro Life and History.

Luther P. Jackson, "Virginia Negro Soldiers and Seamen in the American Revolution," *Journal of Negro History*, July 1942.

Edward A. Johnson, *A History of Negro Soldiers in the Spanish-American War*. Raleigh, Capital Printing, 1899. 147 pp.

Journal of Negro History, "Documents: Thomas Jefferson on the Negro." III, January, 1918.

Journal of Negro History, "Documents: Letters of George Washington Bearing on the Negro," II, October, 1917.

Mimi Cooper Levy, *Whaleboat Warriors*. New York, Viking, 1963. 189 pp. A children's book about Negroes and whites on the whaleboats waging guerrilla war against the British off Long Island, when British forces occupied the area during the Revolutionary War.

James M. McPherson, *The Negro's Civil War: How American Negroes Felt and Acted During the War for the Union*. New York, Pantheon, 1965. 358 pp.

————, *The Struggle for Equality: Abolitionists and the Negro in the Civil War and Reconstruction*. Princeton, Princeton U. Press, 1964. 474 pp.

Samuel A. Madden, *A Brief Consideration of the American Negro Soldier*. Virginia, Works Progress Administration, Public Activities Program, 1942. Traces Negro soldier from French and Indian Wars to World War I.

George H. Moore, *Historical Notes on the Employment of Negroes in the American Army of the Revolution.* New York, Evans, 1862. 24 pp.

William G. Muller, *The Twenty-Fourth Infantry, Past and Present, 1895-1906.* N.p., 1923. 128 pp.

John H. Nankivell, ed., *History of the Twenty-Fifth Regiment, United States Infantry, 1869-1926.* Denver, Smith-Brooks Printing, 1927. 212 pp. Published by the 25th Infantry, U.S. Army, the book reviews activities of Negro soldiers in the Revolutionary War, War of 1812, Civil War, and World War I.

William C. Nell, *The Colored Patriots of the American Revolution.* Boston, Wallcutt, 1855. 396 pp.

A. H. Newton, *Out of the Briars.* Philadelphia, A.M.E. Book, 1910. 269 pp. Personal experiences and reflections of the Negro 29th Regiment of Connecticut volunteers.

John Paynter, *Joining the Navy.* Hartford, American, 1895. 298 pp. Author's experiences as a cabin boy aboard the *Ossipee* and the *Juniata.*

Kenneth Wiggins Porter, "Negroes and the Seminole War, 1817-1818," *Journal of Negro History,* July 1951.

Benjamin Quarles, *The Negro in the American Revolution.* Chapel Hill, U. of North Carolina Press, 1961. 231 pp. *Also in paperback.*
————, *The Negro in the Civil War.* Boston, Little, Brown, 1953. 379 pp.

Emmett J. Scott, *Scott's Official History of the American Negro in the World War.* Chicago, Homewood Press, 1919. 511 pp.

Otis A. Singletary, *Negro Militia and Reconstruction.* New York, Austin, U. of Texas Press, 1957. 181 pp. *Also in paperback.*

T. G. Steward, *The Colored Regulars in the United States Army.* Philadelphia, A.M.E. Book, 1904. 344 pp. Traces Negro soldiers from the Revolutionary War.

Harriet Beecher Stowe, *The Colored Patriots of the American Revolution.* Boston, Wallcut, 1855.

The Negro Soldier (film). U.S. War Department, 1944. Released through U.S. Office of Education, 1949. Contribution of the Negro soldier from Revolutionary days until World War II.

Vanguard Society of America, *The Civil War Centennial and the Negro.* Los Angeles, Vanguard Society of America, 1961. A plea for the correct attitude to be taken in the Centennial of the Civil War and for the proper recognition of the great services performed in that war by Negroes.

Booker T. Washington, *The Colored Soldier in the Spanish-American War.* Chicago, Library and Publication Commission, 1899.

Charles H. Wesley, *Ohio Negroes in the Civil War.* Columbus, Ohio, State University Press, 1962.
————, *The Collapse of the Confederacy.* Washington, Associated,

1937. 225 pp.

George W. Williams, *A History of the Negro Troops in the War of the Rebellion 1861-1865*. New York, Harper, 1888. 353 pp.

Joseph T. Wilson, *The Black Phalanx: The History of the Negro Soldiers of the United States*. Hartford, American, 1888. 528 pp. Wars of 1775, 1812, 1861-65 included.

Association for the Study of Negro Life and History, *Significant Dates for Civil War Centennial of 1961*. Pamphlet reprinted from *Negro History Bulletin*, Washington, Associated, 1961.

Civil War Papers Read Before the Commandery of the State of Massachusetts Military Order of the Loyal Legion of the United States. Boston, 1900.

Military Essays and Recollections: Papers Read Before the Commandery of the State of Illinois, Military Order of the Loyal Legion of the United States. Chicago, 1894. Includes Henry V. Freeman, "A Colored Brigade in the Campaign and Battle of Nashville," and William Elliott Furness, "The Negro as a Soldier."

Personal Narratives of Events in the War of the Rebellion. Soldiers and Sailors Historical Society of Rhode Island. Includes J. M. Addeman, "Reminiscences of Two Years with Colored Troops" (1880); Joseph M. Califf, "Record of Services of Seventh Regiment, United States Colored Troops" (1878); Thomas J. Morgan, "Reminiscences of Services with Colored Troops in the Army of the Cumberland, 1863-65" (1885); James H. Rickard, "Services with Colored Troops in Burnside's Corps" (1894); and George R. Sherman, "The Negro as a Soldier" (1913).

PRIOR TO WORLD WAR II

William S. Braddan, *Under Fire With The 370 Infantry, 8th I.N.G.* Chicago, published by the author. Captain-Chaplain with the 8th Regiment relates experiences in combat.

William S. Braithwaite, *The Story of the Great War*. New York, Stokes, 1919. 371 pp.

John B. Cade, *Twenty-Two Months with Uncle Sam*. Atlanta, published by the author, 1929. Personal experiences of Negro student with the 92nd Division in France during World War I.

Chester D. Heywood, *Negro Combat Troops in the World War*. Worcester, Commonwealth Press, 1928. 310 pp.

Addie W. Hunton and Kathryn M. Johnson, *Two Colored Women with the American Expeditionary Forces*. Brooklyn, Brooklyn Eagle, 1920. 256 pp.

Arthur W. Little, *From Harlem to the Rhine*. New York, Covici, Friede, 1936. 382 pp. World War I and Negro soldiers from the New York area.

W. Irwin McIntyre, *Colored Soldiers*. Macon, Ga., Burke, 1923. Personal experiences of several Negroes as told to the author.

Kelly Miller, *New Pictorial History of the World War for Human Rights; Negro Soldiers in Our War.* Washington, Austin Jenkins, 1919. 480 pp.

Major Warner A. Ross, *My Colored Battalion.* Chicago, published by the author, 1920. 119 pp. Second Battalion of 365th U.S. Infantry.

Emmett J. Scott, *The American Negro in the World War.* Chicago, Homewood, 1919. 511 pp.

W. Allison Sweeny, *The History of the American Negro in the Great World War.* Chicago, Cuneo-Henneberry, 1919. 307 pp.

Charles H. Williams, *Sidelights on Negro Soldiers.* Boston, Brimmer, 1923. 248 pp.

WORLD WAR II AND AFTER

American Battle Monuments Commission, *92nd Division, Summary of Operations in the World War.* Washington, USGPO, 1944. 45 pp. Front-line infantry study with maps and casualty figures included.

John Beecher, *All Brave Sailors.* New York, Fischer, 1945. 208 pp. The story of the *SS Booker T. Washington.*

Earl Brown and George R. Leighton, *The Negro and the War.* Washington, Public Affairs Pamphlet No. 71, 1942. 32 pp.

Charles E. Francis, *The Tuskegee Airmen.* Boston, Humphries, 1956. 225 pp.

Arthur F. Furr, *Democracy's Negroes.* Boston, House of Edinboro, 1947. 315 pp. Facts, figures, statistics, and events related to the Negro's contribution to the war.

Ulysses Lee, *U. S. Army in World War II: The Employment of Negro Troops.* Office of the Chief of Military History, United States Army, Washington, D.C.. 1966.

David G. Mandelbaum, *Soldier Groups and Negro Soldiers.* Berkeley, U. of California Press, 1952. 142 pp.

Thurgood Marshall, *Report of Korea.* New York, NAACP pamphlet, 1951.

Dennis D. Nelson, *The Integration of the Negro into the United States Navy.* New York, Farrar, Straus, 1951. 238 pp.

Lee Nichols, *Breakthrough on the Color Front.* New York, Random, 1954. 235 pp.

Seymour J. Schoenfeld, *The Negro in the Armed Forces: His Value and Status—Past, Present, and Potential.* Washington, Associated, 1945. 84 pp.

John D. Silvera, *The Negro in World War II.* Baton Rouge, Military Press, 1946. Pictorial review.

Walter White, *A Rising Wind.* Garden City, Doubleday, 1945. 155 pp. Report on Negro Troops in World War II.

Ruth Wilson, *Jim Crow Joins Up.* New York, Clark, 1944. 129 pp.

16. SOCIAL AND ECONOMIC ASPECTS OF NEGRO HISTORY

William G. Allen, *The American Prejudice against Color.* London, Cash, 1853. 107 pp.

Herbert Aptheker, *The Negro People in America: A Critique of Gunnar Myrdal's "An American Dilemma."* New York, International, 1966. 80 pp. *Paperback.*

Henry E. Baker, *The Colored Inventor.* New York, Crisis, 1913. 12 pp.

Horace Mann Bond, *The Education of the Negro in the American Social Order.* New York, Prentice-Hall, 1934. 501 pp. Reissued New York, Octagon, 1966.

Arna W. Bontemps and Jack Conroy, *They Seek a City.* New York, Doubleday, 1945. 266 pp. *Also in paperback* under new title, *Anyplace But Here.*

B. A. Botkin, ed., *Lay My Burden Down: A Folk History of Slavery.* Chicago, U. of Chicago Press, 1945. 297 pp. *Also in paperback.*

George F. Bragg, *History of the Afro-American Group of the Episcopal Church.* Baltimore, Church Advocate Press, 1922. 319 pp.

Benjamin G. Brawley, *A Social History of the American Negro.* New York, Macmillan, 1921. 420 pp.

————, *The Negro Genius.* New York, Dodd, 1937. 366 pp.

Brailsford R. Brazeal, *The Brotherhood of Sleeping Car Porters.* New York, Harper, 1946. 258 pp.

Ralph W. Bullock, *In Spite of Handicaps.* New York, Association, 1927. 140 pp.

Wilbur J. Cash, *The Mind of the South.* New York, Vintage, 1961. 440 pp. *Also in paperback.*

Horace R. Cayton and George S. Mitchell, *Black Workers and the New Unions.* Chapel Hill, U. of North Carolina Press, 1939. 473 pp.

Sadie I. Daniel, *Women Builders.* Washington, Associated, 1931. 187 pp.

Martin R. Delany, *The Condition, Elevation, Emigration, and Destiny of the Colored People of the United States.* Philadelphia, 1852.

Frederick G. Detweiler, *The Negro Press in the United States.* Chicago, U. of Chicago Press, 1922. 274 pp.

Jerome Dowd, *The Negro Races*. New York, Macmillan, 1907.

————, *The Negro in American Life*. New York, Century, 1926. 647 pp.

W. E. B. Du Bois, ed., *The Negro in Business*. Atlanta, Atlanta U. Press, Publication No. 4, 1899. 77 pp.

————, ed., *The Negro Artisan*. Atlanta, Atlanta U. Press, Publication Nos. 7 and 17, 1902, 1912. 192 and 114 pp.

————, *The Philadelphia Negro: A Social Study*. Philadelphia, U. of Pennsylvania, 1899. 520 pp.

————, ed., *The Negro Church*. Atlanta, Atlanta U. Press, 1903. 212 pp.

————, *Black Folk Then and Now: An Essay in the History and Sociology of the Negro Race*. New York, Holt, 1939. 401 pp.

————, ed., *Economic Cooperation Among the Negro Americans*. Atlanta, Atlanta U. Press, Publication No. 12, 1907. 184 pp.

————, "The Negro Landholders of Georgia." Washington, *Department of Labor Bulletin*, No. 35, 1901.

————, ed., *Atlanta University Publications*. Atlanta, Atlanta U., 1896–1916. Summaries of the economic and social situation of the Negroes during this period.

———— and Guy B. Johnson, *Encyclopedia of the Negro*. New York, Phelps-Stokes Fund, 1946. 215 pp.

Philip Durham and Everett L. Jones, *The Negro Cowboys*. New York, Dodd, 1965. 278 pp. A chronicle of forgotten men who helped to forge a new land.

Edwin R. Embree and Julia Waxman, *Investment in People: The Story of the Julius Rosenwald Fund*. New York, Harper, 1949. 291 pp.

E. U. Essien-Udom, *Black Nationalism: A Search for an Identity*. Chicago, U. of Chicago Press, 1962. 367 pp. *Also in paperback.* History and appraisal of the Black Muslim movement, with a chapter on the historical development of Black Nationalism.

N. S. Fleischer, ed., *Black Dynamite*. New York, Ring, 1938. The Negro in the fight ring, 1782 to 1938.

G. James Fleming and Christian E. Burckel, *Who's Who in Colored America*. New York, Burckel, 1950. 648 pp.

E. Franklin Frazier, *The Free Negro Family: A Study of Family Origins before the Civil War*. Nashville, Fisk U. Press, 1932. 75 pp.

————, *The Negro Church in America*. New York, Schocken, 1963. 92 pp. *Paperback.*

————, "Traditions and Patterns of Negro Family Life in the United States," in E. B. Reuter, *Race and Culture Contacts*. New York, McGraw, 1934. 253 pp. *Also in paperback.*

————, *The Negro Family in the United States*. New York, Dryden, 1948. 374 pp.

————, *Black Bourgeoisie*. New York, Collier, 1962. 222 pp. *Also in paperback*. The rise of a new middle class.

J. C. Furnas, *Goodbye to Uncle Tom*. New York, Sloane, 1956. 435 pp. *Also in paperback*.

Abram L. Harris, *The Negro as Capitalist: A Study of Banking and Business Among Negroes*. Philadelphia, American Academy of Political and Social Science, 1936. 205 pp.

Melville J. Herskovits, "The Social History of the Negro," in C. Murchison, *Handbook of Social Psychology*. Worcester, Clark U. Press, 1935. 1195 pp.

————, *The American Negro*. New York, Knopf, 1928. 92 pp. *Also in paperback*.

————, *The Myth of the Negro Past*. New York, Harper, 1941. 374 pp. *Also in paperback*.

Dwight Oliver Wendell Holmes, *The Evolution of the Negro College*. New York, Teachers College, Columbia U., 1934. 221 pp.

E. W. Hullinger, *Plowing Through*. New York, Morrow, 1940. 59 pp. Story of the Negro farmer and his contributions to America.

Charles S. Johnson, *Patterns of Negro Segregation*. New York, Harper, 1943. 332 pp.

Guion G. Johnson, *A Social History of the Sea Islands*. Chapel Hill, U. of North Carolina Press, 1930. 245 pp.

Guy B. Johnson, *Folk Culture on St. Helena Island, South Carolina*. Chapel Hill, U. of North Carolina Press, 1930. 183 pp.

James Weldon Johnson, *Black Manhattan*. New York, Knopf, 1930. 284 pp.

————, *God's Trombones*. New York, Viking, 1927. 56 pp. Contains poetic versions of prayers, "folk sermons," etc., which the author remembers from childhood; includes "The Creation" and "The Prodigal Son."

Ruby Funchess Johnston, *The Development of Negro Religion*. New York, Philosophical Library, 1954. 202 pp. Christian religion among American Negroes.

Katharine M. Jones, ed., *The Plantation South*. Indianapolis, Bobbs-Merrill, 1957. 412 pp.

Laurence C. Jones, *Piney Woods and Its Story*. New York, Fleming H. Revell, 1922. 151 pp.

Lewis G. Jordan, *Negro Baptist History, U.S.A.* Nashville, Sunday School Publishing Board, 1930. 394 pp.

Robert H. Kinzer and Edward Sagarin, *The Negro in American Business*. New York, Greenberg, 1950. 220 pp.

J. P. Lichtenberger, ed., "The Negro's Progress in Fifty Years." *Annals*, 49, 1913. Complete issue of the *Annals* of the American Academy of Political and Social Sciences, including contributions to the survey by Booker T. Washington and W. E. B. Du Bois.

A. D. Mayo, *Southern Women in the Recent Educational Movement in the South.* Washington, USGPO, 1892. 300 pp.

Benjamin E. Mays and Joseph W. Nicholson, *The Negro's Church.* New York, Institute of Social and Religious Research, 1933. 321 pp.

Charles M. Melden, *From Slave to Citizen.* New York, Methodist Book Concern, 1921. 271 pp.

Pauli Murray, *Proud Shoes: The Story of an American Family.* New York, Harper, 1956. 276 pp. History of the author's family, using as the central figure her grandfather, Robert G. Fitzgerald, a Northern-born Union Army veteran who went South after the Civil War to establish schools for his race in Durham, North Carolina.

Gunnar Myrdal, *An American Dilemma.* New York, Harper, 1962. 1,483 pp. *Also in paperback.*

H. W. Odum, *Social and Mental Traits of the Negro.* New York, Columbia U. Press, 1910. 302 pp.

John W. Oliver, *History of American Technology.* New York, Ronald, 1956. 676 pp.

Rev. Daniel Alexander Payne, *History of the African Methodist Episcopal Church.* Nashville, A.M.E. Sunday School Union, 1891. 502 pp.

————, *Recollections of Seventy Years.* Nashville, A.M.E. Sunday School Union, 1888. 335 pp.

William Henry Pease, *Black Utopia: Negro Communal Experiments in America.* Madison, State Historical Society of Wisconsin, 1963. 204 pp.

Rev. Owen D. Pelt and Ralph Lee Smith, *The Story of the National Baptists.* New York, Vantage, 1960. The history of the National Baptist Convention, U.S.A., largest Negro denomination in the world.

I. Garland Penn, *The Afro-American Press and Its Editors.* Springfield, Mass., Willey, 1891. 565 pp.

Willard Range, *The Rise and Progress of Negro Colleges in Georgia: 1865–1949.* Athens, U. of Georgia Press, 1951. 254 pp.

Florence Matilda Read, *The Story of Spelman College.* Atlanta, Spelman College, 1961. 399 pp. First college for Negro women which grew out of a school started by two New England white women in an Atlanta church in 1881.

David M. Reimers, *White Protestantism and the Negro.* New York, Oxford U. Press, 1965. Discussion of civil rights, segregation and the Protestant churches from the 18th century to the early 1960's.

Dietrich D. Reitzes, *Negroes and Medicine.* Cambridge, Harvard U. Press, 1958. 400 pp.

John H. Rohrer and Munro S. Edmonson, eds., *The Eighth Generation.* New York, Harper, 1960. 346 pp. *Also in paperback.*

Arnold Rose, *The Negro in America.* Boston, Beacon, 1956. 324 pp.

Also in paperback. A condensed version of Gunnar Myrdal's *An American Dilemma.*

George A. Singleton, *The Romance of African Methodism: A Study of the African Methodist Episcopal Church.* New York, Exposition, 1952. 251 pp.

Mable K. Staupers, *No Time for Prejudice.* New York, Macmillan, 1961. 206 pp. History of the National Association of Colored Graduate Nurses and the part it played in the integration of Negroes in nursing in the United States; contains photograph of Mary Mahoney, first graduate nurse (1879) in America; bibliography and appendices.

Thomas W. Talley, *Negro Folk Rhymes.* New York, Macmillan, 1922. 347 pp.

Frank Tannenbaum, *Slave and Citizen: The Negro in the Americas.* New York, Knopf, 1947. 128 pp. *Also in paperback.*

Julius H. Taylor, ed., *The Negro in Science.* Baltimore, Morgan State College Press, 1955. 192 pp.

Earl E. Thorpe, *Negro Historians in the United States.* Baton Rouge, Fraternal Press, 1958. 188 pp.

U. S. Bureau of the Census, *Negro Population in the United States, 1790–1915.* Washington, USGPO, 1918, 844 pp.

————, *Negroes in the United States, 1920–1932.* Washington, USGPO, 1935. 845 pp.

Harold van Buren Voorhis, *Negro Masonry in the United States.* New York, Emerson, 1940. 132 pp.

Mary Elizabeth Vroman, *Shaped to Its Purpose: Delta Sigma Theta —The First Fifty Years.* New York, Random House, 1965. History of a Negro sorority.

Booker T. Washington, *The Negro in Business.* Boston, Chicago: Hertel, Jenkins, 1907. 379 pp.

Willis Duke Weatherford, *American Churches and the Negro.* Boston, Christopher, 1957. 310 pp. Traces Christian church's attitude toward the Negro from early slavery to the present.

————, *Negro Life in the South.* New York, Young Men's Christian Press, 1910. 183 pp.

Charles H. Wesley, *The History of the Prince Hall Grand Lodge of Free and Accepted Masons of the State of Ohio, 1849–1960: An Epoch in American Fraternalism.* Wilberforce, Ohio, Central State College Press, 1961. An account of Prince Hall, founder of the order of Masons among Negroes, and of the growth of Masonry, particularly in the state of Ohio, sometimes called "The Mother of Masonic Lodges."

————, *Negro Labor in the United States: 1850–1925.* New York, Vanguard, 1927. 343 pp.

E. A. Williams, *History and Manual of the Colored Knights of Pythias.* Nashville, National Baptist Publishing Board, 1917.

James W. Wilson, *Sketches of the Higher Classes of Colored Society in Philadelphia.* Philadelphia, 1841.

Carter G. Woodson, *A Century of Negro Migration.* Washington, Assn. for the Study of Negro Life and History, 1918. 221 pp.

—————, *The Education of the Negro Prior to 1861.* New York, Putnam, 1915. 454 pp.

—————, *Free Negro Heads of Families in the United States in 1830.* Washington, Assn. for the Study of Negro Life and History, 1925. 296 pp. Account of the approximately 500,000 American Negroes who were free before emancipation.

—————, *Free Negro Owners of Slaves in the United States in 1830.* Washington, Assn. for the Study of Negro Life and History, 1924. 78 pp.

—————, *History of the Negro Church,* rev. ed. Washington, Associated, 1945. 322 pp.

—————, *The Negro Professional Man and the Community.* Washington, Assn. for the Study of Negro Life and History, 1934. 365 pp.

A. S. "Doc" Young, *Negro Firsts in Sports.* Chicago, Johnson Publ., 1963. 301 pp.

17. STATE AND LOCAL HISTORIES

James Egert Allen, *The Negro in New York: A Historical-Biographical Evaluation from 1626.* New York, Exposition, 1964. 94 pp.

Irving H. Bartlett, *From Slave to Citizen: The Story of the Negro in Rhode Island.* Providence, Urban League of Greater Providence, 1954. 76 pp.

James H. Boykin, *The Negro in North Carolina Prior to 1861.* New York, Pageant, 1958. 84 pp.

Jeffrey R. Brackett, *The Negro in Maryland.* Baltimore, Johns Hopkins Press, 1889. 268 pp.

Lillian Brandt, *The Negroes of St. Louis.* Boston, American Statistical Assoc. Publications, 1903. Pp. 203–268 of vol. 8.

William Henry Brown, *The Education and Economic Development of the Negro in Virginia.* Charlottesville, Surber-Arundale, 1923. 150 pp.

Howard W. Coles, *The Cradle of Freedom.* Rochester, Oxford Press, 1941. 170 pp. History of the Negro in Rochester, western New York State and Canada.

John Daniels, *In Freedom's Birthplace: A Study of the Boston Negroes.* New York, Houghton, 1914. 496 pp.

W. E. B. DuBois, *The Philadelphia Negro: A Social Study.* Philadelphia, U. of Pennsylvania, 1899. 520 pp.

————, "The Negro Landholders of Georgia." Washington, *Department of Labor Bulletin,* No. 35, 1901.

William Garnett and John M. Ellison, *Negro Life in Rural Virginia: 1865–1934.* Blacksburg, Va., Virginia Polytechnic Institute, Bulletin No. 295, 1934. 59 pp.

Constance McLaughlin Green, *The Secret City, A History of Race Relations in the Nation's Capital.* Princeton, N.J., Princeton U. Press, 1966.

Charles T. Hickok, *The Negro in Ohio, 1802–1870.* Cleveland, Williams, 1896. 182 pp.

Carl G. Hodges and Helene H. Levene, *Illinois Negro Historymakers.* Chicago, Illinois Emancipation Centennial Commission, 1964. 91 pp.

Mary Gibson Hundley, *The Dunbar Story, 1870–1955,* introduction by Robert C. Weaver. New York, Vantage, 1965. An account of a segregated high school in Washington, D.C. from its beginning in 1870 until the public schools were integrated in 1955; the book shows that many Dunbar graduates have made significant contributions to all segments of American life.

Edward Ingle, *The Negro in the District of Columbia*. Baltimore, Johns Hopkins Press, 1893. 110 pp.

Guion G. Johnson, *A Social History of the Sea Islands*. Chapel Hill, U. of North Carolina Press, 1930. 245 pp.

Guy B. Johnson, *Folk Culture on St. Helena Island, South Carolina*. Chapel Hill, U. of North Carolina Press, 1930. 183 pp.

James Weldon Johnson, *Black Manhattan*. New York, Knopf, 1930. 284 pp.

Laurence C. Jones, *Piney Woods and Its Story*. New York, Fleming H. Revell, 1922. 151 pp.

Frenise A. Logan, *The Negro in North Carolina, 1876–1894*. Chapel Hill, U. of North Carolina Press, 1964. 244 pp.

William A. Mabry, *The Negro in North Carolina Politics Since Reconstruction*. Durham, Duke U. Press, 1940. 87 pp.

Joe M. Richardson, *The Negro In The Reconstruction Of Florida, 1865–1877*. Tallahassee, Fla., Florida State U. Press. XII, 255 pp. Florida State U. Studies, No. 46.

Charles B. Roussève, *The Negro in Louisiana*. New Orleans, Xavier U. Press, 1937. 212 pp.

Seth M. Scheiner, *Negro Mecca: A History of the Negro in New York City, 1865–1920*. New York, New York U. Press, 1965. 242 pp.

Mingo Scott, *The Negro in Tennessee Politics and Governmental Affairs, 1865–1965*. Nashville, published by the author, 1965 (Mingo Scott, 1405 Sigler St., Nashville, Tenn.).

Earl Spangler, *The Negro in Minnesota*. Minneapolis, Denison, 1961.

Alrutheus A. Taylor, *The Negro in South Carolina During Reconstruction*. Washington, Assn. for the Study of Negro Life and History, 1924. 341 pp.

———, *The Negro in Tennessee from 1865 to 1880*. Washington, Associated, 1941. 306 pp.

———, *The Negro in the Reconstruction of Virginia*. Washington, Assn. for the Study of Negro Life and History, 1926. 300 pp.

Rosser, H. Taylor, *The Free Negro in North Carolina*. Chapel Hill, North Carolina Historical Society, 1920. 26 pp. *Paperback*.

J. H. Temple, *History of Framingham, Massachusetts*. Framingham, Pub. by the Town, 1887. 794 pp.

Emma Lou Thornbrough, *A Short History of Indiana Negroes, 1863–1963*. Indianapolis, Indiana Division of Emancipation Centennial Authority.

————, *The Negro in Indiana: A Study of a Minority*. Indianapolis, Indiana Historical Bureau, 1957. 412 pp.

Sue Bailey Thurman, *Pioneers of Negro Origin in California*. San Francisco, Acme, 1952. 70 pp.

George B. Tindall, *South Carolina Negroes, 1877–1900*. Columbia, U. of South Carolina Press, 1952. 336 pp.

Edward L. Tinker, *Creole City: Its Past and Its People*. New York, Longmans, 1953. 359 pp.

Edward Raymond Turner, *The Negro in Pennsylvania: Slavery, Servitude, Freedom, 1639–1861*. Washington, American Historical Assn., 1911. 314 pp.

Robert A. Warner, *New Haven Negroes*. New Haven, Yale U. Press, 1940. 309 pp.

Washington Intercollegiate Club, *The Negro in Chicago, 1729–1929*. Chicago, 1948 (2 vols.).

James W. Wilson, *Sketches of the Higher Classes of Colored Society in Philadelphia*. Philadelphia, 1841.

Writers' Program, Virginia WPA, *The Negro in Virginia*. New York, Hastings House, 1940. 380 pp.

Journal of the Illinois State Historical Society—Emancipation Centennial Issue, Autumn 1963. Springfield, Ill. Entire issue deals with the 240 years of history of the Negro in Illinois.

18. LAW, POLITICS AND OTHER GENERAL STUDIES

"A Century of Struggle: Emancipation Proclamation, 1863–1963." *The Progressive*, December 1962. Special issue on the Negro's struggle for civil rights since the Civil War.

Howard Brotz, ed., *Negro Social and Political Thought, 1850–1920: Representative Texts.* New York, Basic Books, 1966. 580 pp.

Fred L. Brownlee, *New Day Ascending.* Boston, Pilgrim, 1946. 310 pp.

Helen H. Catterall, ed., *Judicial Cases Concerning American Slavery and the Negro.* Washington, Carnegie Inst., 1926–37 (5 vols.).

Lucille Arcola Chambers, *America's Tenth Man: A Pictorial Review of One-Tenth of a Nation, Presenting the Negro Contribution to American Life Today.* New York, Twayne, 1957. 351 pp.

John V. Cheney, ed., *Memorable American Speeches.* Chicago, Lakeside, 1907–10 (4 vols.).

Bobbi and Frank Cierciorka, *Negroes in American History: A Freedom Primer.* Atlanta, Ga., Student Voice, Inc. (360 Nelson St., S.W.), 1965. *Paperback.*

Ralph and Carl Creger, *This Is What We Found.* New York, Lyle Stuart, 1960. 64 pp. Began as a history assignment for a twelve-year-old white student at Little Rock's Central High School; grew to be a study of the history of the Negro.

Larry Cuban, *The Negro in America.* Chicago; Scott, Foresman, 1964. 176 pp. *Paperback.*

Karl E. Downs, *Meet the Negro.* Los Angeles, Methodist Youth Fellowship, 1943. 179 pp.

Martin Duberman, *In White America.* Boston, Houghton Mifflin, 1964. *Also in paperback.* Survey of Negro history.

W. E. B. Du Bois, *The Black Flame: A Trilogy.* New York, Mainstream. *The Ordeal of Mansart* (1957, 316 pp.); *Mansart Builds a School* (1959, 367 pp.); *Worlds of Color* (1961, 349 pp.). A trilogy which is a compendium and source book covering more than a hundred years of history of Negro Americans from pre–Civil War times to the present, while examining the problem of the effect of race upon international politics and national diplomacy.

————, *Dark Princess: A Romance.* New York, Harcourt, 1928. 311 pp.

————, *Darkwater: Voices from Within the Veil.* New York, Harcourt, 1920. 276 pp.

————, *The Negro.* New York, Holt, 1915. 254 pp.

Edwin Rogers Embree, *American Negroes: A Handbook.* New York, John Day, 1942. 79 pp.

Eli Ginzberg and Alfred Eichner, *The Troublesome Presence.* New York, Free Press, 1964. 339 pp. History of Negroes and of race relations.

Ralph Ginzburg, ed., *100 Years of Lynchings.* New York, Lancer, 1962. 270 pp. *Paperback.*

Robert A. Goldwin, ed., *100 Years of Emancipation.* Chicago, Public Affairs Conference Center, U. of Chicago, 1963. *Also in paperback.*

Robert J. Harris, *The Quest for Equality.* Baton Rouge, Louisiana State U. Press, 1960. 172 pp.

Roy L. Hill, ed., *The Rhetoric of Racial Revolt.* Denver, Golden Bell Press, 1964. 378 pp. Includes speeches of Negro leaders.

Charles S. Johnson, *The Negro in American Civilization.* New York, Holt, 1930. 538 pp.

Joseph N. Kane, *Famous First Facts: A Record of First Happenings, Discoveries and Inventions in the U.S.* New York, H. W. Wilson, 1950. 888 pp.

Milton R. Konvitz, *A Century of Civil Rights* (With a Study of State Laws against Discrimination, by Theodore Leskes). New York, Columbia U. Press, 1961. 293 pp.

Elizabeth Lawson, *The People's Almanac.* New York, New Century, 1955. *Paperback.*

Paul Levinson, *A Guide to Documents in the National Archives for Negro Studies.* Washington, D.C., American Council of Learned Societies Committee on Negro Studies, Publ. No. 1, 1947.

Paul Lewinson, *Race, Class and Party: A History of Negro Suffrage and White Politics in the South.* New York, Russell, 1963. 302 pp. *Also in paperback.*

Loren Miller, *The Petitioners: The Story of the Supreme Court of the U.S. and the Negro.* New York, Pantheon, 1966. 461 pp.

William Pierce Randel, *The Ku Klux Klan: A Century of Infamy.* Philadelphia, Chilton, 1965. 300 pp.

Clement Richardson, ed., *National Cyclopedia of the Colored Race.* Montgomery, National Publishing Company, 1919. 640 pp.

Joel Augustus Rogers, *Africa's Gift to America,* rev. and enlarged Civil War Centennial ed. New York, published by the author, 1961. 272 pp.

————, *World's Great Men of Color, 3000 B.C. to 1946 A.D.* New York, published by the author, 1946–47 (2 vols.).

John A. Scott, ed., *Living Documents in American History.* Vol. I,

New York, Washington Square, 1963. *Also in paperback*. Reference work containing documents up to 1865 (Vol. II to be published).

Irving J. Sloan, *The American Negro: A Chronological Fact Book*. Dobbs Ferry, N.Y., Oceana, 1965.

Gilbert Sorrentino, *Black and White*. New York, Totem Press, 1964. Unpaged. *Also in paperback*.

David Spitz, *Patterns of Anti-Democratic Thought*. New York, Macmillan, 1949. 304 pp. *Also in paperback*.

The African Repository. Washington, American Colonization Society, 1825–1892 (68 vols.).

The Negro's Progress in Fifty Years. Philadelphia, The American Academy of Political and Social Science, 1913. 244 pp.

Joseph A. Tillinghast, *The Negro in Africa and America*. New York, Macmillan, 1902. 231 pp.

U.S.A. Editorial Staff, *The Negro in American Life*. Washington, *U.S.A.*, 1951.

U.S. Commission on Civil Rights, *Freedom to the Free: Century of Emancipation 1863–1963*. Washington, USGPO, 1963. 246 pp.

John G. Van Dusen, *The Black Man in White America*, rev. ed. Washington, Associated, 1944. Examines attitudes toward the Negro in this country and evaluates Negro contributions to America.

Charles Wagley and Marvin Harris, *Minorities in the New World*. New York, Columbia U. Press, 1958. 320 pp. *Also in paperback*.

Baldwin H. Ward, ed., *Year's Pictorial History of the American Negro*. New York, Year, 1965. 128 pp. *Also in paperback*.

Booker T. Washington, *The Story of the Negro*. New York, Doubleday, 1909. (2 vols.).

Sylvestre C. Watkins, *The Pocket Book of Negro Facts*. Chicago, Bookmark, 1946. 24 pp.

Charles H. Wesley, ed., *The Negro in the Americas*. Washington, Howard U. Press, 1940. 86 pp.

Augusta A. Wheadon, *The Negro from 1863 to 1963*. New York, Vantage, 1964. 91 pp.

Harvey Wish, ed., *The Negro since Emancipation*. Englewood Cliffs, Prentice-Hall, 1964. 184 pp. *Paperback*. History as told by leaders in articles about historical events and experiences, including Douglass, Washington, Du Bois, Baldwin, Muhammed, and others.

Carter G. Woodson, ed., *Negro Orators and Their Orations*. Washington, Associated, 1925. 711 pp.

C. Vann Woodward, *The Burden of Southern History*. Baton Rouge, Louisiana State U. Press, 1960. 205 pp. *Also in paperback*.

Monroe N. Work, *Negro Yearbook*. Tuskegee, Negro Yearbook, 1937–38.

Charles E. Wynes, ed., *The Negro in the South Since 1865*. University, Ala., U. of Alabama Press, 1965.

19. BIOGRAPHIES AND AUTOBIOGRAPHIES

> Full many a flower is born to blush unseen,
> And waste its sweetness on the desert air.
>
> —Thomas Gray

Here are a few of the many books on the lives of Negro men and women in the United States. Others on this subject are listed under young adult and children's books.

Russell L. Adams, *Great Negroes, Past and Present.* Chicago, Afro-Am, 1963. 182 pp.

Stephen Alexis, *American Martyr. John Brown, 1859-1959.* New York, New Century, 1960.

Marian Anderson, *My Lord, What a Morning.* New York, Viking, 1956. 312 pp. *Also in paperback.*

Robert Anderson, *From Slavery to Affluence: Memoirs of Robert Anderson, Ex-Slave.* Hemingford, Nebr., Hemingford Ledger, 1927. 59 pp.

R. McCants Andrews, *John Merrick: A Biographical Sketch.* Durham, Press of the Seaman Printery, 1920. 229 pp.

Pauline K. Angell, *To the Top of the World: The Story of Peary and Henson.* Chicago, Rand McNally, 1964. 288 pp. Matthew Henson, a Negro, and Robert Peary were the first to reach the North Pole with a group of Eskimos in 1909.

Henry Armstrong, *Gloves, Glory and God.* Westwood, Revell, 1956. 256 pp.

Louis Armstrong, *Satchmo: My Life in New Orleans.* Englewood Cliffs, Prentice-Hall, 1954. 240 pp. *Also in paperback.*

Helen Arstein and Carlton Moss, *In Person, Lena Horne.* New York, Greenberg, 1950. 249 pp.

Charles Ball, *Slavery in the United States: A Narrative of the Life and Adventures of Charles Ball, A Black Man.* Lewiston, Pa., J. W. Shugert, 1836. 400 pp.

Rebecca C. Barton, *Witnesses for Freedom.* New York, Harper, 1948. 294 pp.

Denzil Batchelor, *Jack Johnson and His Times*. London, Phoenix Sports Books, 1956. 190 pp.

Daisy Bates, *The Long Shadow of Little Rock*. New York, McKay, 1962. 234 pp.

Delilah L. Beasley, *The Negro Trail Blazers of California*. Los Angeles, Times Mirror, 1919. 323 pp.

Jessie L. Beattie, *Black Moses, The Real Uncle Tom*. Toronto, Ryerson Press, 1957. 215 pp. The story of Josiah Henson.

Lerone Bennett, Jr., *What Manner of Man: A Biography of Martin Luther King*. Chicago, Johnson, 1964. 227 pp. *Also in paperback.*

Mildred Bond, *Negro Heroes of Emancipation*. New York, NAACP, 1964. 22 pp.

T. D. Bonner, *Life and Adventures of James P. Beckwourth, Mountaineer, Scout and Pioneer and Chief of the Crow Nation of Indians*. 1856.

Perry Bradford, *Born with the Blues*. New York, Oak, 1965. 175 pp. A story of pioneer blues singers and musicians.

Sarah Bradford, *Scenes in the Life of Harriet Tubman*. Auburn, New York, W. J. Moses, 1869. 132 pp. *Available in paperback as Harriet Tubman: The Moses of Her People.*

George F. Bragg, *Men of Maryland*. Baltimore, Church Advocate Press, 1925. 160 pp.

Benjamin Brawley, *Paul Laurence Dunbar: The Poet of His People*. Chapel Hill, U. of North Carolina Press, 1936. 159 pp.

Francis L. Broderick, *W. E. B. Du Bois: Negro Leader in a Time of Crisis*. Stanford, Stanford U. Press, 1959. 259 pp.

William Broonzy (as told to Yannick Bruynoghe), *Big Bill Blues*. New York, Grove, 1956. 139 pp. *Also in paperback.* "Big Bill" Broonzy, the folk-blues singer and guitarist.

Hallie Quinn Brown, ed., *Homespun Heroines and Other Women of Distinction*. Xenia, Aldine, 1926. 248 pp.

Henry Box Brown, *Narrative of the Life of Henry Box Brown; Written by Himself*. Manchester, England, 1851.

Jimmy Brown with Myron Cope, *Off My Chest*. Garden City, Doubleday, 1964. 230 pp. The Cleveland Browns fullback.

William Wells Brown, *Narrative of William Wells Brown, A Fugitive Slave*. Boston, Anti-Slavery Office, 1847. 110 pp.

Henry Bruce, *The New Man, Twenty-nine Years a Slave, Twenty-nine Years a Free Man*. York, Pa., P. Anstadt and Sons, 1895. 176 pp.

John Edward Bruce, *Short Biographical Sketches of Eminent Negro Men and Women*. Yonkers, Gazette Press, 1910. Vol. 1.

Helen Buckler, *Dr. Dan: Pioneer in American Surgery*. Boston, Little, Brown, 1954. 381 pp. Life of Dr. Daniel Hale Williams (1856-1931) who in 1893 performed the first successful human heart operation; he organized and directed Chicago's Provident Hospital and was the first Negro admitted to the College of Surgeons.

Henrietta Buckmaster, *Women Who Shaped History.* New York, Macmillan, 1965. Word portraits of six American women whose deeds helped shape history; included are fugitive slave Harriet Tubman and Prudence Crandall, pioneer in equal education for Negroes.

Roy Campanella, *It's Good To Be Alive.* Boston, Little, Brown, 1959. 306 pp.

Poppy Cannon, *A Gentle Knight.* New York, Rinehart, 1956. 309 pp. *Also in paperback.* The author's life with her husband, Walter White.

Ella Kaiser Carruth, *She Wanted to Read: The Story of Mary McLeod Bethune.* Illustrated by Herbert McClure. Nashville, Abingdon Press, 1966. 80 pp.

Gwendolyn Cherry, et al., *Portraits in Color.* New York, Pageant, 1962. 224 pp. Sketches and biographies of Negro women.

Charles Waddell Chesnutt, *Frederick Douglass.* Boston, Small, Maynard & Co., 1899. 141 pp.

Helen M. Chesnutt, *Charles Waddell Chesnutt: Pioneer of the Color Line.* Chapel Hill, U. of North Carolina Press, 1952. 324 pp.

Abraham Chew, *A Biography of Colonel Charles Young.* Washington, Pendleton, 1933. 18 pp.

Ed Clayton, *Martin Luther King: The Peaceful Warrior.* Englewood Cliffs, Prentice-Hall, 1964. 80 pp.

Josephus Roosevelt Coan, *Daniel Alexander Payne, Christian Educator.* Philadelphia, Printed by A.M.E. Book Concern, 1935. 139 pp.

Samuel B. Coles, *Preacher with a Plow.* Boston, Houghton Mifflin, 1957. 241 pp. Autobiography of Samuel B. Coles.

Timothy Mather Cooley, *Sketches of the Life and Character of the Rev. Lemuel Haynes.* New York, Harper, 1837. 345 pp.

Anna J. Cooper, ed., *Life and Writings of the Grimke Family.* Pub. by author, 1951. Archibald H. Grimke, author and rights leader, is the main subject.

James D. Corrothers, *In Spite of the Handicaps: An Autobiography.* New York, Doran, 1916. 238 pp.

Henry and Ellen Craft, *Running a Thousand Miles for Freedom.* London, 1860.

George W. Crawford, *Prince Hall and His Followers.* New York, The Crisis, 1914. 95 pp. Founder of Negro Masonic Order.

Edmund D. Cronon, *Black Moses.* Madison, U. of Wisconsin Press, 1955. 278 pp. *Also in paperback.* Marcus Garvey, the "back to Africa" advocate.

Maud Cuney-Hare, *Norris Wright Cuney: a Tribune of the Black People.* New York, Crisis, 1913. 230 pp.

Wendell P. Dabney, *Maggie L. Walker . . . the Woman and her Work.* Cincinnati, 1927.

John Jay Daly, *A Song in His Heart*. Philadelphia, Winston, 1951. 102 pp. Story of James A. Bland, composer and minstrel singer.

Sylvia G. Dannett, *Profiles of Negro Womanhood*. Yonkers, Educational Heritage, 1964.

Edwin Adams Davis and William Ransom Hogan, *The Barber of Natchez*. Baton Rouge, Louisiana State U. Press, 1954. 272 pp. A slave's story.

Noah Davis, *The Narrative of the Life of Noah Davis, A Colored Man, Written by Himself at the Age Fifty-Four*. Baltimore, John F. Weishampel, 1859.

Sammy Davis, Jr. with Jane and Burt Boyar, *Yes I Can: The Story of Sammy Davis, Jr*. New York, Farrar, Straus and Giroux, 1965. 612 pp.

Beth Day, *Little Professor of Piney Woods*. New York, Messner, 1955. 192 pp. The story of Laurence Jones and the Piney Woods School.

Emily Taft Douglas, *Remember the Ladies: The Story of Great Women Who Helped Shape America*. New York, G. P. Putnam's Sons, 1966. 254 pp.

Frederick Douglass, *Life and Times of Frederick Douglass*. Hartford, Park, 1881. 516 pp. *Also in paperback.*

————, *My Bondage and My Freedom*. New York, Miller, Orton & Mulligan, 1855. 464 pp.

————, *Narrative of the Life of Frederick Douglass, An American Slave*. Boston, Anti-Slavery Office, 1845. 125 pp. *Also in paperback.*

W. E. B. Du Bois, *John Brown*, Philadelphia, Jacobs, 1909. 406 pp. *Paperback.*

————, *Dusk of Dawn: An Essay Toward an Autobiography of a Race Concept*. New York, Harcourt, 1940. 334 pp. Also the story of the NAACP. *Paperback.*

Katherine Dunham, *A Touch of Innocence*. New York, Harcourt, 1959. 312 pp.

Jeanette Eaton, *Trumpeter's Tale: The Story of Young Louis Armstrong*. New York, Morrow, 1955. 191 pp.

Ed Edwin and Neil Hickey, *Adam Clayton Powell*. New York, Fleet, 1965.

Leonard Ehrlich, *God's Angry Man*. New York, Simon and Schuster, 1932. 400 pp. Life of John Brown.

Stanley M. Elkins, *Slavery: A Problem in American Institutional and Intellectual Life*. Chicago, U. of Chicago Press, 1959. 247 pp. *Also in paperback.*

Edwin R. Embree, *Brown Americans*. New York, Viking, 1943. 248 pp.

————, *Brown America: The Story of a New Race*. New York, Viking, 1931. 311 pp.

————, *13 Against the Odds*. New York, Viking, 1944. 261 pp. Stories of famous American Negroes, including Marian Anderson,

Mary McLeod Bethune, George Washington Carver, W. E. B. Du Bois, Langston Hughes, Charles S. Johnson, Mordecai Johnson, Joe Louis, A. Philip Randolph, Paul Robeson, William Grant Still, Walter White, and Richard Wright.

Samuel Epstein, *George Washington Carver: Negro Scientist.* Champaign, Ill., Garrard, 1960. 80 pp.

Finis Farr, *Black Champion: The Life and Times of Jack Johnson.* New York, Scribner, 1964. 245 pp.

Harold W. Felton, *Jim Beckwourth: Negro Mountain Man.* New York, Dodd, Mead, 1966. 173 pp.

Miles Mark Fisher, *The Master's Slave, Elijah John Fisher.* Philadelphia, The Judson Press, 1922. 194 pp.

Henry O. Flipper, *The Colored Cadet at West Point.* New York, Lee, 1878. 322 pp.

Silas Xavier Floyd, *Life of Charles T. Walker, D.D.* ("The Black Spurgeon"). Nashville, National Baptist Publishing Board, 1902. 193 pp.

Albert S. Foley, *God's Men of Color: The Colored Catholic Priests of the United States: 1854-1954.* New York, Farrar, Straus, 1955. 322 pp.

————, *Bishop Healy: Beloved Outcaste.* New York, Farrar, Straus, 1954. 243 pp. The life of James Augustin Healy, (1830-1900) who became Catholic Bishop of Portland, Maine.

Philip Foner, *Frederick Douglass: A Biography.* New York, Citadel, 1964. 444 pp. *Also in paperback.*

Charlotte L. Forten (Mrs. Francis Grimké), *Journal.* New York, Dryden, 1953. 248 pp. *Also in paperback.*

Peter Freuchen, *The Legend of Daniel Williams.* New York, Messner, 1956. 256 pp.

Edmund Fuller, *A Star Pointed North.* New York, Harper, 1946. 361 pp. *Also in paperback.* Biography of Frederick Douglass.

Peter Gammond, ed., *Duke Ellington: His Life and Music.* New York, Roy, 1958.

Amy Jacques Garvey, *Garvey and Garveyism.* Kingston, Jamaica, published by the author (12 Mona Road, Kingston), 1963.

Mifflin W. Gibbs, *Shadow and Light.* Washington, published by the author, 1902. 372 pp. Early Negro pioneer westward, who published first Negro newspaper in California.

Althea Gibson (with Ed Fitzgerald), *I Always Wanted To Be Somebody.* New York, Harper, 1958. 176 pp. *Also in paperback.* Woman athlete and tennis champion.

Robert Goffin, *Horn of Plenty: The Story of Louis Armstrong.* New York, Allen, Towne and Heath, 1947. 304 pp.

Elizabeth Green, *The Negro in Contemporary American Literature.* Chapel Hill, U. of North Carolina Press, 1928. 98 pp.

Dick Gregory (with Robert Lipsyte), *Nigger*. New York, Dutton, 1964. 224 pp. *Also in paperback*. A humorist's autobiography.

Brion Gysin, *To Master—A Long Goodnight: The Story of Uncle Tom*. New York, Creative Age Press, 1946. 276 pp. The story of Josiah Henson.

L. H. Hammond, *In the Vanguard of a Race*. New York, Council of Women for Home Missions, 1922. 176 pp.

W. C. Handy, *Father of the Blues*, ed. by Arna W. Bontemps. New York, Macmillan, 1941. 317 pp. Autobiography of the Negro composer referred to as "Father of the Blues."

Sara Harris, *Father Divine: Holy Husband*. New York, Doubleday, 1953. 320 pp.

Theodore D. Harris, ed., *Negro Frontiersman: The Western Memoirs of Henry O. Flipper, First Negro Graduate of West Point*. El Paso, Tex. Western College.

William E. Hatcher, *John Jasper, the Unmatched Negro Philosopher and Preacher*. New York, F. H. Revell Co., 1908. 183 pp.

William G. Hawkins, *Lunsford Lane* or *Another Helper from North Carolina*. Boston, Crosby, 1863. 305 pp. Story of ex-slave and abolitionist.

Laurence J. W. Hayes, *The Negro Federal Government Worker, 1883-1938*. Washington, Howard U., 1941. 156 pp.

Elizabeth Ross Haynes, *The Black Boy of Atlanta*. Boston, House of Edinboro, 1952. 237 pp. A life of Richard Robert Wright, Sr.

_____, *Unsung Heroes*. New York, DuBois and Dill, 1921. 279 pp.

William H. Heard, *From Slavery to the Bishopric of the A.M.E. Church*. Philadelphia, 1924.

MacKinley Helm, *Angel Mo' and Her Son, Roland Hayes*. Boston, Little, Brown, 1942. 289 pp.

Josiah Henson, *The Life of Josiah Henson*. Boston, Phelps, 1849. 76 pp.

_____, *Father Henson's Story of His Own Life*. Boston, Jewett, 1858. 212 pp. *Also in paperback*. The autobiography of an escaped Negro slave in pre-Civil War days, whose life served as an inspiration for Harriet Beecher Stowe's *Uncle Tom's Cabin*.

Matthew A. Henson, *A Negro Explorer at the North Pole*. New York, Stokes, 1912. 200 pp.

Richard J. Hinton, *John Brown and His Men*. New York, Funk & Wagnalls, 1894. 752 pp.

Helen O. Holdredge, *Mammy Pleasant*. New York, Putnam, 1953. 311 pp. Mary Pleasant, colorful personality of early California days.

Billie Holiday (with William Dufty), *Lady Sings the Blues*. New York, Doubleday, 1956. 250 pp. *Also in paperback*.

Frederic M. Holland, *Frederick Douglass, the Colored Orator*. New York, Funk & Wagnalls, 1891. 423 pp.

Joseph Winthrop Holley, *You Can't Build a Chimney from the Top; the South Through the Life of a Negro Educator.* New York, William-Frederick Press, 1948. 226 pp.

Rackham Holt, *George Washington Carver.* Garden City, Doubleday, 1943. 342 pp.

————, *Mary McLeod Bethune.* Garden City, Doubleday, 1964. 306 pp.

Lena Horne and Richard Schickel, *Lena.* New York, Doubleday, 1965. The singer-actress' own story.

John Hoshor, *God in a Rolls Royce: The Rise of Father Divine, Madman, Menace or Messiah.* New York, Hillman-Curl, 1936.

Elston Howard, *Catching.* New York, Viking, 1966. (Autobiography)

Langston Hughes, *The Big Sea.* New York, Knopf, 1940; Hill and Wang, 1963. 335 pp. Autobiography . . . two parts. *Also in paperback.*

————, *I Wonder as I Wander.* New York, Rinehart, 1956. 405 pp. *Also in paperback.*

William H. Hughes and F. D. Patterson, eds., *Robert Russa Moton of Hampton and Tuskegee.* Chapel Hill, U. of North Carolina Press, 1956. 238 pp.

Zora Neale Hurston, *Dust Tracks on a Road.* Philadelphia, Lippincott, 1942. 294 pp. Autobiography by woman author.

Mahalia Jackson and E. M. Wylie, *Movin' On Up: The Mahalia Jackson Story.* New York, Hawthorn, 1966.

Mary Jenness, *Twelve Negro Americans.* New York, Friendship, 1936. 180 pp.

Jack Johnson, *Jack Johnson in the Ring and Out.* Chicago, National Sports Publishing Co., 1927. 259 pp.

James Weldon Johnson, *Along This Way.* New York, Viking, 1933. 418 pp. Autobiography of a famous poet, attorney, diplomat, college professor, and NAACP Executive Secretary.

T. J. Johnson, *From the Driftwood of Bayou Pierre.* Louisville, 1949. Life of Joseph E. Walker.

Johanna Johnston, *Runaway to Heaven: The Story of Harriet Beecher Stowe.* New York, Doubleday, 1963. 490 pp.

Martin Luther King, *Stride Toward Freedom.* New York, Ballantine Books, 1958. 190 pp. *Also in paperback.*

Ed Kirkeby, *Ain't Misbehavin': The Story of Fats Waller.* New York, Dodd, Mead, 1966. 248 pp.

Eartha Kitt, *Thursday's Child.* New York, Duell, Sloan & Pearce, 1956. 250 pp.

Ralph Korngold, *Citizen Toussaint.* Boston, Little, Brown, 1944. 358 pp. *Also in paperback.*

————, *Thaddeus Stevens,* New York, Harcourt, 1955. 460 pp.

J. Alvin Kugelmass, *Ralph J. Bunche, Fighter for Peace*. New York, Messner, 1952. 174 pp.

Isaac Lane, *Autobiography of Bishop Isaac Lane, LL.D.* Nashville, A.M.E. Church, 1916. 192 pp.

Lunsford Lane, *The Narrative of Lunsford Lane*. Boston, Printed for author by Hewes and Watsons, 1845.

John Mercer Langston, *From the Virginia Plantation to the National Capitol*. Hartford, American, 1894. 534 pp. Congressman from Virginia during Reconstruction.

Elizabeth Lawson, *The Gentleman From Mississippi*. New York, published by the author, 1960. 63 pp. *Paperback*. The story of our first Negro Senator, Hiram R. Revels.

Claude Lewis, *Cassius Clay*. New York, Macfadden-Bartell, 1965. 126 pp. *Paperback*.

Rayford Logan, ed., *Memoirs of a Monticello Slave*. Charlottesville, U. of Virginia Press, 1951. 45 pp. Story of Isaac Jefferson as dictated to Charles Campbell.

J. W. Loguen, *The Rev. J. W. Loguen, as a Slave and as a Freeman*. Syracuse, Truair, 1859. 454 pp.

Alan Lomax, *Mister Jelly Roll*. New York, Duell, Sloan & Pearce, 1950. 318 pp. *Also in paperback*. Controversial jazz-blues singer.

Phillip H. Lotz, ed., *Rising Above Color*. New York, Association Press, 1943. 112 pp.

Joe Louis, *My Life Story*. New York, Duell, Sloan, and Pearce, 1947. 188 pp.

Claude McKay, *A Long Way from Home*. New York, Furman, 1937. 354 pp. A writer and native of Jamaica tells of his life.

F. Alexander Magoun, *Amos Fortune's Choice: The Story of a Negro Slave's Struggle for Self-Fulfillment*. Freeport, Me., Bond Wheelwright, 1964. 237 pp.

Monroe A. Majors, *Noted Negro Women*. Chicago, Donohue & Henneberry, 1893. 365 pp.

John Malvin: *Autobiography*. Cleveland, 1879.

Arthur W. Mann, *The Jackie Robinson Story*. New York, Grosset & Dunlap, 1951. 224 pp.

Herbert Marshall and Mildred Stock, *Ira Aldridge*. New York, Macmillan, 1958. 355 pp. Biography of Ira Frederick Aldridge, one of the greatest Shakespearian actors of his time.

Fletcher Martin, ed., *Our Great Americans: The Negro Contribution to American Progress*. Chicago, Gamma Corp., 1953. 96 pp. *Paperback*.

Basil Mathews, *Booker T. Washington*. Cambridge, Harvard U. Press, 1948. 350 pp.

Marcia M. Mathews, *Richard Allen*. Baltimore, Helicon. Former slave (1760-1831); founder, with Rev. Absalom Jones, of the Free African Society in Philadelphia and first bishop of the African Methodist Episcopal Church which grew out of the Society.

Willie Mays (with Charles Einstein), *Born to Play Ball*. New York, Putnam, 1955. 168 pp.

R. H. Merritt, *From Captivity to Fame: The Life of George Washington Carver*. Boston, Meador, 1929. 196 pp.

Floyd Miller, *Ahdoolo: The Biography of Matthew A. Henson*. New York, Dutton, 1963. 221 pp. Co-discoverer of the North Pole.

Margery Miller, *Joe Louis: American*. New York, Wyn, 1945. 181 pp.

Everett Frederic Morrow, *Black Man in the White House*. New York, Coward-McCann, 1963. 308 pp. *Also in paperback*. Administrative aide to President Eisenhower.

J. H. Moseley, *60 Years in Congress and 28 Out*. New York, Vantage, 1960. 99 pp. Biographies of 28 Negro U.S. Senators and Congressmen.

Robert Russa Moton, *Finding a Way Out: an Autobiography*. Garden City, Doubleday, 1920. 295 pp.

Abigail Mott, *Biographical Sketches and Interesting Anecdotes of Persons of Color*. New York, John Day, 1826. 192 pp.

NAACP, *Black Heroes of the American Revolution*. New York, NAACP, 1965. *Paperback*.

Otto Olsen, *Carpetbagger's Crusade: The Life of Albion W. Tourgée*. Baltimore, Johns Hopkins Press, 1965. 395 pp.

Roi Ottley, *The Lonely Warrior: The Life and Times of Robert S. Abbott*. Chicago, Henry Regnery, 1955. 381 pp.

Mary W. Ovington, *Portraits in Color*. New York, Viking, 1927. 241 pp.

Leroy (Satchel) Paige, as told to David Lipman, *Maybe I'll Pitch Forever*. New York, Grove Press, 1961. 255 pp.

Forbes Parkhill, *Mister Barney Ford: A Portrait in Bistre*. Denver, Sage Books, 1963. 218 pp. Barney Ford, a Negro ex-slave, became an important businessman in the Southwest, especially Colorado, in the nineteenth century. This biography was first published in 1895.

Floyd Patterson (with Milton Gross), *Victory over Myself*. New York, Geis, dist. by Random House, 1962. 244 pp.

Hertha Pauli, *Her Name Was Sojourner Truth*. New York, Appleton-Century, 1962. 250 pp.

Bishop Daniel Alexander Payne, *Recollections of Seventy Years*. Nashville, A.M.E. Sunday School Union, 1888. 355 pp.

James W. C. Pennington, *The Fugitive Blacksmith: or Events in the History of James W. C. Pennington*. London, C. Gilpin, 1850. 84 pp.

James Louis Petigru, *Life, Letters and Speeches of James Louis Petigru, the Union Man of South Carolina*, ed. by James Petigru Carson. Washington, Lowdermilk, 1920. 497 pp.

Thomas Roy Peyton, *Quest for Dignity: An Autobiography of a Negro*

Doctor. Los Angeles, W. F. Lewis, 1950. 156 pp.

William Pickens, *Bursting Bonds.* Boston, Jordan and More, 1923. 222 pp.

M. M. Ponton, *Life and Times of Henry M. Turner.* Atlanta, A. B. Caldwell, 1917. 173 pp.

Gladys L. Porter, *Three Negro Pioneers in Beauty Culture.* New York, Vantage, 1966.

Henry Hugh Proctor, *Between Black and White: Autobiographical Sketches.* Boston, Pilgrim, 1925. 189 pp.

Leslie Harper Purcell, *Miracle in Mississippi: Laurence C. Jones of Piney Woods.* New York, Comet Press Books, 1956. 252 pp.

Frederick Ramsey, Jr., *Been Here and Gone.* New Brunswick, N.J., Rutgers U. Press, 1960. Negro folk music-makers in photographs and prose.

E. A. Randolph, *The Life of Rev. John Jasper.* Richmond, R. T. Hill, 1884. 167 pp.

Reverdy C. Ransom, *The Pilgrimage of Harriet Ransom's Son.* Nashville, Sunday School Union, 1949. 336 pp.

F. T. Ray, *Sketch of the Life of Rev. Charles B. Ray.* New York, Little, 1887. 79 pp.

L. D. Reddick, *Crusader Without Violence.* New York, Harper, 1959. 243 pp. A biography of Martin Luther King.

J. Saunders Redding, *The Lonesome Road.* New York, Doubleday, 1958. 355 pp. The American Negro's difficult struggle for freedom and equality is traced through the lives of thirteen outstanding Negroes: Robert S. Abbott, Frederick Douglass, W. E. B. Du Bois, Marcus Garvey, Joe Louis, Thurgood Marshall, Isaiah Montgomery, Daniel Payne, A. Philip Randolph, Paul Robeson, Sojourner Truth, Booker T. Washington, and Daniel Hale Williams.

Benjamin Franklin Riley, *The Life and Times of Booker T. Washington.* New York, Revell, 1916. 301 pp.

Eslanda Goode Robeson, *Paul Robeson, Negro.* New York, Harper, 1930. 178 pp.

Paul Robeson, *Here I Stand.* New York, Othello Associates, 1958. 128 pp.

Bradley Robinson, *Dark Companion.* New York, McBride, 1947. 266 pp. Life of Matthew Alexander Henson (1866-1955), co-discoverer of North Pole with Peary in 1909.

Jackie Robinson (with Wendell Smith), *My Own Story.* New York, Greenberg, 1948. 170 pp.

James H. Robinson, *Road Without Turning.* New York, Farrar, Straus, 1950. 312 pp. Autobiographical.

Selden Rodman, *Horace Pippin.* New York, Quadrangle Books, 1947. 88 pp.

J. A. Rogers, *World's Greatest Men and Women of African Descent.* New York, published by the author, 1935. 71 pp.

————, *World's Great Men of Color, 3000 B.C. to 1946 A.D.* New York, published by the author, 1946–47 (2 vols).

Frank A. Rollin, *Life and Public Services of Martin R. Delany.* Boston, Lee and Shepard, 1868. 367 pp.

Charlemae H. Rollins, *They Showed the Way.* New York, Crowell, 1964. 165 pp.

————, *Famous American Negro Poets.* New York, Dodd, 1965. 95 pp.

Carl T. Rowan with Jackie Robinson, *Wait Till Next Year.* New York, Random House, 1960. 339 pp.

Mabel Rowland, ed., *Bert Williams, Son of Laughter.* New York, English Crafters, 1923. 218 pp.

Elliott M. Rudwick, *W. E. B. Du Bois, A Study in Minority Group Leadership.* Philadelphia, U. of Pennsylvania Press, 1960. 382 pp.

W. F. Russell and W. McSweeny, *Go Up for Glory.* New York, Coward-McCann, 1966. (Autobiography)

Horace C. Savage, *The Life and Times of Bishop Isaac Lane.* Nashville, National Publication Co., 1958. 240 pp.

Gene Schoor, *Sugar Ray Robinson.* New York, Greenberg, 1951. 119 pp.

Emmett J. Scott and Lyman Beecher Stowe, *Booker T. Washington, Builder of a Civilization.* Garden City, Doubleday, 1916. 331 pp.

Neil Scott, *Joe Louis: A Picture Story of His Life.* New York, Greenberg, 1947. 126 pp. *Paperback.*

Arnold Shaw, *Belafonte.* Philadelphia, Chilton, 1960. 338 pp. *Also in paperback.*

Henry N. Sherwood, *Paul Cuffe.* Washington, Association for Study of Negro Life and History, 1923.

Arthur J. Smith, *The Negro in the Political Classics of the American Government.* Washington, published by the author, 1937. 251 pp. Biographies of 24 Negro congressmen.

Ken Smith, *The Willie Mays Story.* New York, Greenberg, 1954. 94 pp.

Samuel D. Smith, *The Negro in Congress, 1870-1901.* Chapel Hill, U. of North Carolina Press, 1940. 160 pp.

Samuel R. Spencer, *Booker T. Washington and the Negro's Place in American Life.* Boston, Little, Brown, 1955.

Dorothy Sterling and Benjamin Quarles, *Lift Every Voice: The Lives of Booker T. Washington, W. E. B. Du Bois, Mary Church Terrell, and James Weldon Johnson.* Garden City, Doubleday Zenith, 1965. 116 pp.

Charles Emery Stevens, *Anthony Burns.* Boston, Jewett, 1856. 295 pp.

Philip Sterling and Rayford Logan, *Four Took Freedom: The Lives of Harriet Tubman, Frederick Douglass, Robert Smalls, and Blanche*

K. Bruce. Garden City, N.Y., Zenith, 1967. 128 pp. *Also in paper-back.*

Austin Steward, *Twenty-Two Years a Slave.* Rochester, Alling, 1857. 360 pp.

Anson P. Stokes, *A Brief Biography of Booker T. Washington.* Hampton, Va., Hampton Inst. Press, 1936. 42 pp.

Mary Church Terrell, *A Colored Woman in a White World.* Washington, Ransdell, 1940. 436 pp.

Will Thomas, *The Seeking.* New York, A. A. Wyn, 1953. 290 pp.

Era Bell Thompson, *American Daughter.* Chicago, U. of Chicago Press, 1937. 240 pp.

John Thompson, *The Life of John Thompson, a Fugitive Slave.* Worcester, J. Thompson, 1856. 143 pp.

Adah B. Thoms, *Pathfinders.* New York, Kay, 1929. Histories and biographies of Negro graduate nurses.

Ridgely Torrence, *The Story of John Hope.* New York, Macmillan, 1948. 398 pp.

James M. Trotter, *Music and Some Highly Musical People.* New York, Dillingham, 1878. 353 pp. Historical descriptions.

Cornelius V. Troup, *Distinguished Negro Georgians.* Dallas, Royal, 1962. 203 pp. Biographical sketches of 113 Georgians.

Sojourner Truth, *Narrative of Sojourner Truth.* Boston, published by the author, 1875.

Emlen Tunnell with William Gleason, *Footsteps of a Giant.* Garden City, N.Y., Doubleday, 1966.

Barry Ulanov, *Duke Ellington.* New York, Creative Age Press, 1946. 322 pp.

Homer Ulrich, *Famous Negro Singers.* New York, Dodd, Mead.

John G. Van Deusen, *Brown Bomber: The Story of Joe Louis.* Philadelphia, Dorrance, 1940. 163 pp.

Edward Van Every, *Joe Louis: Man and Super-Fighter.* New York, Stokes, 1936. 183 pp.

Gustavus Vassa, *The Interesting Narrative of the Life of Olaudah Equiano, or Gustavus Vassa.* Halifax, Nicholson, 1813. 514 pp.

Kosti Vehanen, *Marian Anderson.* New York, McGraw-Hill, 1941. 270 pp.

Margaret Walker, *Jubilee.* Boston, Houghton Mifflin, 1966. 497 pp. (Novel based on life story of author's great-grandmother on plantation.)

William Jacob Walls, *Joseph Charles Price: Educator and Race Leader.* Boston, Christopher, 1943. 568 pp.

Alexander Walters, *My Life and Work.* New York, Revell, 1917. 272 pp.

Samuel Ringgold Ward, *Autobiography of a Fugitive Negro.* London, J. Snow, 1855. 412 pp.

Booker T. Washington, *My Larger Education.* Garden City, Doubleday, 1911. 313 pp.

——————, *The Story of My Life and Work.* Naperville, Ill., Nichols, 1900. 423 pp.

——————, *Up From Slavery.* Garden City, Doubleday, 1901. 330 pp. *Also in paperback.*

——————, *Frederick Douglass.* Philadelphia, Jacobs, 1907. 365 pp.

Ethel Waters (with Charles Samuels), *His Eye Is on the Sparrow.* Garden City, Doubleday, 1951. 278 pp. *Also in paperback.*

Henry Watson, *Narrative of Henry Watson, a Fugitive Slave.* Boston, Marsh, 1848. 48 pp.

Oscar Wegelin, *Jupiter Hammon, American Negro Poet.* New York, Heartman, 1915.

Charles H. Wesley, *Richard Allen, Apostle of Freedom.* Washington, Associated, 1935. 300 pp.

Walter F. White, *A Man Called White.* New York, Viking, 1948. 382 pp.

Ethel L. Williams, *Biographical Directory of Negro Ministers.* New York, Scarecrow Press, 1966. 421 pp.

Richard Wright, *Black Boy.* New York, Harper, 1945. 228 pp. *Also in paperback.*

Malcolm X. (with the assistance of Alex Haley), *The Autobiography of Malcolm X.* New York, Grove. 455 pp.

Elizabeth Yates, *Howard Thurman, Portrait of a Practical Dreamer.* New York, John Day, 1964. 249 pp. Dean of Marsh Chapel at Boston University.

A. S. Young, *Great Negro Baseball Stars, and How They Made the Major Leagues.* New York, Barnes, 1953. 248 pp.

——————, *Sonny Liston: The Champ Nobody Wanted.* Chicago, Johnson Publishing, 1963. 224 pp. *Paperback.*

Dick Young, *Roy Campanella.* New York, Barnes, 1952. 184 pp.

Who's Who in Colored America. 7 vols. New York, Who's Who in Colored America Corp., 1927-1950.

20. CULTURAL CONTRIBUTIONS

> Ill fares the land, to hastening ills a prey,
> Where wealth accumulates, and men decay.
>
> —Oliver Goldsmith

As in all other areas, the Negro has made his contribution and is active in the cultural development of his country—art, literature, music, theatre, etc. Again, these listings are but partial. Works pertaining to this field are also in the sections on songbooks, phonograph records, and films as well as in books for children and young adults. Lives of individuals in these fields are in the listing of biographies and autobiographies.

LITERATURE

Robert A. Bone, *The Negro Novel in America*. New Haven, Yale U. Press, 1958. 268 pp. (Rev. ed. 1965) Bibliography includes a year-by-year listing of novels and novelettes by Negroes to 1952. *Also in paperback.*

Benjamin Brawley, *The Best Stories of Paul Lawrence Dunbar*. Selected and Edited with an Introduction. New York, Dodd, Mead and Company, 1953. 258 pp.

Benjamin Brawley, ed., *Early Negro American Writers*. Chapel Hill, U. of North Carolina Press, 1935. 305 pp. A selection of the works of several American Negroes who wrote during the period from 1761 to 1865, including representative writings of Richard Allen, Benjamin Banneker, James Madison Bell, William Wells Brown, Alexander Crummell, Martin Robinson Delany, Frederick Douglass, Prince Hall, Jupiter Hammon, Frances W. E. Harper, Josiah Henson, George Moses Horton, Absalom Jones, Daniel A. Payne, Charles L. Reason, George B. Vashon, Gustavus Vassa, David Walker, Phillis Wheatley, James M. Whitfield, and Peter Williams.

Stephen H. Bronz, *Roots of Negro Racial Consciousness, The 1920's: Three Harlem Renaissance Authors*. New York, Libra, 1964. 101 pp. *Paperback.* About James Weldon Johnson, Countee Cullen, and Claude McKay.

Sterling A. Brown, *The Negro in American Fiction.* Washington, Associates in Negro Folk Education, 1937. 209 pp.

Victor F. Calverton, ed., *Anthology of American Negro Literature.* New York, Modern Library, 1929. 535 pp.

John Henrik Clarke, ed., *American Negro Short Stories.* New York, Hill and Wang, 1966. *Also in paperback.*

Conference of Negro Writers, New York, 1959, *The American Negro Writer and His Roots: Selected Papers.* New York, American Society of African Culture, 1960.

D. W. Culp, ed., *Twentieth Century Negro Literature.* Naperville, Ill., J. L. Nichols, 1902. 472 pp.

N. A. Ford, *The Contemporary Negro Novel.* Boston, Meador, 1936. 108 pp.

Hugh Gloster, *Negro Voices in American Fiction.* Chapel Hill, U. of North Carolina Press, 1948. 295 pp. Analysis of the published works of Negro fiction writers from the Reconstruction era to 1948.

Elizabeth Green, *The Negro in Contemporary American Literature.* Chapel Hill. U. of North Carolina Press, 1928. 98 pp.

Herbert Hill, ed., *Anger and Beyond.* New York, Harper & Row, 1966, 227 pp. Essays on American Negro Literature.

John M. Hughes, *The Negro Novelist, 1940–1950.* New York, Citadel, 1953. 288 pp.

David Littlejohn, *Black on White: A Critical Survey of Writing by American Negroes.* New York, Grossman, 1966. 170 pp.

Alain Locke, ed., *The Negro in America.* Chicago, American Library Association, 1933. 64 pp. Anthology of American Negro literature.

Vernon Loggins, *The Negro Author: His Development in America to 1900.* New York, Columbia U. Press, 1931. 480 pp. Reprinted New York, Kennikat, 1964.

Bucklin Moon, ed., *Primer for White Folks.* Garden City, Doubleday, 1945. 491 pp. An anthology of prose writings by and about the American Negro from slavery to the present; contributors include W. E. B. Du Bois, Henrietta Buckmaster, Roi Ottley, Earl Brown, R. C. Weaver, and Lillian Smith; a significant reference work.

Dorothy Porter, *Early American Negro Writings: A Bibliographical Study.* New York, Bibliographical Society of America, 1945. 77 pp.

J. Saunders Redding, *To Make a Poet Black.* Chapel Hill, U. of North Carolina Press, 1939.

Philip Sterling, ed., *Laughing on the Outside: The Intelligent White Reader's Guide to Negro Tales and Humor.* New York, Grosset and Dunlap, 1966. 254 pp.

Sylvestre C. Watkins, ed., *Anthology of Negro Literature.* New York, Modern Library, 1944. 481 pp.

Maxwell Whiteman, *A Century of Fiction by American Negroes, 1853–1952.* Philadelphia, Saifer, 1955. 64 pp. A selective bibliography of some of the Afro-American's contributions to the fictional literature of the land.

Writer's Program, Works Progress Administration, *Cavalcade of the American Negro*. Chicago, Diamond Jubilee Exposition Authority, 1940. 95 pp.

POETRY

Arna Wendell Bontemps, ed., *Golden Slippers: An Anthology of Negro Poetry for Young Readers*. New York, Harper, 1941. 220 pp. Contains 108 poems by 29 different Negro poets—from Paul Laurence Dunbar to Langston Hughes; includes a brief biographical sketch of each poet.

————, ed., *American Negro Poetry*. New York, Hill and Wang, 1963. 197 pp. *Also in paperback.*

Gwendolyn Brooks, *Bronzeville Boys and Girls*. New York, Harper, 1956. 40 pp. A collection of 36 poems about the day-to-day experiences of a group of Negro children in Chicago.

————, *A Street in Bronzeville*. New York, Harper, 1945. 57 pp.

————, *Selected Poems*. New York, Harper, 1963. 127 pp. *Paperback.*

Sterling A. Brown, *Southern Road*. New York, Harcourt, 1932. 135 pp.

————, *Negro Poetry and Drama*. Washington, Associates in Negro Folk Education, 1937. 142 pp.

S. B. Charters, *The Poetry of the Blues*. New York, Oak, 1963. 111 pp. *Paperback.*

Countee Cullen, ed., *Caroling Dusk*. New York, Harper, 1927. 237 pp. An anthology of verse by 38 outstanding Negro poets; contains a biographical sketch of each.

————, *On These I Stand*. New York, Harper, 1927. 197 pp.

Waring Cuney, Langston Hughes, and Bruce Wright, eds., *Lincoln University Poets: Centennial Anthology*. New York, Fine Editions, 1954.

Frank M. Davis, *Black Man's Verse*. Chicago, Black Cat, 1935. 83 pp.

Paul Laurence Dunbar, *Complete Poems*. New York, Dodd, 1947. Complete poems of one of America's most celebrated early Negro poets.

Langston Hughes, *Selected Poems*. New York, Knopf, 1959. 297 pp.

————, *The Dream Keeper and Other Poems*. Illustrated by Helen Sewell. New York, Alfred A. Knopf, 1959. 77 pp.

————, *New Negro Poets*. Bloomington, Indiana U. Press, 1964. 127 pp.

———— and Arna W. Bontemps, ed., *The Poetry of the Negro, 1746-1949*. Garden City, Doubleday, 1949. Contains the selected poems of 66 American Negro poets, plus tributary poems by non-Negroes and poems by native poets of the Caribbean, British Guiana, British Honduras, Barbados, Trinidad, Haiti, Martinique, French Guiana, Cuba, and Africa; with a brief biographical sketch of each poet.

James Weldon Johnson, ed., *The Book of American Negro Poetry*. New York, Harcourt, 1931. 300 pp.

Robert T. Kerlin, *Negro Poets and Their Poems*, 2nd ed. rev. Washington, Associated, 1935. 342 pp.

Armand Lanusse, *Creole Voices*, ed. by Edward M. Coleman. Washington, Associated, 1945. 130 pp. Poems in French by American Negroes.

Victor E. Lawson, *Dunbar Critically Examined*. Washington, Associated, 1941. 151 pp.

Alain Locke, *Four Negro Poets*. New York, Simon and Schuster, 1927. 31 pp. About Cullen, Hughes, McKay, and Toomer.

Walter Lowenfels, ed., *Poets of Today: A New American Anthology*. New York, International, 1964. *Paperback*.

Julian D. Mason, Jr., ed., *The Poems of Phillis Wheatley*. Chapel Hill, N.C., U. of North Carolina Press, 1966. 113 pp.

Claude McKay, *Spring in New Hampshire and Other Poems*. Richards Pub., 1920.

_____, *Selected Poems*. New York, Bookman, 1953. 112 pp.

_____, *A Long Way from Home*. New York, Furman, 1937. 354 pp.

Beatrice M. Murphy, ed., *Negro Voices*. New York, Harrison, 1938. 173 pp. An anthology of poems; some biographies included.

Rosey E. Pool, *Beyond the Blues: New Poems by American Negroes*. Kent, England, Hand and Flower Press, 1962.

Dorothy B. Porter, *North American Negro Poets: A Bibliographical Checklist of Their Writings, 1760-1944*. Hattiesburg, Miss., Book Farm, 1945. 90 pp. Reprinted New York, Burt Franklin, 1963.

J. Saunders Redding, *To Make a Poet Black*. Chapel Hill, U. of North Carolina Press, 1939. 142 pp. Negro poets and poetry related to historical and environmental developments.

Arthur A. Schomburg, *A Bibliographical Checklist of American Negro Poetry*. New York, Heartman, 1916. 57 pp.

Hildegarde Hoyt Swift, *North Star Shining*. New York, Morrow, 1947. 44 pp. A pictorial history of the American Negro in verse form.

Thomas W. Talley, *Negro Folk Rhymes*. New York, Macmillan, 1922. 347 pp.

Oscar Wegelin, *Jupiter Hammon, American Negro Poet*. New York, Heartman, 1915. 51 pp.

Phillis Wheatley, *Phillis Wheatley: Poems and Letters*, ed. by Charles F. Heartman. New York, Heartman, 1915. 111 pp.

Newman I. White, *An Anthology of Verse by American Negroes*. Durham, North Carolina, Trinity College Press, 1924. 250 pp.

MUSIC

Whitney Balliett, *Such Sweet Thunder: 49 Pieces on Jazz*. Indianapolis, Bobbs-Merrill, 1966. 366 pp.

Sidney Béchet, *Treat It Gentle*. New York, Hill and Wang, 1960. 245 pp. Clarinetist relives New Orleans and the jazz era of the twenties.

Rudi Blesh, *Shining Trumpets: A History of Jazz*. New York, Knopf, 1946. 365 pp.

Rudi Blesh and Harriet Janis, *They All Played Ragtime: The True Story of an American Music*. New York, Knopf, 1950. 338 pp.; rev. ed. New York, Grove, 1959. 2nd rev. ed. New York, Oak Publications, 1966. 347 pp.

Perry Bradford, *Born with the Blues*. New York, Oak, 1965. 175 pp. A story of pioneer blues singers and musicians.

Harry O. Brunn, *The Story of the Original Dixieland Jazz Band*. Baton Rouge, Louisiana State U. Press, 1960.

Samuel B. Charters, *Jazz: New Orleans, 1885-1963*, rev. ed. New York, Oak, 1963. Also contains biographical index to Negro musicians in New Orleans. *Paperback*.

_____, *The Country Blues*. New York, Rinehart, 1959. 288 pp.

Samuel Coleridge-Taylor, *Twenty-Four Negro Melodies Transcribed for Piano*. New York, Ditson, 1905. 127 pp.

Maud Cuney-Hare, *Negro Musicians and Their Music*. Washington, Associated, 1936. 439 pp. A descriptive and interpretive study of the history of Negro music and the men who have contributed to it; the book traces Negro music from its African roots to modern times.

Dave Dexter, Jr., *Jazz Cavalcade*. New York, Criterion, 1946. 258 pp.

Lillian Erlich, *What Jazz Is All About*. New York, Messner, 1962. 181 pp.

Leonard Feather, *The Book of Jazz*. New York, Horizon Press, 1957. 280 pp. *Also in paperback*.

_____, *The Encyclopedia of Jazz*. New York, Horizon, 1955. 360 pp.

Sidney Finkelstein, *Jazz: A People's Music*. New York, Citadel, 1948. 278 pp.

Robert Goffin, *Jazz: From the Congo to the Metropolitan*. Garden City, Doubleday, 1944. 254 pp.

Mary A. Grissom, *The Negro Sings a New Heaven*. Chapel Hill, U. of North Carolina Press, 1930. 101 pp.

Richard Hadlock, *Jazz Masters of the 20's*. New York, Macmillan, 1966.

W. C. Handy, *Father of the Blues*, ed. by Arna W. Bontemps. New York, Macmillan, 1941. 317 pp. Autobiography of the Negro composer referred to as "Father of the Blues."

_____ and Abbe Niles, ed., *Treasury of the Blues*. New York, Boni, 1949. 258 pp.

Rex Harris, *The Story of Jazz*. New York, Grossett & Dunlap, 1955. 280 pp.

Roland Hayes, *My Songs*. Boston, Little, Brown, 1948. 128 pp. Arrangements and interpretations of "Aframerican" songs.

MacKinley Helm, *Angel Mo' and Her Son, Roland Hayes.* Boston, Little, Brown, 1942. 289 pp.

Nat Hentoff, *The Jazz Life.* New York, Dial, 1961. 225 pp. With portraits of famous Negro musicians. *Also in paperback.*

Andre Hodeir, *Jazz: Its Evolution and Essence,* trans. by David Noakes. New York, Grove, 1956. 295 pp. *Also in paperback.*

Langston Hughes, *First Book of Jazz.* New York. Watts, 1955. 65 pp. This analysis and history of jazz includes lists of famous jazz musicians and recordings which illustrate jazz history, and Mr. Hughes' 100 favorite jazz, blues, and folk-song recordings.

Uriah P. James, *The Negro Melodist.* Cincinnati, Rulison, 1857. 120 pp. Lyrics; no music.

LeRoi Jones, *Blues People: Negro Music and White America.* New York, Morrow, 1963. 244 pp. *Also in paperback.*

Orrin Keepnews and Bill Grauer, *A Pictorial History of Jazz.* New York, Crown, 1955. 282 pp.; rev. ed. 1966, 293 pp.

Henry Edward Krebhiel, *Afro-American Folksongs: A Study in Racial and National Music.* New York, Schirmer, 1914. 176 pp.

Alain Locke, *The Negro and His Music.* Washington, Associates in Negro Folk Education, 1936. 142 pp.

Donald Myrus, *Ballads, Blues, and the Big Beat.* New York, Macmillan, 1966. 135 pp.

Howard Washington Odum and Guy B. Johnson, *Negro Workaday Songs.* Chapel Hill, U. of North Carolina Press, 1926. 278 pp.

———, *The Negro and His Songs.* Chapel Hill, U. of North Carolina Press, 1925. 306 pp. Lyrics and their historical backgrounds.

Paul Oliver, *Blues Fell This Morning.* New York, Horizon, 1960. 355 pp.

Hugues Panassie, *The Real Jazz,* trans. by Anne Sorelle Williams. New York, Smith and Durrell, 1942. 326 pp.

——— and Madeleine Gautier, *Guide to Jazz,* trans. by Desmond Flower. Boston, Houghton Mifflin, 1956. 312 pp.

F. Ramsey and C. E. Smith, eds., *Jazzmen.* New York, Harcourt, 1959. 360 pp. *Also in paperback.*

George S. Rosenthal (and others), eds., *Jazzways.* New York, Greenberg, 1947. 109 pp.

Winthrop Sargeant, *Jazz: Hot and Hybrid.* New York, Dutton, 1946. 287 pp.

Dorothy Scarborough, *On the Trail of Negro Folk Songs.* Cambridge, Harvard U. Press, 1925. 289 pp. (Reprinted Hatboro, Pennsylvania, Folklore Association, 1963.) Lyrics and historical interpretations.

Nat Shapiro and Nat Hentoff, eds., *Hear Me Talkin' to Ya: The Story of Jazz by the Men Who Made It.* New York, Rinehart, 1955. 432 pp.

Marshall W. Stearns, *The Story of Jazz.* New York, Mentor, 1958. 272 pp. *Paperback.*

Louis (Studs) Terkel, *Giants of Jazz*. New York, Crowell, 1957. 215 pp.

Howard Thurman, *Deep River*. New York, Harper, 1955. 93 pp. Reflective reactions to various spirituals.

Barry Ulanov, *A Handbook of Jazz*. New York, Viking, 1957. 248 pp. *Also in paperback*.

_____, *A History of Jazz in America*. New York, Viking, 1952. 382 pp.

ART

Albany Institute, *The Negro Artist Comes of Age*. A pamphlet.

Benjamin Brawley, *The Negro in Literature and Art in the United States*. New York, Duffield, 1921. 197 pp.

Chicago Public Library, *Subject Index to Literature on Negro Art*. Works Progress Administration, Omnibus Project, State of Illinois, 1941. 49 pp.

Cedric Dover, *American Negro Art*. Greenwich, Conn., New York Graphic Society, 1960. 186 pp. An exceptional survey of creations of American Negro artists from colonial times to the present; includes over 100 reproductions of paintings, drawings, and sculpture; extensive bibliography.

Golden State Mutual Negro Art Collection, 1999 W. Adams, Los Angeles, Calif.

Alain Locke, *Negro Art: Past and Present*. Washington, Associates in Negro Folk Education, 1936. 122 pp. A brief survey of the past, present, and future of Negro art the world over.

_____, *The Negro in Art*. Washington, Associates in Negro Folk Education, 1940. 224 pp. Pictorial history of the Negro artist and of the Negro theme in art; biographical sketches and bibliography.

James A. Porter, *Modern Negro Art*. New York, Dryden, 1943. 272 pp.; reprinted New York, Franklin, 1963. Study of the work of the American Negro artist from pre-Civil War days to the 1940's.

Selden Rodman, *Horace Pippin*. New York, Quadrangle, 1947. 88 pp.

The Portrayal of the Negro in American Painting. Notes on and illustrations of a 1964 exhibition at the Bowdoin College Museum of Art, Brunswick, Maine. 1 vol. unpaged.

THEATRE

Frederick W. Bond, *The Negro and the Drama*. Washington, Associated, 1940. 213 pp.

Randolph Edmonds, *Six Plays for a Negro Theatre*. Boston, Walter Baker, 1934. 155 pp.

Tom Fletcher, *100 Years of the Negro in Show Business*. New York, Burdge, 1954. 337 pp.

Paul Green, *Lonesome Road.* New York, McBride, 1926. 217 pp. Six plays for the Negro theater.

A. W. Grimke, *Rachel.* Boston, Cornhill, 1920. 96 pp.

Lorraine Hansberry, *A Raisin in the Sun.* New York, Random House, 1959. 142 pp. *Also in paperback.*

Du Bose Heyward, *Brass Ankle.* New York, Farrar & Rinehart, 1931. 133 pp.

Langston Hughes and David Martin, *Simply Heavenly.* New York, Dramatists Play Service, 1959. 87 pp. A comedy with music.

Edith J. Isaacs, *The Negro in the American Theatre.* New York, Theatre Arts, 1947. 143 pp. A record of the Negro's contributions to dramatic art in the United States; covers the activities of Negro performers, playwrights, and composers from the early 1800's to 1947.

V. J. Jerome, *The Negro in Hollywood Films.* New York, Masses & Mainstream, 1950.

LeRoi Jones, *The Dutchman and the Slave: Two Plays.* New York, Morrow, 1964. 88 pp.

Alain Locke and Montgomery Gregory, *Plays of Negro Life.* New York, Harper, 1927. 430 pp.

Herbert Marshall and Mildred Stock, *Ira Aldridge.* New York, Macmillan, 1958. 355 pp. Biography of Ira Frederick Aldridge (1805-1867), greatest interpreter of his time of Shakespeare's tragedies.

Peter Noble, *The Negro in Films.* London, S. Robinson, 1948. 288 pp.

George Ralph, *The American Theatre, the Negro, and the Freedom Movement.* Chicago, City Missionary Society, 1964. A biography with detailed references.

Thomas Richardson, *Place: America (a Theatre Piece).* Pamphlet, New York, NAACP, 1939. 51 pp.

Willis Richardson, ed., *Plays and Pageants from the Life of the Negro.* Washington, Associated, 1930. 373 pp.

————— and May Miller, ed., *Negro History in Thirteen Plays.* Washington, Associated, 1935. 333 pp.

Ridgely Torrence, *The Rider of Dreams: Simon the Cyrenean: Plays for a Negro Theatre.* New York, Macmillan, 1917. 111 pp.

GENERAL

Benjamin Brawley, *The Negro Genius.* New York, Dodd, 1937. 366 pp.

—————, *The Negro in Literature and Art in the United States.* New York, Duffield, 1921. 197 pp.

J. Mason Brewer, *Worser Days and Better Times: The Folklore of the North Carolina Negro.* Chicago, Quadrangle, 1965. 192 pp.

Sterling A. Brown, ed., *The Negro Caravan.* New York, Dryden, 1941. 1,082 pp. Contains selections from novels, poetry, folk literature, spirituals, ballads, blues, and protest songs.

Margaret Just Butcher, *The Negro in American Culture*. New York, Knopf, 1956. 294 pp. *Also in paperback.*

Harold Courlander, *Terrapin's Pot of Sense*. New York, Holt, 1957. 125 pp. Contains 31 American Negro folk stories.

Otelia Cromwell, *Readings from Negro Authors, for Schools and Colleges*. New York, Harcourt, 1931. 388 pp.

Herman Dreer, *American Literature by Negro Authors*. New York, Macmillan, 1950. 334 pp.

Ralph Ellison, *Shadow and Act*. New York, Random House, 1964. General field of Negro literature, jazz, etc.

Herbert Hill, ed., *Soon, One Morning: New Writing by American Negroes, 1940-1962*. New York, Knopf, 1963. 617 pp.

Langston Hughes, *The Langston Hughes Reader*. New York, Braziller, 1958. 501 pp.

_____ and Arna W. Bontemps, ed., *The Book of Negro Folklore*. New York, Dodd, Mead, 1958. 624 pp. The Negro's contribution to American literature and folk expression from slavery to jazz.

Charles S. Johnson, *Ebony and Topaz*. New York, Opportunity, 1927. 164 pp. Poems, articles, essays, and stories by Negroes; illustrations by Negro artists.

Alain LeRoy Locke, ed., *A Decade of Negro Self-Expression*. Charlottesville, Va., 1928. 20 pp. Bibliography relating to Negro writing.

Hans Nathan, *Dan Emmett and the Rise of Early Negro Minstrels*. Norman, U. of Oklahoma Press, 1962.

The New Negro: An Interpretation. New York, Boni, 1925. 446 pp. Documentation of the Negro in the cultural arts.

Charlemae Rollins, ed., *Christmas Gif': An Anthology of Christmas Poems, Songs and Stories, Written by and About Negroes*. Chicago, Follett, 1963. 119 pp.

21. BOOKS AND PAMPHLETS ON RACE

> You can't hold the Negro in the ditch without staying in it
> with him.
>
> —George W. Cable

There have been literally hundreds of books written on the question of race. Those listed here represent only a sampling but if properly used are adequate.

Ethel Alpenfels, *Sense and Nonsense About Race*. New York, Friendship, 1957. 64 pp. *Paperback.*

Ruth Benedict, *Race: Science and Politics,* rev. ed. New York, Viking, 1959. Includes *The Races of Mankind. Also in paperback.*

Kenneth B. Clark, *Prejudice and Your Child*. Boston, Beacon, 1963. *Also in paperback.*

Earl W. Count, *This Is Race: An Anthology Selected from the International Literature in the Races of Man*. New York, Abelard-Schuman, 1950.

L. C. Dunn and Theodore Dobzhansky, *Heredity, Race and Society,* New York, Mentor, 1952.

E. Franklin Frazier, *Race and Culture Contacts in the Modern World*. New York, Knopf, 1957. 338 pp. *Also in paperback.*

Mary Ellen Goodman, *Race Awareness in Young Children*. New York, Collier, 1964. *Also in paperback.*

Oscar Handlin, *Race and Nationality in American Life*. Boston, Little, Brown, 1937.

Frank H. Hankins, *The Racial Basis of Civilization: A Critique of the Nordic Doctrine*. New York, Knopf, 1926.

Clyde Kluckhohn, *Mirror For Man*. New York, Whittlesey, 1949. *Also in paperback.*

Marguerite Rush Lerner, *Red Man, White Man, African Chief: The Story of Skin Color*. Minneapolis, Lerner, 1960, unpaged.

Carey McWilliams, *Brothers Under the Skin*. Boston, Little, Brown,

1943. *Also in paperback.*

Ashley Montagu, *Man's Most Dangerous Myth: The Fallacy of Race.* New York, Harper, 1952. *Also in paperback.*

Gustavus Myers, *History of Bigotry in the United States.* New York, Random House, 1943. *Also in paperback.*

Thomas F. Pettigrew, *A Profile of the Negro American.* Princeton, Van Nostrand, 1964. 250 pp. *Also in paperback.*

Toward Better International Understanding. New York, New York Board of Education, 1959. A Teachers' Manual, Curriculum Bulletin 1956-60, Series No. 4.

UNESCO Publications, *The Race Question in Modern Science Series.* Paris, UNESCO, 1956. (Also available through UNESCO Publications Center (317 E. 34th St., New York, N.Y.) *Also in paperback.*

Juan Comas, *Racial Myths.*

Rev. Yves M. J. Congar, O.P., *The Catholic Church and the Race Question.*

L. C. Dunn, *Race and Biology.*

Otto Klineberg, *Race and Psychology.*

Michel Leiris, *Race and Culture.*

Claude Levi-Strauss, *Race and History.*

Kenneth L. Little, *Race and Society.*

G. M. Morant, *The Significance of Racial Differences.*

The Race Concept. Results of an Inquiry.

Racism. (1960)

Arnold M. Rose, *The Roots of Prejudice.*

Harry L. Shapiro, *Race Mixture.*

What Science Says About Race.

22. RACIAL ATTITUDES IN TEXTBOOKS

A number of studies have been made to prove that there has been a virtual exclusion of Negro history from our textbooks. The majority of our textbooks on U.S. history have been written from an Anglo-Saxon point of view, and a great many of the problems that exist, particularly in race relations, have been created and have been maintained by misinformation as well as no information at all. There has been a censorship by omission as well as commission. These few selected listings will at least indicate the depth of the problem.

Astrid C. Anderson, *Treatment of Racial and Cultural Diversity in Elementary School Social Studies Textbooks.* Lincoln Filene Center for Citizenship and Public Affairs.

Herbert Aptheker, "Integrated Education Requires Integrated Textbooks," *Political Affairs,* June 1964, pp. 47-52.

Marie Elizabeth Carpenter, *The Treatment of the Negro in American History School Textbooks.* Wisconsin, 1941. (Or author, 114 Storms Ave., Jersey City, N. J.)

Stanley M. Elkin, "Minorities in Textbooks: The Latest Chapter," (Columbia University) Teachers College Record, March 1965, pp. 502-508.

Lloyd Marcus, *The Treatment of Minorities in Secondary Schoolbooks.* New York, Anti-Defamation League, 1961.

Martin Mayer, "The Trouble With Textbooks," *Harper's,* July 1962, pp. 65-71.

Lawrence D. Reddick, "Racial Attitudes in the South's American History Textbooks" Unpub. M. A. thesis, Fisk University, 1933.

Irving Sloan, *The Negro in Modern American History Textbooks.* Chicago, American Federation of Teachers, AFL-CIO, 1966. 47 pp. A study of the Negro in selected junior and senior high history textbooks as of September, 1966.

Kenneth Stampp and others, "The Negro In American Textbooks," *Integrated Education,* October-November, 1964. Report by a panel of six historians on a review of history textbooks most widely used in California schools.

Bias and Prejudice in Textbooks in Use in New York City Schools. New York, N.Y. Teachers Union, 1960.

"Prejudice in Text Books," *Public Affairs Pamphlet No. 160.* New York, National Conference of Christians and Jews, 1949.

Intergroup Relations in Teaching Materials. Washington, American Council on Education, 1949.

Anti-Negro Propaganda in School Textbooks. New York, NAACP, 1939.

"Common Distortions in the Textbook Treatment of Slavery." *Journal of Negro Education,* 1959.

A Report on the Treatment of Minorities—Elementary School Textbooks. Brooklyn, Assn. for the Study of Negro Life and History, and Emma Lazarus Federation, May 1961.

"Racist Poison in School Books," *Freedomways,* Summer 1961.

23. PAPERBACK BOOKS ON NEGRO HISTORY

> The Constitution does not provide for First and Second
> Class Citizens.—Wendell L. Willkie, *An American Program*

The list of paperback books on Negro history represents an important resource. With the high cost of books and the relatively low budgets of many educational institutions, libraries, and organizations, there is available at relatively low cost a wide variety of titles. These readily available books represent a most important medium through which to dispel myth and create understanding.

James S. Allen, *Reconstruction: The Battle for Democracy*. International.

Ethel Alpenfels, *Sense and Nonsense About Race*. Friendship.

American Oil Company, *American Traveler's Guide To Negro History*. American Oil Company, 910 S. Michigan Ave., Chicago, Ill.

Marian Anderson, *My Lord, What a Morning*. Avon.

Herbert Aptheker, *The Negro in the Civil War*. International.

————, *The Negro in the American Revolution*. International.

————, *Essays in the History of the American Negro*. International.

————, *Negro Slave Revolts in the United States, 1526-1860*. International.

————, *American Martyr: John Brown, 1859-1959*. New Century.

————, *Toward Negro Freedom*. New Century. Historic highlights in the life and struggles of the American Negro people from colonial days to the present.

————, *Documentary History of the Negro People in the United States*. Vol. I: From Colonial Times through the Civil War. Vol. II: From the Reconstruction Era to 1910. Citadel.

————, *American Negro Slave Revolts*. International.

————, *One Continual Cry. David Walker's Appeal to the Coloured Citizens of the World, 1829-1830. Its Setting and Its Meaning*. Marzani & Munsell.

_____, *The Negro in the Abolitionist Movement*. International.

_____, *The Negro People in America* (A Critique of Gunnar Myrdal's *An American Dilemma*). *International*.

_____, *Nat Turner's Revolt: The Environment, the Event, the Effects.* Marzani & Munsell.

Helen A. Archibald, ed., *Negro History and Culture: Selected Material for Use with Children*. Chicago City Missionary Society.

Louis Armstrong, *Satchmo*. Signet.

Ray S. Baker, *Following the Color Line: American Negro Citizenship in the Progressive Era*. Harper Torchbooks.

Richard Bardolph, *The Negro Vanguard*. Vintage.

Gilbert H. Barnes, *The Antislavery Impulse*. Harbinger.

Ruth Benedict, *Race: Science and Politics,* rev. ed. Compass. Includes *The Races of Mankind*.

Lerone Bennett, Jr., *Before the Mayflower: A History of the Negro in America, 1619–1964*. New York, Pelican, 1966.

_____, *What Manner of Man: A Biography of Martin Luther King*. Pocket Books.

Rudi Blesh and Harriet Janis, *They All Played Ragtime: The True Story of an American ʾMusic*. New York, Oak Publications, 1966. 347 pp.

Robert A. Bone, *The Negro Novel in America*. Yale U. Press. rev. ed.

Arna W. Bontemps, ed., *American Negro Poetry*. Hill and Wang.

_____, *Black Thunder*. Seven Seas.

_____ and Jack Conroy, *Anyplace But Here* (originally entitled: *They Seek a City*).

B. A. Botkin, ed., *Lay My Burden Down*. Phoenix Books. A folk history of slavery.

Sarah Bradford, *Harriet Tubman: The Moses of Her People*. Citadel.

Stephen H. Bronz, *Roots of Negro Racial Consciousness: The 1920's; Three Harlem Renaissance Authors*. Libra Publishers. About James Weldon Johnson, Countee Cullen and Claude McKay.

Gwendolyn Brooks, *Selected Poems*. Harper.

William Broonzy (as told to Yannick Bruynoghe), *Big Bill Blues*. Oak

Ina Corinne Brown, *The Story of the American Negro,* 2nd rev. ed. Friendship.

Paul H. Buck, *The Road to Reunion: 1865-1900*. Little, Brown.

Henrietta Buckmaster, *Let My People Go*. Beacon.

W. Hayward Burns, *The Voices of Negro Protest in America*. Galaxy.

George W. Cable, *Old Creole Days*. Signet.

_____, *The Grandissimes*. Hill and Wang.

_____, *The Negro Question*. Anchor.

Poppy Cannon, *A Gentle Knight*. Popular Library.

W. J. Cash, *The Mind of the South*. Vintage.

Samuel B. Charters, *The Poetry of the Blues*. Oak.

————, *Jazz: New Orleans*. Oak.

Bobbi and Frank Cieciorka, *Negroes in American History: A Freedom Primer*. Student Voice, Inc., 360 Nelson St., S.W., Atlanta, Ga.

Kenneth B. Clark, *Prejudice and Your Child*. Beacon.

John Henrik Clarke, ed., *American Negro Short Stories*. New York, Hill and Wang, 1966.

Earl Conrad, *Harriet Tubman: Negro Soldier and Abolitionist*. International.

Harold Courlander, *Negro Songs from Alabama*. Oak.

Edmund Cronon, *Black Moses*. U. of Wisconsin Press. Story of Marcus Garvey.

Larry Cuban, *The Negro in America*. Scott, Foresman.

Richard Current, ed., *Reconstruction, 1865-1877*. Spectrum.

Richard D. Curry, *Abolitionists—Reformers or Fanatics?* Holt.

Carl N. Degler, *Out of Our Past*. Harper.

Lavinia Dobler and Edgar A. Toppin, *Pioneers and Patriots: The Lives of Six Negroes of the Revolutionary Era*. Doubleday Zenith. Biographical sketches of Peter Salem, Jean Baptiste Pointe du Sable, Phillis Wheatley, Benjamin Banneker, Paul Cuffee, and John Chavis.

Frederick Douglass, *Life and Times of Frederick Douglass*. Collier.

————, *Narrative of the Life of Frederick Douglass, An American Slave, Written by Himself*. Dolphin.

Carol Drisko and Dr. Edgar A. Toppin, *The Unfinished March: The Negro in the United States: Reconstruction to World War I*. Zenith.

Martin B. Duberman, *In White America*. Signet. Survey of Negro history.

W. E. B. Du Bois, *An ABC of Color*. Seven Seas. Selections from over a half century of the writings of W. E. Du Bois.

————, *Black Reconstruction in America*. Meridian.

————, *John Brown*. International.

————, *The Souls of Black Folk*. Fawcett.

————, *The World and Africa*. International.

————, *Dusk of Dawn: An Essay Toward an Autobiography of a Race Concept*. Harcourt.

Dwight L. Dumond, *Antislavery Origins of the Civil War in the United States*. Ann Arbor.

Stanley M. Elkins, *Slavery: A Problem in American Institutional and Intellectual Life*. Universal.

E. U. Essien-Udom, *Black Nationalism*. Dell.

Howard Fast, *Freedom Road*. Pocket Books.

Leonard Feather, *The Book of Jazz*. Paperback Library.

Eugene Feldman, *James T. Rapier*. The Southern News Letter, P. O. Box 1307, Louisville, Ky.

_____, ed., *Figures in Negro History*. Museum of Negro History and Art, Chicago, Ill.

Louis Filler, *The Crusade Against Slavery*. Harper Torchbooks.

Miles Mark Fisher, *Negro Slave Songs in the United States*. Citadel.

George Fitzhugh and Hinton R. Helper, *Ante-Bellum: Three Classic Writings on Slavery in the Old South*, ed. by Harvey Wish. Capricorn.

Philip S. Foner, *Frederick Douglass*. Citadel.

_____, ed. *Frederick Douglass: Selections from His Writings*. International.

Charlotte L. Forten, *Journal of a Free Negro in the Slave Era*. Collier. The journal of Charlotte L. Forten, a Negro woman during the time of slavery.

John Hope Franklin, *The Emancipation Proclamation*. Anchor.

_____, *The Militant South*. Beacon.

_____, *Reconstruction: After the Civil War*. U. of Chicago Press.

E. Franklin Frazier, *Black Bourgeoisie*. Collier. The rise of a new middle class in the United States.

_____, *Race and Culture Contacts in the Modern World*. Beacon.

_____, *The Negro Church in America*. Schocken.

_____, "Traditions and Patterns of Negro Family Life in the United States," in E. B. Reuter, *Race and Culture Contacts*. McGraw-Hill.

Wayne A. Frederick, *Slavery and the Breakdown of the American Consensus*. Heath.

Edmund Fuller, *A Star Pointed North*. Harper. Biography of Frederick Douglass.

Althea Gibson (with Ed Fitzgerald), *I Always Wanted To Be Somebody*. Perennial Library.

L. H. Giles and L. F. Holmes, *Color Me Brown*. Johnson. Includes poems and pictures to color of famous Negroes in American history.

Ralph Ginzburg, *100 Years of Lynchings*. Lancer.

Robert A. Goldwin, ed., *100 Years of Emancipation*. Rand McNally.

Mary Ellen Goodman, *Race Awareness in Young Children*. Collier.

Dick Gregory (with Robert Lipsyte), *Nigger*. Pocket Books.

Bella Gross, *Clarion Call: The History and Development of the Negro People's Convention Movement in the United States from 1817-1840*. Bella Gross, 175 W. 93rd St., New York, N.Y.

Ben Haas, *KKK*. Regency.

Oscar Handlin, *Race and Nationality in American Life*. Anchor.

Lorraine Hansberry, *The Movement*. Simon and Schuster.

_____, *A Raisin in the Sun*. Signet.

H. Hawkins, ed., *Booker T. Washington and His Critics: The Problem of Negro Leadership*. Heath.

Josiah Henson, *Father Henson's Story of His Own Life*. Corinth. The autobiography of an escaped Negro slave in pre-Civil War days, whose life served as an inspiration for Harriet Beecher Stowe's *Uncle Tom's Cabin*.

Nat Hentoff, *The Jazz Life*. Apollo.

Melville J. Herskovits, *The Myth of the Negro Past*. Beacon.

————, *The American Negro*. Indiana U. Press.

Thomas Wentworth Higginson, *Army Life in a Black Regiment*. Collier. Adventures of the first slave regiment mustered into the service of the United States during the Civil War.

Andre Hodeir, *Jazz: Its Evolution and Essence*. Grove.

Billie Holiday (with William Duffy), *Lady Sings the Blues*. Popular Library.

Langston Hughes, ed., *An African Treasury*. Pyramid. Articles, essays, stories, poems by black Africans.

————, *Fight for Freedom: The Story of the N.A.A.C.P.* Berkley.

————, *The Big Sea*. Hill & Wang.

————, *I Wonder as I Wander*. Hill & Wang.

Harold R. Isaacs, *The New World of Negro Americans*. Compass.

C. L. R. James, *Black Jacobins*. Vintage. Toussaint L'Ouverture and the San Domingo Revolution.

F. Roy Johnson, *The Nat Turner Slave Insurrection*. Murfreesboro, N.C., Johnson Pub.

James Weldon Johnson, *Autobiography of an Ex-Coloured Man*. Hill and Wang.

LeRoi Jones, *Blues People: Negro Music and White America*. Apollo.

Martin Luther King, *Stride Toward Freedom*. Ballantine.

Clyde Kluckhohn, *Mirror for Man*. Fawcett.

Elizabeth Lawson, *The People's Almanac*. New Century.

————, *Lincoln's Third Party*. International.

————, *The Gentleman from Mississippi*.

Paul Lewinson, *Race, Class and Party: A History of Negro Suffrage and White Politics in the South*. Universal Books.

Claude Lewis, *Cassius Clay*. Macfadden-Bartell.

Leon F. Litwack, *North of Slavery: The Negro in the Free States, 1790-1860*. Phoenix.

Rayford W. Logan, *The Negro in the United States*. Van Nostrand.

————, *The Betrayal of the Negro* (originally *The Negro in American Life and Thought*). Collier.

———— and Irving Cohen, *The American Negro: African Background and New World Experience*. Houghton Mifflin.

Alan Lomax, *Mister Jelly Roll*. Universal.

Louis Lomax, *The Negro Revolt*. Signet.

Walter Lowenfels, ed., *Poets of Today: A New American Anthology*. International.

Agnes McCarthy and Lawrence Reddick, *Worth Fighting For*. Doubleday. A history of the Negro in the Civil War and Reconstruction periods.

Ann McGovern, *Runaway Slave*. Scholastic Books. The story of Harriet Tubman.

Norman McRae and Jerry Blocker, *The American Negro: A History in Biography and Pictures*. Impact.

Grady McWhiney, *Reconstruction and the Freedmen*. Rand McNally.

Carey McWilliams, *Brothers Under the Skin*. Little, Brown.

D. P. Mannix and Malcolm Cowley, *Black Cargoes: History of the Atlantic Slave Trade, 1518-1865*. Compass.

Fletcher Martin, *Our Great Americans: The Negro Contribution to American Progress*. Gamma.

Edith H. Mayer, *Our Negro Brother*. Shady Hill. Biographical information about eight Negroes, ranging from Columbus' pilot, Nino, to union leader A. Philip Randolph, includes Matthew Henson, the only American Negro with Robert E. Peary at the North Pole in 1909.

Enid L. Meadowcroft, *By Secret Railway*. Scholastic Books (reprint). A story of two boys, one Negro, one white, and their adventures in 1860 with the Underground Railway.

August Meier, *Negro Thought in America, 1880–1915: Racial Ideologies in the Age of Booker T. Washington*. U. of Michigan Press.

Milton Meltzer and Dr. August Meier, *Time of Trial, Time of Hope*. Zenith. History of the Negro during World Wars I and II.

Glenford E. Mitchell and William H. Peace, III, eds., *Angry Black South*. Corinth.

Ashley Montagu, *Man's Most Dangerous Myth: The Fallacy of Race*. Meridian.

Everett Frederic Morrow, *Black Man in the White House*. Macfadden.

Hugh Mulzac, *Star to Steer By*. International.

Gustavus Myers, *History of Bigotry in the United States*. Capricorn.

Gunnar Myrdal, *An American Dilemma*. McGraw-Hill. 2 Vols.

NAACP, *Black Heroes of the American Revolution*. NAACP.

J. W. Nordholt-Schulte, *The People That Walk in Darkness*. Ballantine. A history of the Negro in America.

Frederick Law Olmstead, *The Slave States*. Capricorn.

William L. Patterson, ed., *We Charge Genocide*. New York Civil Rights Congress. A petition to the U. N. charging government crimes against the Negro people.

Thomas F. Pettigrew, *A Profile of the Negro American*. Van Nostrand.

Pictorial History of the American Negro, by eds. of *Year* and *News Front*. Hammond.

Benjamin Quarles, *The Negro in the Making of America*. Collier.

_____, *The Negro in the American Revolution*. U. of North Carolina Press.

F. Ramsey and C. E. Smith, eds., *Jazzmen*. Harcourt.

J. Saunders Redding, *On Being Negro in America*. Bantam.

John H. Rohrer and Munro S. Edmonson, eds., *The Eighth Generation*. Harper Torchbooks.

Arnold Rose, *The Negro in America*. Harper Torchbooks. Condensed version of Gunnar Myrdal's *An American Dilemma*.

E. C. Rozwenc, ed., *Slavery as a Cause of the Civil War*. Heath.

Louis Ruchames, ed., *The Abolitionists*. Capricorn. A collection of their writings.

Doris E. Saunders, ed., *The Kennedy Years and the Negro*. Johnson.

John A. Scott, ed., *Living Documents in American History*, Vol. I. Washington Square Press. Reference work containing documents up to 1865. (Vol. II to be published.)

Neil Scott, *Joe Louis: A Picture Story of His Life*. Greenberg.

Edith Segal, *Come with Me*. Citadel.

Arnold Shaw, *Belafonte*. Pyramid.

Samuel Sillen, *Women Against Slavery*. Masses & Mainstream.

Otis A. Singletary, *Negro Militia and Reconstruction*. McGraw-Hill.

G. Sorrentino, *Black and White*. Corinth.

S. R. Spencer, Jr., *Booker T. Washington and the Negro's Place in American Life*. Little, Brown.

David Spitz, *Patterns of Anti-Democratic Thought*. Free Press.

Kenneth M. Stampp, *The Peculiar Institution*. Vintage.

Marshall W. Stearns, *The Story of Jazz*. Mentor.

Dorothy Sterling and Benjamin Quarles, *Lift Every Voice: The Lives of Booker T. Washington, W. E. B. Du Bois, Mary Church Terrell, and James Weldon Johnson*. Zenith.

Philip Sterling and Rayford Logan, *Four Took Freedom: The Lives of Harriet Tubman, Frederick Douglass, Robert Smalls, and Blanche K. Bruce*. Zenith.

Emma Gelders Sterne, *The Long Black Schooner*. Scholastic Book Services, (reprint).

Harriet Beecher Stowe, *Uncle Tom's Cabin*. Collier.

Frank Tannenbaum, *Slave and Citizen: The Negro in the Americas*. Vintage.

Rosser H. Taylor, *The Free Negro in North Carolina*. U. of North Carolina Press.

Jacobus Ten Broek, *Equal Under Law*. Collier. Originally published as *The Anti-Slavery Origins of the 14th Amendment*, U. of California Press.

J. L. Thomas, *Slavery Attacked: The Abolitionist Crusade*. Prentice-Hall.

Barry Ulanov, *A Handbook of Jazz*. Compass.

Richard C. Wade, *The Negro in American Life*. Part One, From Slavery to Citizenship: 1619–1900; Part Two, Toward Full Equality: Since 1900. Houghton Mifflin.

Charles Wagley and Marvin Harris, *Minorities in the New World.* Columbia U. Press.

David Walker's Appeal to the Coloured Citizens of the World. Hill and Wang.

Booker T. Washington, *Up From Slavery.* Bantam Books.

Ethel Waters (with Charles Samuels), *His Eye Is on the Sparrow.* Bantam.

Bernard A. Weisberger, *Abolitionism: Disrupter of the Democratic System or Agent of Progress?* Rand McNally.

Erwin K. Welsch, *The Negro in the United States: A Research Guide.* U. of Indiana Press.

Vernon L. Wharton, *The Negro in Mississippi, 1865-1890.* Harper Torchbooks.

Ann Terry White, *George Washington Carver: The Story of a Great American.* Random House.

Bell I. Wiley, *Southern Negroes, 1861-1865.* Yale U. Press.

Eric Williams, *Capitalism and Slavery.* Andre Deutsch, Limited.

Harvey Wish, ed., *The Negro Since Emancipation.* Prentice-Hall.

————, ed., *Slavery in the South.* Noonday.

C. Vann Woodward, *The Burden of Southern History.* Vintage.

————, *Reunion and Reaction.* Anchor.

————, *The Strange Career of Jim Crow.* Galaxy.

————, ed., *Southern Prophecy: The Prosperity of the South Dependent on the Elevation of the Negro (1889)* by Lewis H. Blair. Little, Brown.

Richard Wright, *Black Boy.* Signet.

Year's *Pictorial History of the American Negro,* Baldwin H. Ward, ed. Year, Inc.

A. S. "Doc" Young, *Sonny Liston: The Champ Nobody Wanted.* Johnson.

B. M. Ziegler, ed., *Desegregation and the Supreme Court.* Heath.

MISCELLANEOUS:

A Guide for the Study of Negro History in the Churches. Commission on Religion and Race, Presbytery of Chicago, 29 East Madison St., Chicago, Ill.

The Race Question in the Modern Science Series. UNESCO Publication Center, 317 E. 34th St., New York, N.Y. Separate booklets on all aspects of the race question.

The Negro in American History: A Curriculum Resource Bulletin for Secondary Schools. Public Schools of the District of Columbia, Washington, D. C. $1.50.

The Negro in American History: Curriculum Bulletin, 1964-65, Series #4. Board of Education, City of New York, 110 Livingston St., Brooklyn, N. Y. $1.00.

24. SELECTED BOOKS FOR CHILDREN AND YOUNG ADULTS

> I have seen a land right merry with the sun, where children sing, and rolling hills lie like passioned women wanton with harvest. And there in the King's Highway sat and sits a figure veiled and bowed, by which the traveler's footsteps hasten as they go. On the tainted air broods fear. Three centuries thought has been the raising and unveiling of that bowed human heart, and now behold a century new for the duty and the deed. THE PROBLEM OF THE TWENTIETH CENTURY IS THE PROBLEM OF THE COLOR LINE.
>
> —W. E. B. Du Bois, *Souls of Black Folk*

One of the most neglected areas is books for children in the early grades of schools. Some are listed here, but this list is primarily for older children. It is often difficult to determine whether books intended for young adults and children are not also of interest to adults. Adults may find some of these books profitable reading.

Merritt Parmalee Allen, *Battle Lanterns*. New York, Longmans, 1949. 278 pp. Historical novel of the Revolutionary War which shows contributions of Negroes in the fight for independence.

Helen A. Archibald, ed., *Negro History and Culture: Selected Material for Use with Children*. Chicago, Chicago City Missionary Society, 1965. *Paperback.*

John L. Becker, *The Negro in American Life*. New York, Messner, 1944. 53 pp. Brief summary of Negro contributions. Grades 5-7.

Laura Benét, *Famous American Poets*. New York, Dodd, 1950. 183 pp.

Sonia Bleeker, *The Seminole Indians*. New York, Morrow, 1954. 156 pp. A history of the Seminole people and their close relationships with the Florida Negroes.

Arna W. Bontemps, *Chariot in the Sky*. Philadelphia, Winston, 1951. 234 pp. Story of an ex-slave who seeks an education and helps build Fisk University. Grades 6-8.

_____, *Famous Negro Athletes*. New York, Dodd, 1964. Ages 12 and up.

_____, ed., *Negro American Heritage*. San Francisco, Century Schoolbook Press, 1965. 136 pp.

_____, *Frederick Douglass: Slave, Fighter, Freeman*. New York, Knopf, 1959. 177 pp. Grades 5-9.

_____, ed., *Golden Slippers: An Anthology of Negro Poetry for Young Readers*. New York, Harper, 1941. 220 pp. This volume contains 108 poems by 29 different Negro poets, from Paul Laurence Dunbar to Langston Hughes; includes brief biographical sketch of each poet. Grades 7-9.

_____, *100 Years of Negro Freedom*. New York, Dodd, 1961. 276 pp. A retrospective study of the American Negro from Reconstruction to the present.

_____, *Story of the Negro*, 3rd ed. rev. New York, Knopf, 1962. 243 pp. A history of the American Negro for young people; contains a chronology of important events in Negro history from 300 to 1955 A.D. Grades 7-10.

_____, *The Story of George Washington Carver*. New York, Grosset, 1954. 181 pp. Sensitively written story about the great agriculturalist. Grades 4-6.

_____, *We Have Tomorrow*. Boston, Houghton, 1945. 131 pp. Biographies, with photographs, of 12 young American Negroes who are making unique contributions. Grades 9-12.

_____ and Langston Hughes, *A Book of Negro Folklore*. New York, Dodd, 1958. The Negro's contribution to American literature and folk expression from slavery to 1933.

Aliki Brandenberg, *A Weed Is a Flower: The Life of George Washington Carver*. Englewood Cliffs, Prentice-Hall, 1966.

Benjamin Brawley, *Negro Builders and Heroes*. Chapel Hill, U. of North Carolina Press, 1937. 315 pp. The lives and achievements of Negroes in the United States from 1770 to 1935. Grades 6-8.

Gwendolyn Brooks. *Bronzeville Boys and Girls*. New York, Harper, 1956. 40 pp. A collection of 36 poems about the day-to-day experiences of a group of Negro children in Chicago. Grades 3 and up.

Francis Williams Brown, *Looking for Orlando*. New York, Criterion, 1961. A thrilling adventure story which also throws light on a heroic movement, the Underground Railroad. Ages 9-11.

Henrietta Buckmaster, *Flight To Freedom: Story of the Underground Railroad*. New York, Crowell, 1958. 217 pp. Grades 7-12.

Ella Kaiser Carruth, *She Wanted to Read: The Story of Mary McLeod Bethune*. Illustrated by Herbert McClure. Nashville, Abingdon Press, 1966. 80 pp. Age 12 up.

John W. Caughey, John Hope Franklin, and Ernest R. May, *Land of the Free—A History of the United States*. New York, Benziger

Brothers, 1966. 658 pp. New integrated textbook for 8th grade.

Bobbi and Frank Cieciorka, *Negroes in American History: A Freedom Primer*. Atlanta, Student Voice (360 Nelson St., S.W.), 1965. *Paperback*.

Earl Conrad, *Harriet Tubman*. Washington, Associated Publishers, 1943. 248 pp. *Also in paperback*. Grades 9-12.

Harold Courlander, *Terrapin's Pot of Sense*. New York, Holt, 1957. 125 pp. Thirty-one American Negro Folk stories. Grades 4-5.

Maud Cuney-Hare, *Negro Musicians and Their Music*. Washington, Associated Publishers, 1936. 439 pp. A descriptive and interpretative study of the history of Negro music and the men who have contributed to it; the book goes back to Africa and traces Negro music up to modern times. Grades 9-12.

Virginia Cunningham, *Paul Laurence Dunbar and His Song*. New York, Dodd, 1947. 283 pp. Extensive bibliography and 12 photographs. Grades 9-12.

Charles C. Dawson, *A.B.C.'s of Great Negroes*. Chicago, Dawson Publishing, 1933. 55 pp.

Elise Palmer Derricotte and others, *Word Pictures of the Great*. Washington, Associated, 1941. 280 pp. Biographical sketches of prominent Negroes, including Ira Aldridge, Benjamin Banneker, Frederick Douglass, Paul Laurence Dunbar, James Weldon Johnson, and Phillis Wheatley. Grades 3-4.

Trella L. Dick, *The Island on the Border*. New York, Schuman, 1963. 160 pp. Wealthy Southern family opposed to the Confederate cause during Civil War was harassed by their neighbors but helped to safety by their Negro servant, Caleb, and a runaway slave, Old Luke. Grades 6-8.

Lavinia Dobler and Edgar A. Toppin, *Pioneers and Patriots: The Lives of Six Negroes of the Revolutionary Era*. Garden City, Doubleday Zenith Books, 1965. 118 pp. *Also in paperback*. Biographical sketches of Peter Salem, Jean Baptiste Pointe du Sable, Phillis Wheatley, Benjamin Banneker, Paul Cuffee, and John Chavis.

Marjory Stoneman Douglas, *Freedom River: Florida, 1845*. New York, Scribner, 1953. 264 pp. Time and place are captured in well-written tale of three boys—a white boy, a Negro, and a Seminole Indian—who find their separate freedoms. Grades 6-8.

Frederick Douglass (adapted by Barbara Ritchie), *Life and Times of Frederick Douglass*. New York, Crowell, 1966. 204 pp.

Esther M. Douty, *Under the New Roof: Five Patriots of the Young Republic*. Chicago, Rand McNally, 1965. The "New Roof" was a frequent epithet for the Constitution of the United States from its ratification through the War of 1812; included in this work is Richard Allen (1760–1831), founder of the African Methodist Episcopal Church, as the Negro patriot.

Carol Drisko and Dr. Edgar A. Toppin, *The Unfinished March: The*

Negro in the United States: Reconstruction to World War I. Garden City, N.Y., Zenith, 1967. 128 pp. *Also in paperback.*

W. E. B. Du Bois, *Quest of the Silver Fleece.* Chicago, McClurg, 1911. 434 pp. One of the earliest novels written by a Negro tells of the struggle for an education by two Negro children on a cotton plantation.

Paul Laurence Dunbar, *Complete Poems.* New York, Dodd, 1940. 289 pp. Complete poems of one of America's most celebrated early Negro poets.

_____, *Little Brown Baby.* New York, Dodd, 1940. 106 pp. Dunbar's poems selected for younger children. Grades 4-5.

Philip Durham and Everett L. Jones, *The Adventures of Negro Cowboys.* New York, Dodd, Mead, 1965–66. 143 pp. A chronicle of forgotten men who helped to forge a new land.

Walter Edmonds, *Cadmus Henry.* New York, Dodd, 1949. 137 pp. Civil War story of young Confederate Army clerk and two Negroes loyal to the Union cause. Grades 6-8.

Samuel and Beryl Epstein, *George Washington Carver: Negro Scientist.* Illustrated by William Moyers. A Discovery Book. Champaign, Illinois, Garrard Publishing Company, 1960. 79 pp. Ages 7–10.

Thomas Fall, *Canalboat to Freedom.* Illustrated by Joseph Cellini. New York, Dial Press, 1966. 214 pp. Ages 9–12.

Arthur Huff Fauset. *For Freedom: A Biographical Story of the American Negro.* Philadelphia, Franklin, 1927. 200 pp. For young people.

_____, *Sojourner Truth: God's Faithful Pilgrim.* Chapel Hill, U. of North Carolina Press, 1938. 187 pp. Well-told biography of a slave woman who became a famous abolitionist.

Harold W. Felton, *John Henry and His Hammer.* New York, Knopf, 1950. 82 pp. Contains a "John Henry Ballad" with words and music. Grades 5-9.

_____, *Jim Beckwourth: Negro Mountain Man.* New York, Dodd, Mead, 1966. 173 pp.

Aileen Fisher, *A Lantern in the Window.* New York, Nelson, 1957. 126 pp. Twelve-year-old Peter goes to live with his Quaker relatives on the banks of the Ohio and learns the farm is a station on the Underground Railroad.

Jean Fritz, *Brady.* New York, Coward-McCann, 1960. 223 pp. Exciting story of the abolitionists and the Underground Railroad. Grades 6-8.

L. H. Giles and L. F. Holmes, *Color Me Brown.* Chicago, Johnson, 1963, 1965. *Paperback.* Includes poems and pictures to color of famous Negroes in American history.

Jean Gould, *That Dunbar Boy.* New York, Dodd, 1958. 247 pp. A fictionalized version of the life of Paul Laurence Dunbar (1872-1906), poet. Grades 10-12.

Shirley Graham, *Booker T. Washington.* New York, Messner, 1955. 192 pp. Grades 6-12.

————, *Jean Baptiste Pointe du Sable*. New York, Messner, 1953. 180 pp. An account of an exceptional man (1745-1818) who was a prosperous trader and recognized as the founder of the City of Chicago. Grades 7-12.

————, *Paul Robeson, Citizen of the World*. New York, Messner, 1946. 264 pp. Grades 8-12.

————, *The Story of Phillis Wheatley*. New York, Messner, 1949. 176 pp. The life of Phillis Wheatley (1753-1784), an African-born slave who was the first Negro poet to receive widespread recognition. Grades 8-12.

————, *There Once Was a Slave: The Heroic Story of Frederick Douglass*. New York, Messner, 1947. 310 pp. Grades 8-12.

————, *Your Most Humble Servant*. New York, Messner, 1949. 235 pp. The story of Benjamin Banneker, Negro surveyor, mathematician, and clock maker. Grades 8-12.

———— and George D. Lipscomb, *Dr. George Washington Carver, Scientist*. New York, Messner, 1944. 248 pp. Grades 6-9.

Margaret Hagler, *Larry and the Freedom Man*. New York, Lothrop, 1959. 175 pp. A 12-year-old white boy and his uncle help a slave boy and his family obtain their freedom when they meet on a journey to Kansas. Ages 9-11.

E. B. Henderson, *The Negro in Sports*, rev. ed. Washington, Associated, 1949. 507 pp. Grades 9-12.

Maurice Hennessy and Edward Sauter, Jr., *A Crown for Thomas Peters*. New York, Ives Washburn, 1964. Thomas Peters was born in Africa in the early 18th century, the son of a chief who was captured and sold into slavery; he escaped in a coffin on the Underground Railroad and eventually returned to Africa to lead his people. A biographical novel, the story is based on the true account of a young African Negro.

Amy Hogeboom, *Audubon and His Sons*. New York, Lothrop, 1956. Grades 6-9.

Elizabeth Howard, *North Winds Blow Free*. New York, Morrow, 1949. 192 pp. An exciting, romantic story of the Underground Railroad. For older girls.

Langston Hughes, *Famous American Negroes*. New York, Dodd, 1954. 147 pp. Contains biographies of 17 Negro men and women who have achieved greatness: Robert S. Abbott, newspaper editor and publisher; Ira Aldridge, Shakespearean actor; Richard Allen, founder of the A.M.E. Church; Marian Anderson, singer; Ralph J. Bunche, United Nations official; George Washington Carver, scientist; Frederick Douglass, orator, writer, and abolitionist; Paul Laurence Dunbar, poet; W. C. Handy, musician; A. Philip Randolph, labor leader; Jackie Robinson, baseball pioneer; Charles C. Spaulding, businessman; Henry Ossawa Tanner, artist; Harriet Tubman, Underground

Railroad conductor; Booker T. Washington, educator; Phillis Wheatley, poet; and Daniel Hale Williams, medical pioneer. Grades 7-11.

—————, *The Dream Keeper and Other Poems*. Illustrated by Helen Sewell. New York, Alfred A. Knopf, 1959. 77 pp. Ages 8–11.

—————, *Famous Negro Heroes of America*. New York, Dodd, 1958. 202 pp. Contains biographies of 16 Negro men and women: Crispus Attucks, Revolutionary War martyr; James B. Beckwourth, frontiersman; Paul Cuffee, seaman and colonizer; Benjamin O. Davis, Jr., Air Force general; Frederick Douglass, orator, writer, and abolitionist; Jean Baptiste Pointe du Sable, founder of Chicago; Estevanico, discoverer of Arizona; Matthew A. Henson, explorer; Henry Johnson, World War I soldier; Dorie Miller, World War II sailor; Hugh N. Mulzac, ship captain; Gabriel Prosser, slave insurrection leader; Robert Smalls, captor of Confederate ship, congressman; Harriet Tubman, Underground Railroad conductor; Ida B. Wells, social reformer; and Charles Young, soldier. Grades 7-10.

—————, *Famous Negro Music Makers*. New York, Dodd, 1955. 179 pp. Biographical history of the Negro's contribution to American music.

—————, *The First Book of Jazz*. New York, Watts, 1955. 65 pp. Simple explanation of the history of jazz from African drums to Calloway and Gillespie; companion record is Folkways FP 712. Grades 6-8.

—————, *The First Book of Negroes*. New York, Watts, 1952. 64 pp. Traces the U.S. Negro's history from Africa to 1952. Grades 4-8.

—————, *The First Book of Rhythms*. New York, Watts, 1954. 63 pp. Grades 1-6.

————— and Milton Meltzer, *A Pictorial History of the Negro in America*. New York, Crown, 1963. 337 pp. Concise text and illustrations from prints, engravings, woodcuts, and photographs cover the history of the American Negro.

Altona Trent Johns, *Play Songs of the Deep South*. Washington, Associated, 1944. 33 pp. A collection of singing games and play songs for children, all originating with the Negro. Grades 4-5.

Johanna Johnston, *Together in America*. New York, Dodd, 1965. 158 pp.

Ruth Fosdick Jones, *Escape to Freedom*. New York, Random House, 1958. 236 pp. Using the true adventures of her grandparents, the author has written a lively story about two boys who join in the exciting work of running a "station" on the Underground Railroad.

John and Margaret Kieran, *John James Audubon*. New York, Random House, 1954. The story of the wandering naturalist-artist told by another naturalist and his wife. Grades 5-10.

Beatrice Landeck, *Echoes of Africa in Folk Songs of the Americas*. New York, McKay, 1961. 184 pp. A well-known musicologist traces folk music and jazz from Africa to the Americas. For older boys and girls.

Mimi Cooper Levy, *Corrie and the Yankee*. New York, Viking, 1959. 189 pp. An exciting story of how Corrie, a little slave girl, saved a young Yankee soldier from the patrollers. Grades 4-5.

————, *Whaleboat Warriors*. New York, Viking, 1963. 189 pp. Children's book about Negroes and whites on whaleboats waging guerrilla war against the British off Long Island, when British forces occupied this area during the Revolutionary War.

Agnes McCarthy and L. D. Reddick, *Worth Fighting For: A History of the Negro in the United States During the Civil War and Reconstruction*. New York, Doubleday, 1965. 118 pp. *Also in paperback.* Grades 5-6.

Ann McGovern, *Runaway Slave*. New York, Scholastic, 1965. *Also in paperback.* The story of Harriet Tubman. Grades 4-6.

Else McKean, *Up Hill*. New York, Shady Hill, 1947. 63 pp. Biographies of Ernest Everett Just, scientist; Paul Robeson, singer; Richard Wright, author; Charles Richard Drew, blood plasma pioneer; Mordecai W. Johnson, educator; and Mrs. Emma Clarissa Clement, "American Mother of the Year" for 1946. Grades 4-8.

Norman McRae and Jerry Blocker, *The American Negro: A History in Biography and Pictures* (includes Teacher's Manual). Chicago, Rand McNally, 1966. *Also in paperback.*

Elaine Mardus, *Five Who Served America*. New York, Dial, 1965. Biographies of unusual women who fought for moral and social justice in the last 100 years; included is Ida Wells, Negro journalist.

Edith H. Mayer, *Our Negro Brother*. New York, Shady Hill, 1948. 39 pp. *Paperback.* Biographical information about eight Negroes, ranging from Columbus' pilot, Nino, to union leader A. Philip Randolph; includes Matthew Henson, the only American Negro with Robert E. Peary at the North Pole in 1909.

Enid Meadowcroft, *By Secret Railway*. New York, Crowell, 1948. 275 pp. A Chicago boy and his friend, a runaway slave, share adventures on the Underground Railroad in 1860. Grades 4-5.

Florence Means, *Carvers' George*. Boston, Houghton, 1952. 176 pp. A sensitive interpretation of the Negro scientist for younger readers. Grades 5-6.

Milton Meltzer, ed., *In Their Own Words: A History of the American Negro*. 2 Vols.; Vol. I, 1619-1865, New York, Crowell, 1964. 195 pp. Vol. II, 1865-1916, Crowell, 1965. *Vol. III, 1916–1966*. Crowell, 1967. 213 pp. Ages 12-16.

Milton Meltzer and Dr. August Meier, *Time of Trial, Time of Hope*. Garden City, N.Y., Zenith, 1966. 128 pp. (History of the Negro during World Wars I and II.) *Also in paperback.*

Earl Schenck Miers, *Freedom*. New York, Grosset and Dunlap, 1965.

_____, *The Story of the American Negro*. New York, Grosset and Dunlap, 1965.

Dharathula H. Millender, *Crispus Attucks: Boy of Valor*. Illustrated by Gray Morrow. Indianapolis, Bobbs-Merrill, 1965. 200 pp. Ages 10–12.

Hugh Mulzac, *A Star to Steer By*, as told to Louis Burnham and Norval Welch. New York, International, 1963. *Paperback*. Autobiography of the first Negro in U.S. history to win his Master's license (1918) and command his own ship, the *Booker T. Washington* Liberty Ship during World War II (1942).

Donald Myrus, *Ballads, Blues, and the Big Beat*. New York, Macmillan, 1966. 135 pp. Age 12 up.

Shirlee Newman, *Marian Anderson: Lady from Philadelphia*. Philadelphia, Westminster, 1965.

Anne Parrish, *A Clouded Star*. New York, Harper, 1948. 242 pp. Story of Harriet Tubman.

Lillie G. Patterson, *Booker T. Washington: Leader of His People*. Champaign, Ill., Garrard Press, 1962. 80 pp. Grades 3-7.

_____, *Frederick Douglass: Freedom Fighter*. Illustrated by Gray Morrow. Champaign, Illinois, Garrard Publishing Company, 1965. 80 pp. 8–10.

Catherine Peare, *Mary McLeod Bethune*. New York, Vanguard, 1951. 219 pp. A well-written biography about an outstanding American personality who was known as "the first lady of the Negro people." Grade 7.

Ann Petry, *Harriet Tubman, Conductor on the Underground Railroad*. New York, Crowell, 1955. 247 pp. Grades 7-11.

_____, *Tituba of Salem Village*. New York, Crowell, 1964. 254 pp. Very readable, sympathetic story of Tituba's relation to the Salem witch trials. Ages 12-16.

Benjamin Quarles, *Frederick Douglass*. Washington, Associated, 1948. 378 pp. Grades 9-12.

Ben Richardson, *Great American Negroes*, rev. ed. New York, Crowell, 1956. 339 pp. Sketches of the lives of 26 Negroes who have achieved greatness in music: Marian Anderson, Louis Armstrong, Dean Dixon, Duke Ellington, and William Grant Still; the theater: Katherine Dunham and Bill Robinson; art: Richard Barthe and Jacob Lawrence; literature: Langston Hughes, James Weldon Johnson, Ann Petry, and Richard Wright; education: Mary McLeod Bethune and Mordecai W. Johnson; religion: Adam Clayton Powell, Sr.; civic leadership: Ralph J. Bunche, A. Philip Randolph, and Walter F. White; science: Charles Drew and George Washington Carver; sports: Joe Louis, Willie Mays, and Jesse Owens; and the armed forces: Benjamin O. Davis, Jr., and Dorie Miller. Grade 7.

Willis Richardson, *Plays and Pageants from the Life of the Negro.* Washington, Associated, 1930. 373 pp. Crispus Attucks, Sojourner Truth, Nat Turner, Harriet Tubman, William and Ellen Craft, Frederick Douglass, Samory of Soudan, Menolik of Abyssinia, Antonio Maceo of Cuba, Christophe and Toussaint L' Ouverture of Haiti. Grades 7-8.

Bill Roeder, *Jackie Robinson.* New York, Barnes, 1950. 183 pp.

Charlemae Rollins, ed., *Christmas Gift: An Anthology of Christmas Poems, Songs and Stories, Written by and About Negroes.* Chicago, Follett, 1963. 119 pp. Grades 4-7.

————, *They Showed the Way.* New York, Crowell, 1964. Short biographies of 40 Negroes who led the way in various fields. Grades 6 and up.

Jessie H. Roy and Geneva C. Turner, *Pioneers of Long Ago.* Washington, Associated, 1951. 316 pp. Includes Negro adventurers who accompanied the Spanish discoverers and explorers, Negro heroes who aided the British in America, and others who helped to extend the American frontier to the Pacific. Grades 3-4.

Edith Segal, *Come With Me.* New York, Citadel, 1963. 63 pp. *Also in paperback.* A delightful book of poems with instructions for dancing games; for Negro and white children.

Jane Dabney Shackelford, *The Child's Story of the Negro,* rev. ed. Washington, Associated, 1956. 222 pp. Grades 2-5.

————, *My Happy Days.* Washington, Associated, 1944. 121 pp. Life of a child in a typical struggling Negro family in an environment where the race has not many difficulties and takes advantage of the opportunities at hand. Grades 2-3.

Irwin Shapiro, *John Henry and the Double-Jointed Steam Drill.* New York, Messner, 1945. 55 pp. Grades 5-8.

Milton J. Shapiro, *The Hank Aaron Story.* New York, Julian Messner, 1961.

————, *Jackie Robinson of the Brooklyn Dodgers.* New York, Messner, 1963.

————, *The Roy Campanella Story.* New York, Messner, 1958.

————, *The Willie Mays Story.* New York, Messner, 1963.

Beatrice Steinman, *This Railroad Disappears.* New York, Watts, 1958. 181 pp. Historical fiction: abolitionists and a 13-year-old conductor of an Underground Railroad.

Dorothy Sterling, *Captain of the Planter.* Garden City, Doubleday, 1958. 264 pp. The fascinating story of slave Robert Smalls (1839-1915), a South Carolina seaman who fled to freedom with his family by "taking" a Confederate paddlewheel steamer and delivering it to the Union Navy; Smalls then fought in the Union Army, and after the war eventually became a member of the U.S. House of Representatives from his native state. Grades 7-8.

_____, *Forever Free: The Story of the Emancipation Proclamation.* New York, Doubleday, 1963. 208 pp. Also a history of slavery in the U.S., including a documented chapter on the "Negro Fort" of the Negro maroons and Seminole Indians in Florida during and after the War of 1812; the federal government's troops massacred Negro women and children in the fort; for more than 20 years the government fought to re-enslave the Negro maroons and transport the Indians to lands west of the Mississippi River. Grades 6-8.

_____, *Freedom Train.* Garden City, Doubleday, 1954. 191 pp. Fictionalized account of the exciting and daring life of Harriet Tubman. Grades 4-12.

_____ and Benjamin Quarles, *Lift Every Voice: The Lives of Booker T. Washington, W. E. B. Du Bois, Mary Church Terrell, and James Weldon Johnson.* Garden City, Doubleday Zenith, 1965. 116 pp. *Also in paperback.*

Philip Sterling and Rayford Logan, *Four Took Freedom: The Lives of Harriet Tubman, Frederick Douglass, Robert Smalls, and Blanche K. Bruce.* Garden City, N.Y. Zenith, 1967. 128 pp. *Also in paperback.*

Emma Gelders Sterne, *I Have a Dream.* New York, Knopf, 1966. 228 pp. (History of the Negro Civil Rights Movement including biographical sketches of Negro freedom fighters.)

_____, *Mary McLeod Bethune.* New York, Knopf, 1957. 268 pp. Founder and former president of Bethune-Cookman College in Florida, a leader in the movement for equal rights for women, born of slave parents on a South Carolina plantation . . . the young reader gets a dynamic view of American history during the past century. Ages 12–16.

_____, *The Long Black Schooner.* New York, Scholastic, 1964. The voyage of the *Amistad. Paperback.* Grades 5-8.

Augusta Stevenson, *Booker T. Washington: Ambitious Boy.* Indianapolis, Bobbs-Merrill, 1950. 199 pp. Childhood of Booker T. Washington. Grades 3-6.

_____, *George Carver: Boy Scientist.* Indianapolis, Bobbs-Merrill, 1952. 202 pp. Grades 3-6.

Maxwell Stewart, *The Negro in America.* Washington, Public Affairs Committee, 1962. 28 pp. Summary of Gunnar Myrdal's outstanding sociological study, *An American Dilemma.* For older boys and girls.

Harriet Beecher Stowe, *Uncle Tom's Cabin.* New York, Edward McCann, 1929. 446 pp. *Also in paperback.* The old classic in an attractive edition; has historic value, but must be used with other books about the Negro.

Madeline R. Stratton, *Negroes Who Helped Build America.* Boston, Ginn, 1965. 165 pp.

Hildegarde Hoyt Swift, *North Star Shining.* New York, Morrow, 1947.

44 pp. Pictorial history of the American Negro in verse form. Grades 7-9.

————, *The Railroad to Freedom*. New York, Harcourt, 1932. 364 pp. A biography of Harriet Tubman and her work in the Underground Railroad. Grades 7-10.

Henry Thomas, *George Washington Carver*. New York, Putnam, 1958. 126 pp. Biography of the great scientist and humanitarian. Grades 4-8.

Richard C. Wade, *The Negro in American Life*. Part One, From Slavery to Citizenship: 1619–1900; Part Two, Toward Full Equality: Since 1900. New York, Houghton Mifflin, 1966. *Also in paperback.*

Booker T. Washington, *Up from Slavery: An Autobiography*. New York, Doubleday, 1915. 330 pp. *Also in paperback.* For older children.

Ann Terry White, *George Washington Carver: The Story of a Great American*. New York, Random House, 1953. 182 pp. Grades 4-6.

Helen Adele Whiting, *Negro Art, Music, and Rhyme*. Washington, Associated, 1938. 38 pp. For younger children.

————, *Negro Folk Tales for Pupils in the Primary Grades*. Washington, Associated, 1938. 28 pp. Grades 1-3.

Carter G. Woodson and Charles H. Wesley, *Negro Makers of History*, rev. ed. Washington, Associated, 1958. 406 pp. Grades 6-9.

————, *The Story of the Negro Retold*, rev. ed. Washington, Associated, 1959. 472 pp. Grades 9-12.

Hildreth Wriston, *Susan's Secret*. New York, Ariel, 1957. 126 pp. Story of an 11-year-old Vermont girl whose family aids the Underground Railroad. Ages 8-12.

Elizabeth Yates, *Amos Fortune, Free Man*. New York, Aladdin, 1950. 181 pp. An African-born prince who was sold into slavery, purchased his freedom, and dedicated his life to freedom for himself and others. Grades 4-9.

Edna Yost, *American Woman of Nursing*. Philadelphia, J. B. Lippincott, 1953. 197 pp. Young adults.

————, *Famous American Pioneering Women*. New York, Dodd, Mead, 1961. 158 pp. Age 12 up.

25. PHONOGRAPH RECORDS, SONG BOOKS AND FILM STRIPS

These lists are but samples of materials available in these media. There are many albums of folk music which are not included, but are part of the history of any people. One may well check his local library and centers of learning to see if other audio and visual aids are available. Refer also to the selections covering visual materials and teaching guides.

Phonograph Records

Adventures in Negro History, Vol. I: *Adventures in Negro History.* Vol. II: *The Frederick Douglass Years: 1817–1895.* Pepsi-Cola Company, New York, N.Y. Two records, filmstrip and manual.

Adventures in Negro History, New York, City Commission on Human Rights, 80 Lafayette St., New York, N. Y. (20-minute tape.)

An Anthology of Negro Poetry for Young People, compiled and read by Arna Bontemps. New York, Folkways Records.

Anthology of Negro Poets, reading from their own works, Folkways Records, New York, N. Y. Includes Langston Hughes, Claude McKay, Countee Cullen, Margaret Walker, Gwendolyn Brooks, and others.

Anthology of Negro Poets, read by Arna Bontemps. Folkways Records, New York, N. Y. Includes Paul Laurence Dunbar, Phillis Wheatley, Countee Cullen, and others.

The Autobiography of Frederick Douglass, read by Ossie Davis, ed. and text by P. Foner. Folkways Records, New York, N.Y. 5522.

W. E. B. Du Bois, Folkways Records, New York, N. Y. A recorded autobiography, interviewed by Moses Asch; early college years (Fisk), Harvard, Germany, Atlanta University, NAACP, "The Crisis," World War I, Pan-American Conference, Africa, U.S.A. & Russia, NAACP and the U.N., Peace Congresses and the Trial, The Negro and Young People, The Negro and Africa of Today. With complete text.

Evolution of the Blues Song, narrated by Jon Hendricks, as presented at Monterey Jazz Festival (1960), Columbia Records.

Exploding the Myths of Prejudice, WaSP-Warren Schloat Productions, Inc., Palmer Lane West, Pleasantville, N.Y. 10570. Record and two color filmstrips.

First Jazz, Langston Hughes, FC7312.

George Washington Carver. Enrichment Records, 246 Fifth Ave., New York, N.Y., 1965. Grades 7-12. Tells of his origin and trials and tributes.

God's Trombones, James Weldon Johnson, read by Bryce Bond, music by William Martin, Folkways Records, New York, N. Y.

Great Negro Americans, narrated by Hilda Simms and Frederick O'Neil, World Specialties, Inc., 140 W. 31st St., New York, N. Y.

Huddie Ledbetter (Leadbelly) Memorial Album, Folkways Records, New York, N. Y. Work songs and spirituals, notes and text included.

In White America, Columbia Records.

Langston Hughes and Sterling Brown read from their poetry, Folkways Records, New York, N. Y.

Minorities Have Made America Great. WaSP-Warren Schloat Productions, Inc., Palmer Lane West, Pleasantville, N.Y. 10570. Six records and six color filmstrips.

Negro Folk Music of Africa and America, Folkways Records, New York, N. Y. Two records.

Negro Folk Music of Alabama, Folkways Records, New York, N. Y. Six records, notes by Harold Courlander.

Negro Folk Symphony, Decca Records. Written by Negro composer, W. L. Dawson; American Symphony, Stokowski conducting.

Negro Folksongs and Tunes, sung by Elizabeth Cotten. FG 3526.

Negro Folksongs for Young People. Leadbelly. FC 7533.

Negro Poetry — FC 7114.

Negro Poetry for Young People, LangArts Elementary, In-Service-CD, #946. Oakland, Oakland Public Schools, 1964. Read by Arna Bontemps. Poems by Paul L. Dunbar, Beatrice Murphy, Claude McKay, Helen Johnson, Fenton Johnson, and others.

The Negro Woman, Speeches and Writings of Negro Pioneers. Folkways Records, New York, N.Y. 5523.

Negro Work Songs and Calls, Library of Congress, Music Division, Washington, D. C.

Poetry of the Negro, read by Sidney Poitier and Doris Belack, Glory Records.

Singers in the Dusk, poems by Negro poets, read by Charles Lampkin with accompanying piano music.

Songs of American Negro Slaves, sung by Michel LaRue, Folkways Records, New York, N.Y. Notes included. 5252

The Banjo, and other Creole Ballads, Negro Songs and Caprices, Vanguard Records. Eugene Liszt, piano.

The Dream Keeper, Folkways Records, New York, N.Y. 1965. Langston Hughes reads a children's selection of his own poetry.

The Glory of Negro History, Langston Hughes. Folkways Records, New York, N.Y.

The Negro in American History, National Education Association, 1201-16th St., N.W., Washington, D.C. Record, 2 color filmstrips, script and presentation guide on the Negro in American History.

The Negro People Through Their Songs and Ballads, Heirloom Records, Wiscasset, Me. A program planned, written, and executed by high school students of the Fieldston School, Yonkers, N.Y.

The Negro Spiritual, Roger Wagner Chorale, Capital Records. Notes included.

Who Built America. Folkways Records, New York, N.Y. American history through folksongs.

Library of Congress, Music Division, Recording Laboratory, Washington, D.C.

Song Books

W. F. Allen, C. P. Ware, and Lucy Garrison, *Slave Songs of the United States.* New York, P. Smith, 1868 (reprinted by Oak, New York, 1965).

Moses Asch and Alan Lomax, ed., *The Leadbelly Songbook.* New York, Oak Publications, 1962. A collection of more than 70 blues, ballads, and folksongs by Huddie Ledbetter, one of the greatest interpreters of Negro folksongs. Biographical chapters supplied by Pete Seeger, Woodie Guthrie, Fred Ramsay, and Charles Smith.

Rev. W. E. Barton, *Old Plantation Hymns, with Historical and Descriptive Notes.* Boston, Lamson, Wolfee, 1899. 45 pp.

Harold Courlander, *Negro Folk Music U.S.A.* New York, Columbia U. Press, 1963.

_____, *Negro Songs from Alabama.* New York, Oak, 1963. *Paperback.*

R. Nathaniel Dett, ed., *Negro Spirituals.* London, Blandford, 1959.

Miles Mark Fisher, *Negro Songs in the United States.* New York, Citadel, 1963. *Also in paperback.*

J. Rosamond Johnson, *Rolling Along in Song.* New York, Viking, 1937. Music and words in a chronologically arranged survey.

James Weldon Johnson, ed., *Books of American Negro Spirituals.* New York, Viking, 1940. Words and music of many well-known spirituals; the book is two volumes in one, including: *The Book of American Negro Spirituals* and *The Second Book of American Negro Spirituals.*

John A. Lomax, compiler, *American Ballads & Folk Songs.* New York, Macmillan, 1949.

———— and Alan Lomax, *Negro Folk Songs as Sung by Leadbelly.* New York, Macmillan, 1936. Lyrics only.

Howard Washington Odum and Guy B. Johnson, *The Negro and His Songs: A Study of Typical Negro Songs in the South.* Chapel Hill, U. of North Carolina Press, 1925. 306 pp.

————, *Negro Workaday Songs.* Chapel Hill, U. of North Carolina Press, 1926.

Walter Raim, ed., *The Josh White Song Book.* Chicago, Quadrangle, 1963.

Altona Trent-Johns, *Play Songs of the Deep South.* Washington, Associated, 1944.

Clarence C. White, *Forty Negro Spirituals.* Philadelphia, Presser, 1927.

N. I. White, *American Negro Folk Songs.* Hatboro, Pa., Folklore Associates, 1965.

John W. Work, *American Negro Songs.* New York, Soskin, 1940.

————, ed., *American Negro Songs and Spirituals.* New York, Crown, 1940.

————, *Folk Songs of the American Negro.* Nashville, Fisk U. Press, 1915. 131 pp.

Films and Film Strips

Visual Materials Center, The Chicago Public Library, Chicago, Ill. Film Strips:

    A-720 Booker T. Washington.

    A-138 George Washington Carver, the plant doctor.

    A-650 Crossroad at Cedarmont.

    A-762 George Washington Carver, Biologist.

16mm Sound Films:

    Booker T. Washington (18 m.).

    George Washington Carver (12 m.—color).

    The House on Cedar Hill (Frederick Douglass) (17 m.·).

    Marian Anderson (30 m.).

    The Negro Soldier (40 m.).

    Hands That Made America (20 m.)

    Helen Tamiris in Her Negro Spirituals.

Society for Visual Education, Inc., 1345 Diversey Pkwy., Chicago, Ill. Film Strip Set A242SR, *Leading American Negroes.* Mary McLeod Bethune, George Washington Carver, Robert Smalls, Benjamin Banneker, Frederick A. Douglass, Harriet Tubman. Includes Teacher's Guide, reading script and 3 LP records (one side to each filmstrip).

Anti-Defamation League of B'nai B'rith, 315 Lexington Ave., New York, N.Y. 10016.

Epitaph for Jim Crow (series of film-lectures):
Tale of Two Ladies, emphasizes the history of Negro protest against racial discrimination.
14th Generation Americans, review history of the Negro in America.
George Washington Carver Story. 72 frames, color, silent script.

The Negro Soldier. U.S. War Department, released through U.S. Office of Education in 1949. Contribution of the Negro soldier from Revolutionary days until World War II.

Negro History Associates, P.O. Box 583, Manhattanville Station, New York, N.Y.

The Revolutionary Period, 1770-1790. Color, 32 frames. Teacher's manual and script included. Records persons and events, including some hitherto unknown Negroes; reveals how independence was won by teamwork of people from many different lands.
Early American Inventors, 18th and 19th centuries. Color, 35 frames. Manual and script describes patents and inventions and includes early Negro inventors who made great contributions to mankind.
The Story of Lewis Latimer. A true story of the son of fugitive slaves who became one of the creators of the electric industry, aided Alexander Graham Bell by executing the drawings with which he obtained the telephone patent, and was a poet, musician, linguist, draftsman, inventor and author. Dramatic script included.

Educational Heritage, Inc., 733 Yonkers Ave., Yonkers, N.Y. Negro Heritage Library Film Strip Series; Section II—The New World, Slavery to Emancipation:
Part 1. Africa to America; Colonial Times; the Slave Trade, 1719-1770.
Part 2. The Revolutionary War; Anti-Slave Agitation.
Part 3. Abolitionists: the Uiderground Railroad.
Part 4. Civil War, 1861-1865.
Approximately forty single frames per strip, with commentary.

Oakland Public Schools, Oakland, Calif.

Outstanding Americans of Negro Origin. Color, 35 slides. Grades 8-12. Series of portraits in color include artists, writers, scientists, musicians, and civic leaders—DuBois, Bethune, Carver, M. Johnson, Bunche, Robeson, Randolph, Joe Louis, Turner, Campbell, Fauset, Houston, Tobias, Alexander, Bolin, Work, Terrell, Hastie, Drew, Anderson, and others.

Pepsi-Cola Company, 500 Park Ave., New York, N.Y. 10022. *Adventures in Negro History,* Vol. I. Filmstrip, record and manual. *Adventures in Negro History,* Vol. II: *The Frederick Douglass Years: 1817–1895.* Filmstrip, record and manual.

The History of the American Negro Series, McGraw-Hill film strip series (8 film strips, average length of each 37 frames). Text-Film Division, McGraw-Hill Book Company, 327 W. 41st St., New York, N.Y.

Harriet Tubman and the Underground Railroad. 16 mm, 54 minute sound film, produced by C.B.S. Text-Film Division, McGraw-Hill Book Company, 327 W. 41st St., New York, N.Y.

National Educational Television.

History of the Negro People, a series of nine half-hour programs exploring the Negroes' little-known and long-ignored heritage. *Viewer's Handbook,* containing a synopsis of these programs, is obtainable from National Educational Television; can be used for house group discussion guides, etc. Tapes may be rented or bought from NET Film Service, Audio-Visual Center, Indiana U., Bloomington, Ind.

WaSP Film Strips, Palmer Lane West, Pleasantville, N.Y.

Exploding the Myths of Prejudice, by Dr. Ethel J. Alpenfels. Two color film strips and one 12 inch record.

Minorities Have Made America Great, consultant Dr. Ethel J. Alpenfels. Six color film strips and 6 records.

OTHER ORGANIZATIONS WITH FILMS AND FILM STRIPS:

American Film Center, Committee on Mass Education in Race Relations, 45 Rockefeller Plaza, New York, N.Y. 10010.

Brandon Films, 200 W. 57th St., New York, N.Y.

Harmon Foundation, 140 Nassau St., New York, N.Y.

Carlton Moss, P.O. Box 1827, Hollywood, Calif., film strip work on the Negro.

National Conference of Christians and Jews, 43 W. 57th St., New York, N.Y.

National Education Association, 1201-16th St., N.W., Washington, D.C. *The Negro in American History.* 2 color filmstrips, record, script, and presentation guide on the Negro in American History.

United World Films, Inc., 1445 Park Ave., New York, N.Y. 10029.

A sampling of some of the available publications that carry material on the Negro—both past and present.

Afro-American, 628 W. Utah St., Baltimore, Md. Weekly newspaper.

A.M.E. Review, Board of Education of the African Methodist Episcopal Church, 414 Eighth Ave. S., Nashville, Tenn. Quarterly.

American Historical Review, American Historical Association, 400 "A" St., S.E., Washington, D.C. Quarterly.

Atlanta World, 210 Auburn Ave. N.E., Atlanta, Ga. Daily newspaper.

Chicago Defender, 2400 S. Michigan Ave., Chicago, Ill. Daily newspaper.

Ebony Magazine, Johnson Publishing Co., 1820 S. Michigan Ave., Chicago, Ill. Monthly.

Freedomways, Freedomways Associates, Inc., 799 Broadway, New York, N.Y. 10013. Quarterly.

Harvard Journal of Negro Affairs, Harvard U., Cambridge, Mass.

Integrated Education, Integrated Education Associates, 343 S. Dearborn St., Chicago, Ill. Bi-monthly magazine.

Interracial Review, Catholic Interracial Council of New York, 233 Broadway, New York, N.Y. Monthly.

Jet, Johnson Publishing Co., 1820 S. Michigan Ave., Chicago, Ill. Weekly pocket-size news magazine.

Journal of American History, Box 432, Abilene, Kans. 67410. Quarterly.

Journal of Negro Education, Bureau of Educational Research, Howard U., Washington, D.C. Quarterly.

Journal of Negro History, Association for the Study of Negro Life and History, 1538 Ninth St., N.W., Washington, D.C. Quarterly.

Journal of Southern History, Bennett H. Wall, U. of Kentucky, Lexington, Ky. Quarterly.

Liberator, 244 E. 46th St., New York, N.Y. 10017. Monthly.

Negro Digest, Johnson Publishing Co., 1820 S. Michigan Ave., Chicago, Ill. Monthly.

Negro Heritage, P.O. Box 8153, Chicago, Ill. Bi-weekly newsletter.

Negro History Bulletin, Association for the Study of Negro Life and History, 1538 Ninth St., N.W., Wash., D.C. Monthly.

New York Amsterdam News, 2340 Eighth Ave., New York, N.Y. Weekly newspaper.

Phylon, Atlanta U., Atlanta, Ga. Quarterly journal.

Pittsburgh Courier, Centre Ave. at Francis St., Pittsburgh, Pa. Weekly newspaper.

Sepia, 1220 Harding St., Fort Worth, Tex. Monthly picture magazine.

Southern School News, Southern Education Reporting Service, Box 6156, Acklen Station, Nashville, Tenn. Monthly.

The Crisis, Crisis Publishing Co., 20 W. 40th St., New York, N.Y. 10018. Official publication of NAACP, monthly.

The Southern Patriot, Southern Conference Educational Fund, Inc., 822 Perdido St., New Orleans, La. Monthly.

Tuesday, Tuesday Publications, 605 Third Ave., New York, N.Y. Monthly roto supplement.

27. BIBLIOGRAPHIES

Many organizations, schools, libraries, churches, and individuals have prepared bibliographies on Negro history and/or materials relevant to the activities of the Negro in the U.S. This list represents some of the available compilations.

A Bibliographical Checklist of American Negro Poetry, by Arthur A. Schomburg. New York, Heartman, 1916.

A Bibliography of Anti-Slavery in America, by Dwight Lowell Dumond. Ann Arbor, U. of Michigan Press.

A Bibliography of Negro Migrations, by Frank A. Ross and Louise V. Kennedy. New York, Columbia U. Press, 1934.

A Bibliography of the Negro in Africa and America, by Monroe N. Work. New York, Wilson, 1928. Reissued New York, Octagon Books, 1965.

About 100 Books: A Gateway to Better Group Understandings (by age groups). American Jewish Committee, Institute of Human Relations, 165 E. 56th St., New York, N.Y. 10022.

Adventuring With Books, National Council of Teachers of English, 508 S. 6th St., Champaign, Ill.

An Annotated Bibliography of Biographies and Autobiographies of Negroes, 1839-1961, by Juanita B. Fuller, ACRL Microcard, Rochester, N.Y., U. of Rochester Press, for The Association of College and Research Libraries, 1964.

Bibliographic Survey: *The Negro in Print*. Washington, The Negro Bibliographic and Research Center, Inc., May 1965. Vol. 1, No. 1. (Published every two months.)

Bibliographical Essay, pp. 280-303, *North of Slavery: The Negro in the Free States, 1790-1860*. By Leon F. Litwack. Chicago, U. of Chicago Press, 1961. *Also in paperback.*

Bibliography: *A Decade of Negro Self-Expression,* by Alain LeRoy Locke. Charlottesville, N.C., 1928. Bibliography relating to Negro writing.

Bibliography. Urban Education Collection, Auburn Library, Union Theological Seminary, 3041 Broadway, New York, N.Y.

Bibliography of Negro History, compiled by Earl Spangler. Minneapolis, Ross & Haines, 1963. This limited edition is a selected, annotated listing of books, pamphlets, periodicals, Negro newspapers, public documents, unpublished materials and clipping files relating to the Negro generally in the U.S. but mostly about the Negro in Minnesota. He also published *The Negro in Minnesota* in 1961.

Nancy Block Award Book List, 1955-1963. New York, The Nancy Bloch Intercultural Library of the Downtown Community School, 235 E. 11th St., New York, N.Y. 10003.

Books for Friendship. A list of books recommended for children. 3rd ed., *Books are Bridges.* Prepared by the American Friends Service Committee.

Books to Grow On: Helping the Very Young Explore Their World and Its People. M. P. Anderson, American Jewish Committee, 1961.

Books About Negro Life for Children. Augusta Baker, Publications Division, New York Public Library, 5th Ave. & 42nd St., New York, N.Y. 10018.

Books about the Negro: An Annotated Bibliography, by Dorothy R. Homer and Ann M. Swartout. New York, Praeger (in cooperation with the Anti-Defamation League of B'nai B'rith), 1966. 148 pp.

Books for Negro History Week. Division of Libraries, Chicago Public Schools, 1963. Chicago, Ill.

"Early American Negro Writings: A Bibliographical Study," by Dorothy B. Porter. *The Papers of the Bibliographical Society of America,* XXXIX, 1945, pp. 192-268.

Elementary Library Books About Negroes in the U.S. Oakland Public Schools, Oakland, Calif. Office of the Coordinator of Library Services, 1964.

Negro Life and History. Boston Public Library, Copley Square, Boston. A selected book list for children.

North American Negro Poets: A Bibliographical Checklist of Their Writings, 1760-1944, by Dorothy B. Porter, Hattiesburg, Miss., Book Farm, 1945. Reprinted New York, Burt Franklin, 1963.

100 Years of Freedom: A Selected Bibliography of Books About the American Negro. Compiled by Preston E. Amos, Milwaukee Public Library, Milwaukee, Wis. The Association for the Study of Negro Life and History, 1538 Ninth St., N.W., Washington, D.C.

Resource Handbook of Human Relations. Council on Human Relations, 281 The Arcade, Cleveland, Ohio.

Selected Bibliography On The Negro. New York, National Urban League Dept. of Research, 14 E. 48th St., New York, N.Y.

Selected Reading List for Adults and Children on Negro History. George C. Hall Branch, Chicago Public Library, 4801 South Michigan Ave., Chicago.

That All Men May Be Free. The Free Library of Philadelphia, Philadelphia, Pa. Selected readings on the Negro in America.

The American Theatre, The Negro, and The Freedom Movement, by George Ralph. Bibliography, Chicago City Missionary Society.

The Negro in America, by Alain LeRoy Locke. Chicago, American Library Association, 1933. Bibliographical.

The Negro in America: A Bibliography. Compiled by Elizabeth W. Miller. Cambridge, Mass., Harvard U. Press, 1966. (Books, documents, articles and pamphlets written since 1954.)

The Negro in American Life: A Selected Bibliography . . . 1960 to 1963. Department of Education, Div. of Library Extension, Mass., 1963.

The Negro—Books for Young People: Bibliographies Compiled by the Secondary School Librarians of the Oakland Public Schools. Oakland Public Schools, Oakland, Calif., 1963.

The Negro—A List of Significant Books. Compiled by Dorothy R. Homer, Publications Div., New York Public Library, Fifth Ave. & 42nd St., New York, N.Y. 10018, 1960.

The Negro in the United States: A Research Guide. Compiled by Erwin K. Welsch. Bloomington, Indiana U. Press, 1964.

28. VISUAL MATERIALS

(For recordings, films, and film strips see the section on Phonograph Records, Song Books and Film Strips.)

Calendar: Pictures and Important Dates in Negro History. Educational Heritage, Inc., 733 Yongers Ave., Yonkers, N.Y.

Council Against Intolerence in America, 17 E. 42nd St., New York, N.Y. 10017. "The Negro in American Life," a set of 25 placards, 20" x 33", showing contributions of Negroes. Also, "Pictures for Democracy."

Educational Photo Series, Johnson Publishing Co., 1820 S. Michigan Ave., Chicago, Ill.

Golden State Mutual Murals. Depicting the history of the Negro in California and the West. Lobby of Golden State Mutual Life Insurance Co., 1999 W. Adams Blvd., Los Angeles, Calif.

Great Negroes, Past and Present. Posters, Afro-Am Pub. Co., 1727 S. Michigan Ave., Chicago. Portfolio No. 1, Historical Negro Contributors; Portfolio No. 2, Modern Negro Contributors.

Human Rights Exhibition Album. UNESCO Publications Center, 317 E. 34th St., New York, N.Y. 10016.

Important Early Negro Inventors. Set of 6 photos, 8x10. Negro History Associates, P.O. Box 583 Manhattanville Station, New York 10027. Negro Heroes and Heroines of the American Revolution (artists' conceptions).

Norman McRae and Jerry Blocker, *The American Negro: A History in Biography and Pictures* (includes Teacher's Manual). Chicago, Rand McNally, 1966. *Also in paperback.*

Place Mats. Friendship Press, 475 Riverside Dr., New York, N.Y. Set of 12, 75¢. Reduced version of picture map (above), with selected poems on reverse side.

Portraits of Outstanding Negroes, Friendship Press, 475 Riverside Dr., New York, N.Y. A collection of 24 photographs, each approximately 11" x 14".

Series of Individual Photos of Negroes in U.S. History. Associated, 1538 Ninth St., N.W., Washington, D.C. Includes Crispus Attucks, Benjamin Banneker, Booker T. Washington, Paul Laurence Dunbar, Mary McLeod Bethune, Ralph Bunche, Carter G. Woodson, Frederick Douglass, Langston Hughes, Charity Bailey, John Henry, George Washington Carver, Phillis Wheatley.

Twentieth Century Americans of Negro Lineage. Friendship Press, 475 Riverside, New York, N.Y. In tube: $2.00; folded flat: $1.50. Picture map featuring photographs of outstanding Negro leaders, against a colorfully illustrated map of the United States.

29. TEACHING MATERIALS AND GUIDES

In programming for the teaching of Negro history, the following list represents some of the available aides developed in the field.

A Guide for the Study of Negro History in the Churches, Edward A. White. Commission on Religion and Race, Presbytery of Chicago, 29 E. Madison St., Chicago, Ill.

A Guide to Documents in the National Archives for Negro Studies, by Paul Levinson. Washington, D.C., American Council of Learned Societies Committee on Negro Studies, Publ. No. 1, 1947.

A Guide to the Study of the Negro in American History, by Merl R. Eppse. Nashville, National Educational Publishing Co., 1937. A manual or guide suggesting sources and activities relating to study of American history.

A Suggestive Outline for the Study of the Negro in History. A pamphlet prepared by the Missouri State Department of Education, 1941.

Cultural Diversity: Library and Audio-Visual Materials for In-Service Education, Oakland Public Schools. Catalog by Mrs. Helen Syr, Coordinator of Library Services; Miss Barbara Baker, Librarian, Teachers Professional Library; Mr. George Noone, Acting Supervisor, Audio-Visual Department. March 1964.

Guide for Teachers on Contributions of Afro-Americans to the American Culture: Grades—Kindergarten to 6th Grade. Guide for Teachers, 114-53 207th St., Cambria Heights, Queens, N.Y.

Intergroup Relations: A Resource Book for Elementary School Teachers. N.Y. State Department of Education, Publications Distribution Unit, Education Bldg., Albany, N.Y. Emphasis on Negro History and Culture for Grades 4, 5, and 6.

" 'Let My People Go,' A Unit on the Negro for High School English Classes," by Virginia Joki, in *Journal of Education,* Boston U. School of Education, 765 Commonwealth Ave., Boston, Mass., December 1964, pp. 96-109.

Norman McRae and Jerry Blocker, *The American Negro: A History in Biography and Pictures* (includes Teacher's Manual). Chicago, Rand McNally, 1966. *Also in paperback.*

Negro American Heritage, ed. by Arna Bontemps. San Francisco, Century Schoolbook Press, 1965. 136 pp.

Negro History Week. Teacher News, Teachers' Union, City of New York, 206 W. 15th St., New York, N.Y.

Negro History and Culture: Selected Material for Use with Children, ed. by Helen A. Archibald. Chicago City Missionary Society, Department of Curriculum Development, 19 S. LaSalle St., Chicago, Ill.

Negro History Study Kit. Associated Publishers, 1538 9th St., Wash., D.C.

Pamphlets, Periodicals, Audio-Visual Aids and *Articles and Selected Bibliography Books.* Annual Institute of Race Relations, Race Relations Department, United Church Board for Homeland Ministries, Fisk University, Nashville, Tenn.

Racial Integrity, by Arthur A. Schomburg. A pamphlet prepared in 1913 for the Negro Society for Historical Research, discussing the need for the study of the Negro and his history in high schools and colleges.

Sources of Instructional Materials on Negroes. Pamphlet published by Federal Security Agency, U.S. Office of Education, Washington, D.C., 1951. Suggestions for a curriculum in Negro History.

The American Negro. Commission on American Citizenship, Catholic U. of America Press, Washington, D.C., 1962. A unit expanded from the *Eighth Grade Social Studies Guiding Growth in Christian Social Living.*

The American Negro as a Politician. Southern Christian Leadership Conference, Atlanta, Ga., 1965.

The Negro in American History, by Louis R. Harlan. Publication No. 61, American Historical Association, Washington, D.C., 1965.

The Negro in American History: A Curriculum Resource Bulletin for Secondary Schools. Department of History, Public Schools of the District of Columbia, Carl F. Hansen, Superintendent of Schools, Washington, D.C.

The Negro in American History: Curriculum Bulletin, 1964-65, Series #4. Board of Education, City of New York (July 1964), 110 Livingston St., Brooklyn 1, N.Y.

The Negro in American History and Culture: A List of Resources for Teaching. Union Theological Seminary, 3041 Broadway, New York, N.Y.

The Struggle for Freedom and Rights: The Negro in American History. Detroit Public Schools, Information Service, 5057 Woodward Ave., Detroit, Mich., 1964. A guide for teachers of the eighth grade.

The Washington Afro-American. August 29, 1964, Back-To-School Supplement, "Negro History in the United States."

We Build Together, by Charlemae Rollins. Chicago, The National Council of Teachers of English, 1941. A reader's guide to Negro life and literature for elementary and high school use.

30. ORGANIZATIONS

This list includes some of the many organizations which are involved with the Negro and have developed or maintain historical information.

American Friends Service Committee, 160 N. 15th St., Philadelphia, Pa.

Congress of Racial Equality (CORE), 38 Park Row, New York, N.Y.

Moorland Foundation, Howard University, Washington, D.C.

National Association for the Advancement of Colored People—20 W. 40th St., New York, N.Y. 10018.

National Urban League, 14 E. 48th St., New York, N.Y. 10017.

Schomberg Collection, 103 W. 135th St., New York, N.Y. 10030; Wendell Wray, curator.

Southern Christian Leadership Conference (SCLC), 334 Auburn Ave. N.E., Atlanta, Ga.

Southern Conference Educational Fund, Inc., 822 Perdido St., New Orleans, La. 70112.

Student Nonviolent Coordinating Committee (SNCC), 360 Nelson St., S.W., Atlanta, Ga.

The American Society of African Culture, 15 E. 40th St., New York, N.Y. 10016.

The Anti-Defamation League of B'nai B'rith, 315 Lexington Ave., New York, N.Y. 10016.

The Association for the Study of Negro Life and History, 1538 Ninth St., N.W., Washington, D.C.

The Department of Racial and Cultural Relations of the National Council of Churches of Christ, 475 Riverside Dr., New York, N.Y. 10027.

The Museum of Negro History and Art, 3806 S. Michigan Ave., Chicago, Ill.

The National Conference on Religion and Race, 150 Fifth Ave., New York, N. Y. 10011.

The Negro Heritage Library, 733 Yonkers Ave., Yonkers, N.Y.

Unesco Publication Center, 317 E. 34th St., New York, N.Y. 10016.

University Place Bookshop, 69 University Pl., New York, N.Y. An extensive collection of books by and about Negroes, for sale.

31. LIBRARIES

1. Tuskegee Institute, Hollis Burke Frissell Library, Washington Collection, Tuskegee, Ala. 11,000 volumes.
2. Philander Smith College Library, 812 W. 13th St., Little Rock, Ark.
3. University of California (Santa Barbara), Wyles Collection, Goleta, Calif. 13,153 volumes. Emphasis primarily on the Negro as a slave and implications of slavery and the Civil War.
4. Yale University Library, James Weldon Johnson Memorial Collection of Negro Arts and Letters. New Haven, Conn. (manuscripts and pictures)
5. Howard University Library, Negro Collection. Washington, D.C. 70,000 volumes.
6. Paine College, Warren A. Chandler Library, Augusta, Ga., 396 volumes. (Shelf list only, especially race problem as it concerned churches in the Old South)
7. Fort Valley State College, Henry Alexander Hunt Memorial Library, Fort Valley, Ga. 861 volumes.
8. Savannah State College Library, Savannah, Ga., 1,000 volumes. Includes pamphlet and clipping file.
9. Johnson Publishing Co. Library, 1820 S. Michigan Ave., Chicago, Ill. 2500 volumes. (pictures, photostats, microfilm)
10. Dillard University Library, 2601 Gentilly Blvd., New Orleans, La. (Card index on Negroes in New Orleans, from newspapers covering the period 1850–65)
11. Xavier University Library, Palmetto and Pine Sts., New Orleans, La. (Restricted use, closed August; manuscripts, maps, pictures, photostats, microfilm)
12. Detroit Public Library, 5201 Woodward, Detroit, Mich. 849 volumes. (Includes music, recordings, dance, drama)
13. St. Augustine Seminary Library (Divine Word Seminary), Bay St. Louis, Miss. 500 volumes. Maintained for missionary endeavor among Negroes.
14. Rust College Library. Magee Memorial Library. Holly Springs, Miss., 3,659 volumes. (Includes books by Negroes)

15. Tougaloo College. Eastman Library. Tougaloo, Mississippi
16. Bronxville Public Library, 201 Pondfield, Bronxville, N.Y. (Books by and about the Negro, presented in honor of Dr. Ralph Bunche)
17. Columbia University Libraries, Special Collections Dept., Alexander Gumby Collection, New York 27, N.Y.
18. New York Public Library Branch, Schomburg Collection, 103 W. 135th St., New York 27, N.Y. 33,500 volumes. (A library of books, periodicals, manuscripts, clippings, pictures, prints, records, sheet music attempting to record the entire experience of peoples of African descent—historical and contemporary; restricted use: materials must be used on the premises)
19. University of North Carolina, Louis Round Wilson Library, Chapel Hill, N. C.
20. Western Carolina College Library, Cullowhee, N. C.
21. Duke University Library, Durham, N. C.
22. Bennett College, Thomas F. Holgate Library, Greensboro, N. C. 1,481 volumes.
23. Richard B. Harrison Public Library, 214 S. Blount St., Raleigh, N. C. 3,500 volumes. (Mimeographed bibliographies available)
24. The Rutherford B. Hayes Library, 1337 Hayes Ave., Fremont, Ohio. 65,000 volumes.
25. Wilberforce University, Carnegie Library, Daniel Alexander Payne Collection, Wilberforce, Ohio. 4,500 volumes. (Includes manuscripts and pictures)
26. Lincoln University, Vail Memorial Library, Lincoln University. Penna. 2,900 volumes. (Includes African materials)
27. The Free Library of Philadelphia, Social Science and History Dept. Negro Collection. Logan Square, Philadelphia, Penna. 900 volumes.
28. Starks Library, Benedict College, Taylor and Harden Streets, Columbia 4, S. C. 28,100 volumes. (Includes manuscripts, maps, pictures, slides)
29. Fisk University Library, Erastus Milo Cravath Memorial Library, Nashville 8, Tenn. 10,000 volumes. (Includes manuscript collection) Restricted use, noncirculating.
30. Texas Southern University Library, Heartman Collection, 3201 Wheeler, Houston 4, Texas. 11,428 volumes. (Includes maps and photographs)
31. Hampton Institute, The Collis P. Huntington Memorial Library, George Foster Peabody Collection. Hampton, Virginia. 9,289 volumes.
32. Virginia State College Library, Norfolk Division, 2401 Corprew Ave., Norfolk, Va.
33. Virginia Union University, William J. Clark Library, 1500 Lombardy St., Richmond 20, Va. 1,650 volumes.

ADDENDA

CHAPTER 9. BOOKS ON THE GENERAL HISTORY OF THE NEGRO IN THE UNITED STATES

Lulamae Clemons, Erwin Hollitz, Gordon Gardner, *The American Negro*. New York, McGraw-Hill. 138 pp. *Also in paperback*.

Joseph E. Coleman and Mary E. Walls, *Another Chosen People— American Negroes*. Philadelphia, Coleman, 1963.

The Negro in American Life and History: A Resource Book for Teachers (Preliminary Ed.). San Francisco Unified School District, 1965. 367 pp.

The Negro in American Life and History, a resource book with a teacher's guide for 8th grade. San Francisco Unified School District.

Drs. Harry A. Ploski and Roscoe C. Brown, Jr., eds., *Negro Almanac*. New York, Bellwether Publ., 1967. 1012 pp.

CHAPTER 11. PRE–CIVIL WAR AMERICA: SLAVERY AND ABOLITION, 1789–1860.

Alfred H. Conrad and John R. Meyer, *The Economics of Slavery*. Chicago, Aldin, 1967.

William Styron, *The Confessions of Nat Turner*. New York, Random House, 1967.

CHAPTER 14. THE TWENTIETH CENTURY

Francis Broderick and August Meier, eds., *Negro Protest Thought in the Twentieth Century*. Indianapolis, Bobbs-Merrill, 1965. 444 pp.

Flint Kellogg, *NAACP: A History of the National Association for the Advancement of Colored People, Vol. I, 1909–1920*. Baltimore, Johns Hopkins.

CHAPTER 15. NEGROES IN WARS

William H. Leckie, *The Buffalo Soldiers: A Narrative of the Negro Cavalry in the West*. Norman, U. of Oklahoma Press, 1967. 290 pp.
Irvin H. Lee, *Negro Medal of Honor Men*. New York, Dodd, Mead, 1967. 139 pp.

CHAPTER 16. SOCIAL AND ECONOMIC ASPECTS OF NEGRO HISTORY

James A. Atkins, *The Age of Jim Crow*. New York, Vantage, 1964.
James O. Buswell, *Slavery, Segregation and Scripture*. Grand Rapids, Eerdmans, 1964.
Seymour L. Gross and Edward Hardy, eds., *Images of the Negro in American Literature*. Chicago, U. of Chicago Press, 1967.
Brion Gysin, *To Master—A Long Goodnight: The Story of Uncle Tom*. New York, Creative Age, 1946.
Louis E. Lomax, *The Reluctant African*. New York, Harper, 1960.
Arthur M. Ross and Herbert Hill, eds., *Employment, Race and Poverty*. New York, Harcourt, Brace, 1967. 598 pp. A critical study of the disadvantaged status of Negro workers from 1865 to 1965.
Alan H. Spear, *Black Chicago: The Making of a Negro Ghetto, 1890–1920*. Chicago, U. of Chicago Press, 1967.
Joseph R. Washington, Jr., *Black Religion. The Negro and Christianity in the United States*. Boston, Beacon, 1964.

CHAPTER 17. STATE AND LOCAL HISTORIES

Hugh V. Brown, *A History of the Education of Negroes in North Carolina*. Raleigh, Irwin-Swain Press, 1961.
Edward T. Clayton, *The Negro Politician, His Success and Failure*. Chicago, Johnson, 1964.
Frederick A. McGinnis, *The Education of Negroes in Ohio*. Wilberforce, published by the author, 1964.
Roi Ottley and William J. Weatherby, eds., *The Negro in New York: An Informal Social History*. New York, New York Public Library and Oceana, 1967. 352 pp.

CHAPTER 19. BIOGRAPHIES AND AUTOBIOGRAPHIES

Charlotta A. Bass, *Forty Years, Memoirs from the Pages of a Newspaper*. Los Angeles, published by author, 1960.
Harold Cruse, *The Crisis of the Negro Intellectual*. Clifton, New Jersey, William Morrow, 1967.

Lawrence Elliott, *George Washington Carver: The Man Who Overcame*. Englewood Cliffs, Prentice-Hall, 1967. 256 pp.

James W. English, *Handyman of the Lord: The Life and Ministry of the Rev. William Holmes Borders*. New York, Meredith, 1967, 177 pp.

Blanche E. Ferguson, *Countee Cullen and the Negro Renaissance*. New York, Dodd, Mead, 1967. 206 pp.

Henry O. Flipper, *Negro Frontiersman*. El Paso, Western College Press, 1963.

Roy L. Hill, *Who's Who in the American Negro Press*. New York, Royal, 1960.

Langston Hughes and Milton Meltzer, *Black Magic: A Pictorial History of the Negro in American Entertainment*. Englewood Cliffs, New Jersey, Prentice-Hall, 1967.

LeRoi Jones, *Black Music*. Clifton, New Jersey, William Morrow, 1967.

Jack Olsen, *Black is Best: The Rule of Cassius Clay*. New York, Putnam's, 1967, 255 pp.

William L. Patterson, *Ben Davis: Crusader for Negro Freedom and Socialism*. New York, New Outlook, 1967, 48 pp., *Paperback*.

Allan Peskin, ed., *North into Freedom: The Autobiography of John Malvin, Free Negro, 1795–1880*. Cleveland, Western Reserve Press, 1967, 87 pp.

George S. Schuyler, *Black and Conservative: The Autobiography of George S. Schuyler*. New Rochelle, Arlington, 1966.

A. B. Spellman, *Four Lives in the Bebop Business*. New York, Pantheon, 1967.

CHAPTER 20.   CULTURAL CONTRIBUTIONS

LITERATURE

Abraham Chapman, *The Negro in American Literature*. Oshkosh, Wisconsin Council of Teachers of English, Wisconsin State U., 1967. 135 pp. *Paperback*.

Seymour L. Gross and Edward Hardy, eds., *Images of the Negro in American Literature*. Chicago, U. of Chicago Press, 1967.

Langston Hughes, ed., *The Best of Stories by Negro Writers*. Boston, Little, Brown, 1967. 508 pp.

Langston Hughes, ed., *The Book of Negro Humor*. New York, Dodd, Mead, 1966. 265 pp.

Norman V. McCullough, *The Negro in English Literature*. Devon, Stockwell, 1962.

POETRY

Blanche E. Ferguson, *Countee Cullen and the Negro Renaissance*. New York, Dodd, Mead, 1967. 206 pp.

Richard Walser, *The Black Poet*. New York, Philosophical Library, 1966. 120 pp.

MUSIC

Tim Dennison, Sr., *The American Negro and His Amazing Music*. New York, Vantage, 1963.

Ira Gitler, *Jazz Masters of the 40's*. New York, Macmillan, 1966. 290 pp.

Le Roi Jones, *Black Music*. Clifton, N.J., William Morrow, 1967.

Neil Leonard, *Jazz and the White Americans*. Chicago, U. of Chicago Press, 1962.

J. Overton Rogers, *Blues and Ballads of a Black Yankee*. New York, Exposition Press, 1965.

A. B. Spellman, *Four Lives in the Bebop Business*. New York, Pantheon, 1967.

ART

T. V. Roelof-Lanner, ed., *Prints by American Negro Artists*. Los Angeles, Cultural Exchange Center of Los Angeles, Calif.

THEATRE

Loften Mitchel, *Black Drama: The Story of the American Negro in the Theatre*. New York, Hawthorn.

GENERAL

Freda De Knight, *The Ebony Cookbook: A Date with a Dish*. Chicago, Johnson, 1962.

Langston Hughes and Milton Meltzer, *Black Magic: A Pictorial History of the Negro in American Entertainment*. Englewood Cliffs, Prentice-Hall, 1967.

CHAPTER 21.   BOOKS AND PAMPHLETS ON RACE

Carleton S. Coon, *The Origin of Races*. New York, Knopf, 1962.

Milton Gordon, *Assimilation in American Life. The Role of Race, Religion and National Origins*. New York, Oxford U. Press, 1964.

CHAPTER 23.   PAPERBACK BOOKS ON NEGRO HISTORY

Abraham Chapman, *The Negro in American Literature*. Oshkosh, Wisconsin Council of Teachers of English, Wisconsin State U., 1967. 135 pp.

Lulumae Clemons, Erwin Hollitz, Gordon Gardner, *The American Negro*. New York, McGraw-Hill. 138 pp.

William L. Patterson, *Ben Davis: Crusader for Negro Freedom and Socialism*. New York, New Outlook, 1967. 48 pp.

CHAPTER 24.   SELECTED BOOKS FOR CHILDREN
AND YOUNG ADULTS

Adele de Leeuw, *John Henry: Steel-Drivin' Man.* Champaign, Ill., Garrard, 1966. 40 pp. Ages 8-10.

David Namber, *Wizard of Tuskegee: The Life of George Washington Carver.* New York, Crowell-Collier, 1967. 168 pp. Ages 12-16.

Sheldon N. Ripley, *Matthew Henson: Arctic Hero.* Boston, Houghton Mifflin, 1967. 191 pp. Ages 8-11.

CHAPTER 25.   PHONOGRAPH RECORDS, SONG BOOKS
AND FILM STRIPS

Film Associates (Vignette Films), 11559 Santa Monica Blvd., Los Angeles, Calif. 90025
   Paul Laurence Dunbar, biography, 14-minute color sound film, 1965.
   American Negro Pathfinder Series, 6 filmstrips for upper elementary, junior and senior high school:
      Dr. Ralph Bunche: Missionary of Peace, 48 frames.
      Judge Thurgood Marshall: Mr. Civil Rights, 45 frames.
      Gen. Benjamin O. Davis, Jr.: American Guardian, 44 frames.
      A. Philip Randolph: Elder Statesman, 35 frames.
      Dr. Mary McLeod Bethune: Courageous Educator, 41 frames.
      Dr. Martin Luther King, Jr.: Non-violent Crusader, 44 frames.

Frederick Douglass, 2 parts, sound film 25 minutes each, Profiles in Courage, Series II, No. 1. NBC, made and released by Robert Saudek Associates, 1965.

From Slavery 'Til Now, Vee-Jay Records. Anthology of Negro gospel and spiritual music; helpful in understanding the sociological development of Negro thought and communications, particularly during the slave period.

McGraw-Hill Book Company, Text-Film Division, 327 W. 41st St., New York, N.Y.
   A History of the Negro in America, 1619–1860; Out of Slavery
   A History of the Negro in America, 1861–1877; Civil War and Reconstruction, sound films, 20 minutes each, Niagara Films, 1965.
   The Boston Massacre, 27-minute sound film, You Are There Series. Includes Crispus Attucks.

The Negro Worker in the City, Negro labor situation since the Civil War discussed by Rayford Logan. U. of Colorado National Tape Repository. (U. of Colorado will duplicate this tape for a nominal fee when blank tapes are submitted: Bureau of Audio Visual, University Extension Div., Folsom Stadium, Boulder, Colo.) 30-minute tape.

CHAPTER 26.   PERIODICALS

Interracial Books for Children, 9 E. 40th St., New York, N.Y. Quarterly.

CHAPTER 27.   BIBLIOGRAPHIES

The Negro American in Paperback. National Education Association, Washington, D.C. A selected list of paperbound books compiled and annotated for secondary-school students.

CHAPTER 28   VISUAL MATERIALS

Americans of Negro Origin. 22 Study Prints (10 x 12) B&W. Harmon Foundation.

Important Dates in the History of the Negro People In Our Country. 1 chart, (17 x 22) in color, and information sheet. Cultural and economic events of American Negro History, and achievements of Negro leaders. Artisan Productions.

Two small booklets and 5 bronze busts of Negroes in American history. National Distillers Products Company, 99 Park Ave., New York, N.Y.

CHAPTER 29.   TEACHING MATERIALS AND GUIDES

Recommendations, Resources, Activities for Integrating the History and Culture of Negro Americans into the Existing Social Studies Curriculum, by the Teachers of Washington Elementary School in cooperation with Illinois Commission on Human Relations. Board of Education, District 89, 1133 S. Eighth St., Maywood, Ill., John Prater, Superintendent.

The Negro in American Life and History: A Resource Book for Teachers (Preliminary Ed.). San Francisco Unified School District, San Francisco, Calif., 1965. 367 pp.

The Negro in American Life and History, a resource book with teacher's guide for 8th grade. San Francisco Unified School District, San Francisco, Calif.

ABOUT THE AUTHOR

Erwin A. Salk is a leader in business, civic, and interracial affairs and president of Salk, Ward & Salk, Inc., one of the nation's leading mortgage banking institutions. Mr. Salk received his M.A. in political science at the University of Chicago and is a graduate of the School of Military Governors for the Far East. Formerly Chief of Wages, Hours and Working Conditions Policy for Japan and a chief of section for UNESCO in Paris, he is now chairman of the housing committee and a member of the executive board of the Chicago Conference on Religion and Race and the Evanston Community Relations Commission. He frequently addresses civic organizations on housing, economic, and international affairs, is a member of the speakers bureau of the United Nations Association and a seminar lecturer for the Mortgage Bankers Association of America. He also serves as a consultant on curriculum on American history for several school districts. Mr. Salk's avid interest in Negro history led him to compile this invaluable book.